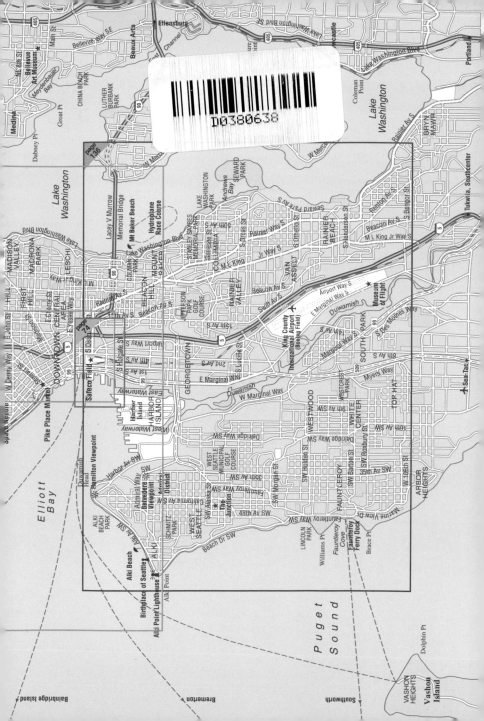

Other Insight Guides available:

Alaska
Amazon Wildlife
American Southwest
Amsterdam
Argentina
Arizona & Grand Canyon
Asia, East
Asia, Southeast
Asia's Best Hotels
Australia
Austria
Bahamas
Bali & Lombok
Baltic States
Bangkok
Barbados
Belgium
Belize
Berlin
Bermuda
Brazil
Brittany
Buenos Aires
Bulgaria
Burgundy
Burma (Myanmar)
Cairo
California
California, Southern
Canada
Caribbean
Caribbean Cruises
Channel Islands
Chicago
Chile
China
Colorado
Continental Europe
Corsica
Costa Rica
Crete
Cuba
Cyprus
Czech & Slovak Republic
Delhi, Jaipur & Agra
Denmark
Dominican Rep. & Haiti
Dublin
East African Wildlife
Eastern Europe
Ecuador
Edinburgh
Egypt
England
Finland
Florida
France
France, Southwest
French Riviera
Gambia & Senegal
Germany
Glasgow
Gran Canaria
Great Britain
Great Railway Journeys
   of Europe

Great River Cruises
   of Europe
Greece
Greek Islands
Guatemala, Belize
   & Yucatán
Hawaii
Hungary
Iceland
India
India, South
Indonesia
Ireland
Israel
Istanbul
Italy
Italy, Northern
Italy, Southern
Jamaica
Japan
Jerusalem
Jordan
Kenya
Korea
Laos & Cambodia
Lisbon
Madeira
Malaysia
Mallorca & Ibiza
Malta
Mauritius Réunion
   & Seychelles
Melbourne
Mexico
Miami
Morocco
Namibia
Nepal
Netherlands
New England
New Mexico
New Orleans
New York State
New Zealand
Nile
Normandy
North American and
   Alaskan Cruises
Norway
Oman & The UAE
Oxford
Pacific Northwest
Pakistan
Peru
Philippines
Poland
Portugal
Provence
Puerto Rico
Rajasthan
Rio de Janeiro
Romania
Russia
Sardinia
Scandinavia
Scotland

Sicily
South Africa
South America
Spain
Spain, Northern
Spain, Southern
Sri Lanka
Sweden
Switzerland
Syria & Lebanon
Taiwan
Tenerife
Texas
Thailand
Trinidad & Tobago
Tunisia
Turkey
Tuscany
Umbria
USA: On The Road
USA: Western States
US National Parks: West
Utah
Venezuela
Vienna
Vietnam
Wales

INSIGHT CITY GUIDES
(with free restaurant map)

Athens
Barcelona
Beijing
Boston
Bruges, Ghent & Antwerp
Brussels
Cape Town
Florence
Hong Kong
Kuala Lumpur
Las Vegas
London
Los Angeles
Madrid
Montreal
Moscow
New York
Paris
Philadelphia
Prague
Rome
St Petersburg
San Francisco
Seattle
Singapore
Sydney
Taipei
Tokyo
Toronto
Vancouver
Venice
Walt Disney World/Orlando
Washington, DC

INSIGHT GUIDES
SEATTLE

Discovery CHANNEL

APA PUBLICATIONS **L**
Part of the Langenscheidt Publishing Group

INSIGHT GUIDE
SEATTLE

Project Editor
Martha Ellen Zenfell
Art Editor
Ian Spick
Picture Editor
Hilary Genin
Cartography Editor
Zoë Goodwin
Production
Kenneth Chan
Editorial Director
Brian Bell

Distribution

United States
Langenscheidt Publishers, Inc.
36–36 33rd Street 4th Floor
Long Island City, NY 11106
Fax: (1) 718 784-0640

UK & Ireland
GeoCenter International Ltd
Meridian House, Churchill Way West,
Basingstoke, Hants RG21 6YR
Fax: (44) 1256-817988

Australia
Universal Publishers
1 Waterloo Road
Macquarie Park, NSW 2113
Fax: (61) 2 9888 9074

New Zealand
Hema Maps New Zealand Ltd (HNZ)
Unit D, 24 Ra ORA Drive
East Tamaki, Auckland
Fax: (64) 9 273 6479

Worldwide
Apa Publications GmbH & Co.
Verlag KG (Singapore branch)
38 Joo Koon Road, Singapore 628990
Tel: (65) 6865-1600. Fax: (65) 6861-6438

Printing

Insight Print Services (Pte) Ltd
38 Joo Koon Road, Singapore 628990
Tel: (65) 6865-1600. Fax: (65) 6861-6438

©2008 Apa Publications GmbH & Co.
Verlag KG (Singapore branch)
All Rights Reserved

First Edition 1993
Fourth Edition 2007
Reprinted 2008

ABOUT THIS BOOK

The first Insight Guide pioneered the use of creative and full-color photography in guidebooks in 1970. Since then, we have expanded our range to cater for our readers' need not only for reliable information about their chosen destination but also for a real understanding of that destination. Now, when the internet can supply inexhaustible (but not always reliable) facts, our books marry text and pictures to provide that much more elusive quality: knowledge. To achieve this, they rely heavily on the authority of locally based writers and photographers.

How to use this book

The book is carefully structured to convey an understanding of Seattle:
◆ To understand the city today, you need to know something of its past. The first section covers its history, people, culture and nature in lively essays written by local specialists.
◆ The main Places section provides a full run-down of all the attractions worth seeing. The main places of interest are coordinated by number with full-color maps. Margin notes provide background information and tips on special places and events.
◆ Photographs are chosen not only to illustrate the city and its buildings but also to convey the moods of Seattle and the life of its people.
◆ A special section of photographic features highlights the Experience Music Project, shopping in Seattle, and the Pacific Northwest's Native American tribes, volcanic mountains and wonderful wildlife.
◆ The Travel Tips listings section provides a point of reference for infor-

while the sun was out in Seattle! – and looked through 4,500 digital images before Zenfell did the final selection from the 1,000 images she submitted. **Jerry Dennis** and Puget Sound-based **Tim Thompson** also supplied fine photographs.

The text was given a make-over, too. Chief supervisor was **Giselle Smith**, who has worked with Insight since the first Seattle edition. Smith launched *Seattle Magazine* as a bimonthly, and is currently editor of *Seattle Homes & Lifestyle*s magazine. She holds degrees in English and journalism from the University of Washington, and lives in Fremont.

Assisting Smith was **Anna Chan,** a freelance editor who has lived in the city her entire life and has no desire to move. She wrote our chapter on Seattle Center. A contributor to the *Seattle Times* and *Seattle Magazine,* **Matthew Amster-Burton** has been selected three times for the annual Best Food Writing anthology; he penned our new essay on food, while girl-about-town **Allison Lind** wrote our essay on culture. **Steve Wainwright** is a longtime newspaper editor who has lived in 12 different city neighborhoods over the past decades. He was perfectly placed, obviously, to write our piece on Seattleites.

Thanks to previous contributors **John Wilcock, Scott Rutherford** and many, many others; in London, special thanks to **David Whelan, Mary Pickles, Sylvia Suddes,** and **Helen Peters**.

mation on travel, hotels, shops and festivals. Information may be located quickly by using the index printed on the back cover flap – and the flaps are designed to serve as bookmarks. ◆ A separate pull-out map highlights more than 50 restaurants carefully chosen by our local experts.

The contributors

Martha Ellen Zenfell was the project editor of the first Insight book to Seattle, and is also this edition's project editor. The first thing Zenfell did was to engage the services of **Catherine Karnow**, who has worked with Zenfell on Insight Guides to Los Angeles and Las Vegas, among others. After the photographer gained unprecedented access in order to document the city in the 21st century, she and Zenfell hunkered down in a dark hotel room –

CONTACTING THE EDITORS

We would appreciate it if readers would alert us to errors or outdated information by writing to:
Insight Guides, P.O. Box 7910, London SE1 1WE, England.
Fax: (44) 20 7403-0290.
insight@apaguide.co.uk

www.insightguides.com
In North America:
www.insighttravelguides.com

Contents

Maps

Travel Tips

TRANSPORTATION

ACCOMMODATIONS

ACTIVITIES

A–Z

WHAT TO READ

THE BEST OF SEATTLE

Setting priorities, saving money, unique attractions...
here, at a glance, are our recommendations, plus some
tips and tricks even Seattleites won't always know

WORLD-FAMOUS COMPANIES

- **Starbucks** started here in 1971. *See page 87.*
- **Microsoft** has headquarters in Redmond. *See page 152.*
- **Amazon.com** is situated in an Art Deco building. *See page 140.*
- **Adobe** software has offices in Fremont. *See page 123.*

ABOVE: Microsoft's Visitor Center in Redmond. **ABOVE RIGHT:** the downtown area and harbor. **BELOW RIGHT:** Seattle by night; Smith Tower is the building on the far left.

BEST VIEWS

- The 360° bird's-eye view of the entire region from the top of the **Space Needle**. *See pages 104–105.*
- Boats headed for the locks from the deck at **Ray's Boathouse**. *See page 132.*
- Mount Rainier from **Kerry View Point Park** on Queen Anne Hill. *See pages 10–11 and 119.*
- The Downtown view from **West Seattle**. *See page 134.*
- The city from the deck of a **Washington State Ferry**. *See page 99.*
- Puget Sound from the observation deck of the **Smith Tower**. *See page 78.*
- Downtown from the top of **Beacon Hill**. *See pages 58 and 139.*

BEST OUTDOOR CITY PLACES

- **Green Lake** is circled by a paved trail for walking, jogging or skating. *See page 129.*
- **Seward Park** has wilderness, a waterfront, a long, paved trail and an art studio. *See page 141.*
- The **Burke-Gilman Trail** carries cyclists along parks and a lake. *See page 123.*
- The city's best sandy beaches are in **Alki** in West Seattle. *See page 136.*
- **Volunteer Park** is home to the Seattle Asian Art Museum as well as a conservatory. *See page 114.*
- **Discovery Park** has beaches, sand dunes, forest trails and sea cliffs. *See page 119.*

BEST FESTIVALS AND EVENTS

- **Bumbershoot** This annual Labor Day weekend festival includes top-name concerts, a small film festival, comedy, author readings, lectures, crafts and more. *See page 106.*
- **Fremont Solstice Parade** Held on the closest Saturday to summer solstice. Naked bicyclists, political satire, street theater and more. *See page 222.*
- **Bite of Seattle** Local restaurants and food companies offer tastes of their goods, while famous chefs demon-strate secrets of the kitchen. *See page 223.*
- **Seafair** A month-long mid-summer event that brings the entire community together. Great boats. *See page 223.*

LEFT: Chinese New Year in the International District is one local festival not to miss.

LEFT: the Space Needle was built for the 1962 World's Fair. It takes 43 seconds to reach the top.

ONLY IN SEATTLE

- The **Space Needle** has been an icon for over four decades. It even featured in the Austin Powers movie, *The Spy Who Shagged Me. See page 103.*
- Bruce Lee and his son, Brandon Lee, both died young and are buried at **Lake View Cemetery** on Capitol Hill. *See page 114.*
- The **Fremont** sculp-tures include a giant troll clutching a VW automobile, and com-muters waiting for a trolley. *See pages 127 and 128.*
- Watch out for the "fly-ing fish" at **Pike Place Market**. When you buy a salmon, vendors put on a boisterous show as they weigh and package it. *See pages 12–13 and 96.*
- Legend Jimi Hendrix is buried in Renton's **Greenwood Ceme-tery**. *See page 168.*
- In 1962, the city coun-cil turned an old gas plant on the north shore of Lake Union into a public park. The bigger draw at **Gas Works Park** is the hill that's perfect for kite flying. *See page 126.*
- **Experience Music Project/Science Fiction Museum** EMP is an interactive music museum with rock-star memeobilia. SFM features artifacts from movies and authors. *See pages 110–111 and 105.*
- **Washington State Ferries** are the largest US passenger fleet. *See page 98.*

SEATTLE FOR FAMILIES

- **Seattle Center** This place is a great spot for the entire family. Enjoy the amusement rides and games at the Fun Forest, then go to the Pacific Science Center, IMAX Theater or the Children's Museum. *See page 103.*

BELOW: future tech genius at the Children's Museum.

- **Waterfront Activities Center** Rent a canoe or a rowboat and enjoy the wildlife on Union Bay. Paddle through the arboretum, then pull up on shore and have a picnic in the park. *See page 126.*
- **Seattle Aquarium** See, touch and marvel at sea mammals and scaley underwater creatures of the deep. The aquarium is right on the waterfront. *See page 97.*
- **Woodland Park Zoo** Watch nearly 300 species of animals in a huge and lovely park. Don't miss the Day and Night exhibits of reptiles and nocturnal mammals, Butterflies & Blooms or the Rose Garden. *See page 129.*

ABOVE: Shrunken heads in Ye Olde Curiosity Shop.

FREE (ALMOST) SEATTLE

- In downtown Seattle and Pioneer Square, **First Thursdays** are when galleries stay open late and introduce new shows. The Seattle Art Museum is free. Look for **First Fridays** in Fremont, or **Second Saturdays** in Ballard.
- Admission is always free at the interesting and privately owned **Frye Art Museum**. *See page 83.*
- Many of Puget Sound's **wineries** offer free tours and tastings. If there's a fee, it's often refunded with a purchase. *See page 154.*
- Part gift shop, part museum, **Ye Olde Curiosity Shop** has quirky souvenirs and spooky oddities. *See page 98.*
- Bring a blanket to the **Fremont Outdoor Movies**, on summer Saturdays at dusk. Suggested donation.
- Many of the city's prolific coffeehouses offer **free Wi-Fi**. For a fee, you can even have Wi-Fi on a ferry.
- During summer, Wednesday outdoor **Brown Bag Lunch** concerts are free at Olympic Plaza in downtown Seattle.

BEST COFFEEHOUSES

Coffeehouses are everywhere in Seattle – and they're not all owned by Starbucks. Here are some (mostly) independent places. Capitol Hill is the best area.

- Trendy **Vérité Coffee** claims to "hand craft each cup" for the best coffee; don't miss their delicious cupcakes. (West Seattle, Ballard, Madrona)
- **Café Zoka** roasts its beans on site and brews them in small batches. (Green Lake)
- Dunk one of Seattle's best doughnuts into a good cup at **Top Pot Coffee and Doughnuts**. (Capitol Hill)
- Get comfortable with a book and good espresso in **Bauhaus Books & Coffee**. (Capitol Hill)
- Have your coffee with a slice of edgy culture: **The Aurafice** has live music on occasion, local art and board games. (Capitol Hill)
- Sip espresso while browsing through LPs at **Cranium's Coffee and Collectibles**. (Lake City)
- For a taste of Seattle's caffeine history, stop by the small, original **Starbucks** – where the empire began. (Pike Place Market)

BELOW: Espresso Vivace in Capitol Hill may serve the best coffee in town. Be sure to check out the "latte art."

BEST TOURS

- **Underground Tour** An inspection of the shops and rooms that were abandoned when Seattle caught fire in 1889. *See page 75.*
- **Argosy Cruises** Choose to tour the Seattle harbor or Lake Washington; either way, the city is at its best from the water. *See page 230.*
- **Washington Wine Tours** No drinking and driving with this tour. *See page 231.*

- **Market Ghost Tours** Hear the legends of Pike Place Market. Be afraid; be very afraid. *See page 96.*
- *Spirit of Washington* **Dinner Train** Have dinner in a 1900s railroad car and watch Lake Washington roll by. *See page 231.*
- **Safeco Field Tours** Take me out to the ballgame and visit one of the most modern stadiums in America. *See page 80.*

ABOVE: Excursions out of Seattle by road, ferry, train or clipper ship are one of the delights of the city's location.
BELOW LEFT: Boeing's Future of Flight and tour offers the chance to really get inside the workings of an airplane.

BEST EXCURSIONS

Part of Seattle's appeal is its proximity to other places in the Pacific Northwest. Here are some excursions long and short that are not to be missed.

- Visit one of the only rainforests in America, on the Olympic Peninsula. *See page 192.*
- Ride the handsome *Victoria Clipper* to old-English **Victoria, BC**. *See page 198.*
- Journey to **Mount Rainier** for excellent hiking. *See page 203.*
- Take a passenger ferry or a seaplane to the **San Juan Islands**. *See page 195.*

- Explore the lava tubes at **Mount St Helens**. *See page 203.*
- Stroll the charming streets of Victorian **Port Townsend**. *See page 187.*
- Take a 35-minute ferry ride to **Bainbridge Island** to visit pretty towns and a winery. *See page 181.*
- Take the train from Seattle to **Vancouver, BC**. *See page 204.*

MONEY-SAVING TIPS

If you're planning to visit most or all of the city's main attractions, purchase a **Seattle CityPass**. This book of tickets will get you into the Woodland Park Zoo, Museum of Flight, Pacific Science Center, Seattle Aquarium and Argosy Cruises for a fraction of the price of individual tickets. Go to www.citypass.com.
Go Seattle is a similiar scheme for saving money if you plan to visit several attractions. For more information, go to www.gocardusa.com.

Twenty-Five for $25 is a great way to save money while sampling the fare at 25 of Seattle's best restaurants. The promotion, which runs every March and November, offers diners prix-fixe three-course lunches ($12.50) or dinners ($25), Sunday through Thursday. Prices do not include drinks, tax or tips. Go to www.nwsource.com/25for25.

Interested in catching a show? **Ticket/Ticket** offers half-price tickets on the day of or day before each show. Ticket/Ticket windows are located at Broadway Market, Pacific Place and Meydenbauer Center; no service charge for walk-up cash sales. For more information, go to www.ticketwindowonline.com.

For traveling around Downtown, forget the cabs and hop on a Metro bus. The King County bus service offers a **Ride-Free Zone** between 6am and 7pm every day that extends south from Battery Street to South Jackson Street, and west from 6th Avenue to the waterfront. For more information, go to transit.metrokc.gov.

SEATTLE AND SEATTLEITES

Seattleites are cool – in every sense of the word.
Climate and geography are said to affect behavior,
and this is definitely the case in the Emerald City

Had Dorothy landed in this modern-day Emerald City of Seattle, she might have taken a wide-eyed look around and said, "Wow, Toto! The heck with Kansas!"

In this local update of *The Wizard of Oz*, she would have turned left off the yellow brick road and gone for a run around Green Lake, a tree-lined jogging/strolling/people-watching jewel in the middle of the city, which "won" the Emerald City nickname in a tourism contest in the 1980s.

Later that day, Dorothy might have sent Auntie Em an e-mail to say she had just been hired as a project analyst at Microsoft and is putting a deposit on a new condo near the Pike Place Market, where she can pick up organic *biscotti* for her rock-climbing club's vegetarian picnic: "The commute will be a drag, Auntie Em, but I can buy a hybrid if I cut back to one chai latte a day."

The place and the people

Anthropologists theorize that climate and geography help shape behavior. The Northwest's moss greens, muted blues and overcast grays, combined with the gently persistent rains and the rounded hills that define many Seattle neighborhoods all contribute to a subdued, cool populace.

Seattle is a come-as-you-are city. Even

PRECEDING PAGES: watching from Kerry View Point Park as dusk descends on Mount Rainier; the famous flying fish of Pike Place Market.
LEFT: University of Washington cheerleaders.
RIGHT: Seattleite at work.

local billionaires dress in khakis and sweaters. It wouldn't be unusual to see opera fans in jeans and windbreakers. To understand Seattleites, consider how they have learned to dress for fickle Northwest weather – in layers.

Though many visitors never get past the smooth outer layer that sheds both rain and rudeness, under that is a second layer that keeps essential warmth close to the fleece vest, so to speak

It's not that Seattleites aren't interested in getting to know outsiders; it's more that their emotional "No vacancy" sign is lit because their lives are pretty full already. But if you inquire about their kayaking club or an upcoming Democratic fundraiser, they might offer detailed directions and even invite you to join their car pool.

Seattleites' political views tend to reflect the weather – moderate. Fact is, the past five Seattle mayors have been Democrats.

The high (tech) life

Not many barrel-chested lumberjacks are clomping around Seattle these days, but commercial fishermen can still be spotted unloading their catch at Fishermen's Terminal in Magnolia, not far from Queen Anne Hill. More and more, though, Seattle's economy is based on technology; it's got lots of sharp

and biotech companies. Microsoft alone has about 30,000 employees in the Puget Sound area, which accounts for half of the area's information-technology workers.

Seattle has a lot of wealth, but not a lot of bling. You won't catch Microsoft co-founders Bill Gates and Paul Allen or Amazon.com's Jeff Bezos riding around in stretch Bentley limos, flashing gold chains – or even wearing neckties most of the time. Seattle has no shortage of dotcom millionaires who live very well indeed, but their mansions tend to be nestled discreetly and anonymously behind a curtain of fir trees.

Stabled in their three-car garages are under-

minds, but not many sharp edges. In fact, Seattle tops the list of America's most educated cities, according to a Census Bureau study, with more than half of the city's population 25 years and older holding at least a bachelor's degree, and often more.

Up until 15 or 20 years ago, being an "engineer" in Seattle meant someone who worked at Boeing. The aviation company wings still cast a giant shadow across the region, where Boeing employs more than 64,000, but the job title nowadays is more often preceded by "software" and means he or she works for Microsoft, Amazon, Adobe, Expedia, Nintendo or one of dozens of other local internet

stated Audis, BMWs, Lexuses and an occasional Porsche rather than lipstick-red Maseratis or purple Dodge Vipers.

Many of those who are doing well are also doing good. The Bill & Melinda Gates Foundation, for example, is focused on global issues such as AIDS, tuberculosis and education. Charity auctions have no trouble raising generous sums to help organizations such as the Fred Hutchinson Cancer Research Center, which trains physicians from around the world in bone-marrow and stem-cell transplants, and Children's Hospital & Regional Medical Center, which leads the field in research on birth defects and gene therapy.

Manners matter

Seattleites enjoy a good rant but tend to vent considerately, via letters to the editor or call-in radio shows rather than in-your-face confrontations. One of their most frequent complaints is about *rudeness*, whether on the highway or in a restaurant.

Like the over-hyped rain that softens the edges of their city, Seattleites are generally well-mannered. They don't come on like hailstorms or hurricanes. If they tell you to get out, it's an encouragement to "go outside and *do* something."

In eclectic neighborhoods such as Capitol Hill, tolerance is an everyday thing – blue-

Road rage? Here, it's more like road *aggravation*. Tailgating and other angry behavior are increasingly common on Seattle freeways, but mayhem is minimal. Again, it's a relative thing – drivers from other parts of the country comment, "This is nothing like Phoenix/LA/Miami ..."

Fully half of Seattle drivers use their turn signals – it's not considered a display of weakness here – and they allow fellow drivers into their lanes if they *request* rather than demand room to move over. They let pedestrians cross the street, but blatant jaywalkers may receive a disapproving shake of the head – or a ticket. (Seattleites have

haired matrons share the busy sidewalk with blue-haired mohawks without so much as a raised eyebrow, plucked or pierced. The city's Gay Pride parade draws no more than a handful of protestors, vociferous but not venomous.

Seattleites *can* be rude when the situation warrants, such as when the Seahawks' football foes are trying to score at Qwest Field, or when the State Legislature votes to cut funding for maintenance of hiking trails in the Cascade Mountains.

FAR LEFT AND LEFT: Seattleites are even-tempered, understated and overtly concerned about nature. **ABOVE:** boys with their tech toys.

learned to wait for the "Walk" signal even when there's no traffic in sight, due to local law enforcement's propensity for slapping tickets on offenders.)

It's absolutely true that many Seattle motorists will choose to fume in silence behind a driver snoozing at a green light rather than honk and possibly cause the other person to be upset. It's not that they're all that serene and accepting, rather the fact that they just don't want to be rude. One local driver admitted that "I know it's been at least 20 years since I honked my horn, because that's when we got the Subaru, and I don't even know where the horn *is*."

Hey, growth happens

The Space Needle remains a proud if kitschy landmark, but Seattleites have grown up a lot since *It Happened at the World's Fair* with Elvis Presley more than 40 years ago. For example, the locals don't get all giddy now when Hollywood celebrities touch down at Boeing Field. After Elvis (1962), the Beatles (1964), starring roles in *Sleepless in Seattle* (1993) and the TV series *Frasier* (1993–2004) and *Grey's Anatomy* (2005–present), celebs aren't a big deal anymore.

There was a time when Seattleites blamed Californians for just about everything bad ("Californication," they called it): freeway congestion that is among the nation's worst, and spiraling housing prices, and property taxes. But with people moving in from *every* state, as well as China, Russia, Mexico, the Philippines, Vietnam, India and the Pacific Islands, their fingers couldn't point in all directions at once and the grumble evolved into a resigned sigh.

These days, the fingers tend to point at developers, who are accused of flattening forests to make way for "McMansions" and bulldozing neighborhood character by slapping together cookie-cutter condos.

Seattleites aren't in denial about the city's daily struggle with population growth, tangled

SEATTLEITES

According to local columnist and councilwoman Jean Godden, Seattleites never carry umbrellas, never shine their shoes and never turn on windshield wipers unless it's absolutely pouring. Godden also wrote that Seattleites seldom visit the Space Needle unless accompanied by visitors, seldom hail taxis, can describe 42 shades of gray, and think that a perfect day is 68°F (20°C), partly sunny, with a light breeze from the north. Seattleites also buy more sunglasses than residents of any other city in the United States, perhaps because they never expect to use them – only 50 days' sun on average each year – and so invariably have left them at home.

traffic and crime. Seattle is no Pleasantville, they will admit, but then add, "If so many people want to come here, we must be doing something right." They might remind you (politely) that Seattle was named the most-livable large city by the US Conference of Mayors in 2005, and according to a recent Gallup poll, 80 percent of those surveyed consider Seattle a safe place to live or visit.

Newcomers and natives

Finding a true, born-in-Seattle native is a challenge. It has gotten to the point where some now say that 20 years' residency qualifies a person to be an honorary native.

In a changing city where the population grew from 494,000 in 1980 to an estimated 572,600 in 2004, being new in town is no big deal. Ask a "local" for directions, however, and you may hear one of two apologies:

"Gee, I don't know. I just moved here last summer myself."

Or, "It's near the place that used to be a shoe-repair shop they tore down to build the apartments that aren't there anymore."

Either way, Seattleites aren't unwilling to help – for example, if you're lost, they may offer to lead you to your destination since they're headed in that general direction anyway. Or, if a dollar bill falls from your pocket

TRAVEL TIP

In Seattle, it is illegal to carry an aquarium or a fishbowl onto a bus, because the sound of the water sloshing may disturb other passengers.

● Can distinguish between resident orcas (not "killer whales," please) and transient visitors swimming in Puget Sound (hint: check their menu; residents prefer salmon, while the transient pods are fond of fresh seal and seabirds).
● Steps on a slug barefoot for the first time.
● Discovers that cotton is worthless when wet and invests in a serious rain parka.
● Can order the following coffee drinks with a

at the supermarket, they might follow you out to the parking lot to return it.

A newcomer becomes a Seattleite when he or she...

● First sets foot inside the REI flagship store, gazes up at the 65-ft (20-meter) indoor climbing pinnacle, then perhaps invests in that first rain-resistant microfiber jacket spun from recycled soda bottles.

FAR LEFT: father, son and Puget Sound.
LEFT: a lingering moment on Lake Washington.
ABOVE: Seattleites rarely dine at the Space Needle's restaurant, but they will be very polite when you do.

straight face: "harmless" (decaf espresso); "skinny" (non-fat milk), and "skinny harmless" (decaf, non-fat latte, also called a "Why Bother"). Or maybe a "double tall skinny foamless almond": two shots, tall cup, non-fat milk, no foam, with a shot of almond syrup.
● Is buoyed by a weather forecast of "sun breaks" and a chance to rush outside for a few fleeting minutes of Vitamin D before the clouds close in again.
● Can confidently pronounce Alki (AL-kye, rhymes with "pie"), Puyallup (pyoo-AL-up) and geoduck (GOO-ee-duck, a kind of clam with an obscenely long neck).
● Gently helps visitors understand that al-

though Puget Sound is saltwater, it is *not* the Pacific Ocean, and the ferries *Walla Walla* and *Spokane* do not actually *go* to those towns.

● Knows that a "mountain slowdown" traffic alert means morning commuters are easing up to let a massive, pink-and-silver Mount Rainier fill their windshields. "The mountain is out" is local shorthand for "Mount Rainier is clearly visible today."

Seattleites care about:

● Their environment, especially the water that rewards them with fresh food, fun and fantastic views. The long-term health of Puget Sound, in particular, is a major concern.

Charles and Ernestine Anderson to Woody Guthrie, Nirvana, Soundgarden, Pearl Jam, Kenny G, Sir Mix-a-Lot and Alice in Chains.

● And, yes, coffee. All those high-rpm minds need premium-grade fuel. The cliché about a coffeehouse on every Seattle street corner isn't far from fact, but only two-thirds of them are Starbucks, which leaves a lot of independents.

Half the patrons go to these places to share a latte with friends, while others plug into their social network via the city's free and plentiful Wi-Fi connections. (An Intel Corp. survey in 2005 named Seattle "the most unwired city in America," based on the availability of wireless internet – even the ferries have Wi-Fi.)

● Safe schools, state-of-the-art libraries, miles of bicycle paths and well-maintained parks with off-leash areas for their Golden Retrievers.

● The welfare of animals, both domestic and wild (urban dwellers find it a bit unsettling but also kind of cool to count raccoons, coyotes – and even an occasional befuddled black bear – among their neighbors).

● Recycling: Seattleites are slow to complain about sorting plastic, paper, glass and yard waste for curbside pickup. The city estimates that 40 percent of all garbage is being recycled now, heading toward a goal of 60 percent.

● The city's eclectic musical connections that range from Jimi Hendrix, Quincy Jones, Ray

It's true that Seattleites tend to be cool rather than warm, subdued rather than noisy. They value brain power and civility. They may not give you a bear hug and insist you come to dinner but they will give you the time of day, recommend their favorite restaurant and, with a polite but genuine smile, encourage you to enjoy your stay.

A local grade-schooler's advice, posted on a supermarket bulletin board, captures the Emerald City essence: "When in doubt, be nice." Dorothy herself couldn't have said it better. ❏

ABOVE: vintage vehicle, with view, West Seattle.

Seattlespeak

Mukilteo. Sequim. Humptulips. Enumclaw. Influenced especially by local Native American names, cartographers have made the state of Washington a minefield of barely pronounceable monikers. Skookumchuck? Puyallup? Pysht? The days when men spoke "with forked tongues" may be gone, but they've been surviving in Seattle in the era of the twisted tongue.

The most colorful place names have been taken from Chinook jargon, a mishmash of Native dialects that white settlers used to communicate with the previous stewards. Alki, for instance, which is a beach and an area of West Seattle, means "by and by." La Push, referring to a town at the mouth of the Quillayute River ("river with no head"), is at least geographically correct: it means, simply, "mouth." The language is still is use.

Other names are simply garbled versions of Native words. Snohomish, which refers to a city, a river and a county north of Seattle, does not exist in any known Native language, according to linguists. Its suffix, however – *ish*, which translates as "people" – is everywhere on local road maps. Sammamish means "the hunting people." Skykomish translates as "the inland people." Stillaguamish, Duwamish... these words come from different Native dialects, but they both mean "people living on the river."

So prominently did rivers and other bodies of water figure in the language of Northwest Indians that if someone were to ask you what a peculiar-sounding Washington name means, you could say "water" and stand a chance of being right.

Lucile McDonald, a prolific historian who lived east of Seattle in Redmond and Kirkland wrote that "Skookumchuck, Entiat, Cle Elum and Skamania all have to do with strong, swift or rapid water. Walla Walla and Wallula mean small, rapid river; Washougal is rushing water; Tumwater, a waterfall; Wenatchee, a river issuing from a canyon; Selah, still water; Pilchuck, red water;

Newaukum, gently flowing water; Paha, big water. Yakima is lake water. Sol Duc is magic water. Chelan is deep water." Which is exactly what outsiders find themselves in when trying to pronounce these names. When in doubt, refer to the book *Washington State Place Names*, by Doug Brokenshire, which offers not only the source of local appellations, but pronunciations, too.

Locals sometimes look at these mispronounceable monikers as their special revenge against the accents in other parts of the country. After all, as linguists are wont to remind Seattleites, Northwesterners have no discernible accent.

The Northwest's language differences are subtle. In New England, men who used to risk their lives cutting down forests were called "lumberjacks." In the Northwest, they're known as "loggers." Call somebody on a horse in eastern Washington a "cowpoke" and you're liable to earn a mean stare at best, a poke in the nose at worst. They prefer the name "buckaroo," pardner.

Despite its tenuous connections with the Old West of legend, Washington has appropriated a few discernible Westernisms. For instance, it's not uncommon in farming country to hear someone say "That's as useless as tits on a boar hog." ❑

RIGHT: the motto of Bulldog News is "where your neighborhood meets the world."

THE MAKING OF SEATTLE

The natural beauty of the Pacific Northwest,
rich with fish, fruit, produce and lumber,
nourished the nation for centuries. Then it gave
us the aerospace and software industries

The impression that visitors receive of Seattle today – a self-confident, prosperous, and eminently livable city – belies the eccentricity and gritty character that mark its earlier history. Dating from 1851 and carved from the primeval forests, Seattle has come into its own as a great American metropolis, but in the earliest days it resembled more the Native American village of "seven ill-looking houses" that Meriwether Lewis and William Clark found "at the foot of the high hill" when they concluded their transcontinental expedition of the Pacific Coast in 1805.

First inhabitants

The mild climate of Puget Sound, abundant with fish, wildlife and crops, was inhabited by peaceful tribes like the Salish and Duwamish. Fishing and hunting only their own lands, with seashells for currency, they bought dressed deer and elk skins from easterly inland tribes.

The Duwamish were enthusiastic about celebrating almost any occasion. The first salmon of each spring heralded a feast, as did the first deer, berries or fowl. In summer, eastern inland tribes came from the mountains to trade for seafood to help them survive the winter. Fishing, hunting, and berry-picking grounds were tribal territory. Using these lands without permission was seen as an invasion and frequently led to war.

The first Europeans to see this area landed under the command of an Englishman, Capt.

George Vancouver, near what is now Everett, north of Seattle, in 1792. The Hudson's Bay Company was based to the south in Fort Vancouver on the Columbia River, along the present-day border between Washington and Oregon. A rag-tag group of social outcasts was engaged to bring in the pelts of sea otters and beavers and deal with the indigenous peoples. Sir George Simpson was sent in the 1820s to organize the company's holdings, and he wrote of "The very scum of the earth, and the most unruly and troublesome gang to deal with in this, or perhaps any other part of the World." For three decades, the distant landlords of the Hudson's Bay Company dom-

LEFT: native village, Alert Bay.
RIGHT: Chief Sealth, for whom the city is named.

inated the Northwest, but the mid-19th century gold strike in northern California and the opening of new trails to the West pushed out the corporate bureaucrats and fur traders.

Pristine regions of the Pacific Coast were carved up by zealous city builders and entrepreneurs, and there were already a handful of settlers in Puget Sound when David Denny

reached the sandy spit of Alki Point – south of present-day downtown Seattle – in September 1851. The settlers at the newly named Alki-New York (*alki* meaning "by-and-by" in Chinook, and New York for Denny's home) came by way of Illinois, and through Portland, a burg already congested by 2,000 people. The Denny group decided to go farther north to Puget Sound, and the history of Seattle began.

Flattery and fraud

City building was a booming enterprise of the American 19th century. A determined developer laid claim to a location with promise, devised a town plan, then enticed settlers and investors, using any means at his disposal – from bribery and exaggeration to flattery and fraud. Thus began the towns of Steilacoom, Olympia, Whatcom, Port Townsend, Tacoma and, most successfully, Seattle.

A dismal winter showed Alki-New York was an unsuitable site for a cabin, let alone a city. Denny realized that a deep-water harbor would be needed, so he borrowed a clothesline, tied horseshoes to it, and took a dugout canoe along the coastline, plumbing the depths until he found deep water in Elliott Bay. The site for present-day Seattle had been chosen.

Denny, Charles Boren and William Bell staked out claims on the waterfront and were soon joined by Dr David Swinson Maynard. Medical doctor, merchant, lumberman, blacksmith, entrepreneur and all-around visionary, Maynard – like thousands of pioneer settlers – had come by the Oregon Trail, a 2,000-mile (3,200-km) trek, fraught with dangers of death and disease, from the Mississippi River through the Rocky Mountains to the mouth of the Columbia River.

Maynard searched Puget Sound for a place to open a business. The few still at Alki-New York and the Denny trio on Elliott Bay both wanted Maynard to join them "for the benefit," as one wrote, "a good man brings." Maynard thought the new town on Elliott Bay more likely to succeed, and it didn't hurt that Boren, Bell and Denny shifted their claims an eighth of a mile (200 meters) north to make room for his.

The first store

Maynard measured out about 300 yards (270 meters) of the most southerly deep-water frontage and took the rest of his claim in marsh and hill side. He hired local tribal men to build near the Sag, as they called the land by the water, and within a few days his new store was selling "a general assortment of dry goods, groceries, hardware, etc., suitable for the wants of immigrants just arriving."

In Olympia, Maynard had befriended an Indian *tyee* (chief) named Sealth (pronounced *see-alth* and sometimes *see-attle*), leader of the tribe at the mouth of the Duwamish River, where it entered Elliott Bay. In a breechcloth and faded blue blanket, the 6ft-tall (1.8-meter) chief with steel-gray hair hanging to his shoulders caused quite a stir among the settlers.

Europeans in the region considered him among the most important *tyee* in the territory. They were certainly more impressed with Sealth than his fellow people were. The tribes had their differences but they agreed on one thing: a chief had little personal authority, and his opinions carried little more weight than any other tribesman. Even so, in naming the new city Maynard's suggestion of Seattle – in honor of his noble friend – it replaced the native name used by the local authorities: Duwamps.

Two years earlier, a ship captained by G.W. Kendall had nosed past the Strait of Juan de Fuca in search of ice to cool drinks on the Barbary Coast of California. He settled for a load of piling, and timber became the region's first cash crop. Maynard employed Natives to cut a stand of fir behind the store into shakes, square logs, and cordwood, while others caught salmon and made rough barrels. When the ship *Franklin Adams* docked in October, the entrepreneur had 1,000 barrels of brined salmon, 30 cords of wood, 12,000 ft (3,700 meters) of squared timbers, 8,000 ft (2,400 meters) of piling and 10,000 shingles ready for shipping.

The salmon spoiled, which ruined most of his profits, but "Doc" Maynard's enthusiasm wasn't dimmed. What was good for Seattle was good for Maynard, so when Henry Yesler arrived scouting the Sound to locate a steam-driven sawmill, Maynard and Boren both contributed land at the water frontage.

Sawmills

The rugged residents built a log cookhouse and started on "Skid Road," a log slide for the timber to slip down the hill to the sawmill. When Yesler returned from San Francisco and set up his equipment, Seattle took a large step forward. "Huzza for Seattle!" said the paper in Olympia. "The mill will prove as good as a gold mine to Mr Yesler, besides tending greatly to improve the fine town site of Seattle and the fertile country around it, by attracting thither the farmer, the laborer, and the capitalist. On with improvement!"

Seattle became the government seat for King County, and Doc Maynard's little store became the site not only of the post office but even the Seattle Exchange.

Though the local tribes had at first welcomed the outsiders – and their wonderful tools, blankets, liquor, guns, and medicines – they soon rued new diseases; a religion that called Indian ways wicked (for reasons less than clear); and most perniciously, the notion of private property. By the time Doc Maynard helped broker a deal to buy their land, they were in a weak bargaining position. In 1854, a proposal, the Port Elliott treaty, was put to the Indians by a drunken Governor Stevens in Chinook Creole, a bastard tongue used by fur traders, more suited to rough commerce than diplomacy.

The US government offered the Native American tribes $150,000, paid over 20 years in goods, and a reservation, for 3,000 sq miles (8,000 sq km) of land. Chief Seattle, 12 inches (30 cm) taller than Stevens, answered on behalf of all the Indians in his language, Duwamish. Recalling the speech over three decades later, Dr. Henry Smith was taken "with the magnificent bearing, kindness and paternal benignity" of Chief Seattle.

"The Big Chief at Washington sends us word that he wishes to buy our lands but is willing to allow us enough to live comfortably," goes Smith's version of Chief Seattle's speech. "His people are many. They are like

LEFT: Dr David Swinson Maynard established the first store in 1853 and promoted the city enthusiastically.
RIGHT: sawmills dominated the streets of early Seattle.

the grass that covers vast prairies. My people are few. They resemble the scattering trees of a storm-swept plain. Every part of this soil is sacred in the estimation of my people. Every hill side, every valley, every plain and grove has been hallowed by some sad or happy event in days long vanished, and when the last Red Man shall have perished and the memory of my tribe shall have become a myth among the White Men, these shores will swarm with the invisible dead of my tribe."

The next year the treaty was signed and most Indians moved to reservations across Puget Sound. In 1856 though, some rebelled. There were few casualties on either side, and

daughter of Chief Seattle, worked as domestic help. "A good worker," said Sophie Frye Bass, niece of founder David Denny, "but when she had a fit of temper she would leave, even though she left a tub full of clothes soaking."

Racial problems

The mid-1880s were difficult times in Seattle. The city was hard hit by an economic depression afflicting the entire country. Out-of-work fishermen, lumber workers and miners competed for jobs – not only with unemployed city clerks and carpenters – but also with the many Chinese laborers discharged after completion of the railroads. The Chinese workers became

the US Army easily defeated the small group. Leschi was a rebel Indian leader, caught by the perfidy of a nephew, tried and convicted of murdering an officer during the war, and hanged. The so-called Indian War was over and the whites had won, but many issues, like territorial fishing rights, remain disputed to this day. Leschi became a regional hero, with a neighborhood, a park and a statue dedicated to his memory.

Seattle became an industrious village. Yesler's sawmill sent lumber to San Francisco, and sawdust filled the swampy lowland. Venison was sold for 10 cents a pound, where 8 ft- (2.5 meter-) thick trees still grew. Angeline, the

a scapegoat for the area's problems. Hard-working and uncomplaining, the Asian immigrants were resented by many unemployed Seattleites. The Knights of Labor, a white fraternal organization, wanted them ejected from the Northwest by force. In 1885, about 30 Chinese were driven out of nearby Newcastle.

In early 1886 Seattle exploded in racial violence. Five men were shot, Chinese stores and homes were demolished, and 200 Chinese were forced aboard a San Francisco-bound steamer. By March, when federal troops restored order, the Chinese community of about 500 had been eliminated.

By 1890, Seattle's population had more

than quadrupled, from 11,000 a decade before to 50,000. Three years later, the surge was over, but the city had become a very different place. Seattle was developing a sense of place, a personality and an identity.

An 1882 visitor had found it a "self-reliant, determined, well-governed" community with "exceptional public spirit." Observers stressed the "marvelous enterprise" of the city's inhabitants, calling it a virtual "paradise" for anyone willing to work hard. One New Englander found, "few flowers, less laughter, and a scarcity of tennis courts," but said Seattle's, "dogged determination and energetic push reminds me most strongly of Chicago."

The Great Fire and Skid Row

Nothing demonstrates Seattle's "can-do" attitude better than the city's reaction to John Back's blunder on June 6, 1889. Back, a handyman, threw a bucket of water on a flaming pot of glue in the middle of a paint store. The building exploded into flames, and 12 hours later the entire commercial district – 60 city blocks – was consumed. "Oh, lighthearted, industrious Seattle," a reporter wailed in Friday's *Seattle Daily Press*, "to be reduced to ashes in a single afternoon."

Before the "Great Fire," the commercial section of Seattle had become a pestilential morass. The downtown area was built on mudflats, and sewers backed up when the tide came in. Chuckholes and pools of mud would open up at intersections, swallowing a schoolboy, horses and even carriages. Typhoid and tuberculosis were rampant.

The fire allowed the overhaul of the municipal systems, and the city was rebuilt. Civic improvement began three days after the blaze, while the embers were still warm. Three years later, a new Seattle of brick and stone stood ready to lead the Pacific Northwest. New, higher roadways now reached the second stories of the buildings; people crossed the street by ladders. But the sidewalks and the ground levels 12 ft (4 meters) below needed to remain accessible. This two-tier city is now the sub-ject of a rambling, entertaining "Underground Seattle" tour *(see page 75).*

New wharves, railroad depots, freight sheds, coal bunkers and warehouses lined the mile-long waterfront strip. The sawmills moved out of town, leaving behind the name of Skid Road (now called Yesler Way). In later years, as this part of town became the haunt of homeless men and women, "Skid Row" became a term used in other US cities to describe poor and urban neighborhoods of broken dreams.

For much of the 1890s, Seattle was in decline. Skid Road was becoming dangerous and derelict, and business slumped – until the

arrival from Alaska of the SS *Portland* in July of 1897. Headlines screamed across the country the next day that the *Portland* docked bearing "A Ton of Gold Aboard." Seattle's then-mayor, W.D. Wood, heard news of the Yukon gold strike while visiting San Francisco, wired his resignation, and headed straight for gold country.

Yukon Gold Rush

The mania swept the Western world, as men from Sydney to Switzerland uprooted their lives and headed to the frozen fields of the Yukon, far to the north. Many of these treasure seekers needed to pass through Seattle.

LEFT: the Great Fire of 1889 allowed the city fathers to rebuild a safer, better metropolis.
RIGHT: miners pose on a Downtown street; the Yukon Gold Rush of 1897 made local merchants wealthy.

Tens of thousands of prospectors and unprepared fortune hunters hit the city, wanting supplies for their northbound adventure. Schwabacher's Outfitters rose to the top of the provisioning industry, and supplies for the trek north were stacked on the boardwalk 10 ft (3 meters) high. By the spring after the SS *Portland*'s arrival, Seattle merchants raked in some $25 million, against the previous year's revenues of $300,000. Hotels and restaurants were overbooked and Seattle banks filled with Yukon gold. Schools taught mining and classes were even given in dog-sled driving. This, in a city that rarely saw a snowflake.

The transient Gold-Rush population craved

entertainment. John Considine, patriarch of the famous acting family, opened up the People's Theater and brought in famed exotic dancer Little Egypt, who, clad in diaphanous harem clothes, gave a lesson in international culture – the muscle dance, the Turkish dance and the Damascus dance – for appreciative crowds almost every night of the year. Boxhouses – so-called for the private alcoves at the sides of the theater – were a feature of Seattle's nightlife.

Prostitution was a natural product of the mostly male lumber town. As early as 1861, an enterprising rake by the name of John Pennell established the Illahee (Salish for "homeland") over the mudflats, close by the mill – for its male workers. In view of arriving ships, Pennell's bordello was a landmark. The demographic discrepancy between men and women led Asa Mercer, a carpenter on the newly built Territorial University (and its first president), to secure a $300 fee from lonely Northwest bachelors with the promise of marriageable young maidens from the East Coast. He aimed to bring 500 women, but returned to Seattle a year later with just 100. But Mercer managed to placate his male clients, married one of his imports and moved inland.

The Klondike Gold Rush also confirmed Seattle as the Northwest's trade center, surpassing the older city of Portland, to the south. The boom raised Seattle's population to 80,000 by 1900; with three railroad lines and a road over the Cascades, numbers rose to a quarter of a million by 1910. Swedes populated the then-separate sawmill city of Ballard (now part of North Seattle). Laborers from Japan came in large numbers in the late 1890s, foreshadowing Seattle's later role as a shipping link to Asia and the Pacific.

The downtown area was regraded to reduce the inclines of the hills. Areas like Capitol Hill became neighborhoods of the utmost propriety. The high-class bordellos and cheaper "crib-houses" were closed, and John Considine moved from his first box-house theater on Skid Road into a vaudeville-theater chain that soon extended across the United States. Alexander Pantages, who began as a bartender in a Dawson saloon and also ran a box-house theater, rivaled Considine's chain. By 1926, Pantages owned the largest theater chain in the country. He later sold the chain, but his name lives on in film theaters.

The birth of Boeing

Seattle dominated the Alaskan shipping routes of the West Coast, and when the Panama Canal opened in 1914 and World War I brought increased demand for navy vessels, Seattle saw its future in shipbuilding and the sea. In 1910, at a makeshift airport south of Los Angeles, one wealthy Seattlite set his sights higher. The scion of a wealthy Minnesota iron-and-timber family with his own fortune from local timber, William Boeing was at the US's first international flying meet.

Boeing's initial interest in flying may have been on a par with his purchase of the Heath shipyards just in order to finish a yacht, but over Lake Washington, while testing a Curtiss-type hydroplane he built with friend and fellow Yale graduate Conrad Westervelt, he found a profession and a mission. In 1916, the company was incorporated in Seattle.

In the early 1930s, the economic body blow that followed the Great Depression hit Seattle harder than most cities. Skid Road saw an ever-growing population of the haggard and the hungry. A meal cost only 20 cents, but few on Skid Road could afford it. Still, there was order among the destitute.

The city's so-called Hooverville (Depression-era shantytowns were named after then-President Hoover), built on the tide flats in an abandoned shipyard, was among the largest temporary communities in the US. It had its own self-appointed vigilante committee to enforce a sanitation code. The Unemployed Citizens' League reached a peak membership of 50,000 in 1931, and formed a separate community – called the Republic of the Penniless – with a system of work and barter to feed and house its members. Those lucky enough to hold jobs were members of a network held in lock step with the powerful teamsters.

When non-union beer from the East Coast appeared in the Seattle area, teamsters refused to move it from warehouses. Local breweries benefited, helping to establish the strong Seattle tradition of regional breweries.

Big bombers and the Jet Age

World War II brought Seattle's next great economic boom. Although based partly on shipbuilding, this time the recovery was centered predominantly on one industry – aircraft – and one company – Boeing. Borne on the wings of Boeing's mass-produced B-17 Flying Fortress and B-29 Super Fortress bombers, the 1940 metropolitan population of about 450,000 grew another 50 percent by 1950. But the burgeoning economy was out of reach for the local Japanese population.

LEFT: Bill Boeing's industry dominated the region; be in a picture with him at the Future of Flight museum.
RIGHT: the World's Fair of 1962 was responsible for Seattle's most prominent landmark, the Space Needle.

WOMAN MAYOR

Bertha Knight Landes was elected mayor in 1926. She was the first female-elected executive in a major American city, and the only woman to date who has held the position of Seattle's mayor.

When President Franklin D. Roosevelt signed Executive Order 9066 in February 1942, 110,000 Japanese were summarily removed from their jobs and homes and interned in camps along the West Coast, Wyoming and Idaho. In Seattle, 7,000 Japanese lost everything they owned and spent the next three years in an Idaho camp.

SEATTLE WORLD'S FAIR
SEATTLE, WASH., U.S.A.
April 21-October 21
1962

Yet, like the Chinese before them, many Japanese returned to Seattle after the end of the war, even though their property was taken and despite the often overt racism they encountered almost daily.

Seattle also gained from the Korean War, with growing demand for B-47 and B-52 bombers. The civilian 707 launched Seattle's confident entry into the Jet Age. Nothing symbolized this better than the landmark of the skyline, the Space Needle, built for the 1962 World's Fair in Seattle.

Despite the massive lay-offs at Boeing in the late 1960s, Seattle continued to be a draw for newcomers. By 1970, the population had

Bill Gates and Microsoft

Every year since 1993, *Forbes* magazine has rated Microsoft chairman Bill Gates as the richest person in the world, mostly from his skill in training so many of the world's eyes on the Windows operating system.

By the year 2000, Gates had grown his locally based company to a valuation of $500,000,000,000 – which is more than all the US currency in circulation. In 2006, Gates' personal worth was estimated to be around $53 billion, and that's after $29

Bill Gates and Paul Allen

Bill Gates and Paul Allen, Microsoft's founding partners, in the early 1970s.

billion he endowed to scores of charities.

William H. Gates III, the son of a successful Seattle attorney, was born on October 28, 1955. Prodigious in math and science, he gained programing experience at the city's posh Lakeside School. At the age of 19, taking time out from Harvard, he founded Microsoft with an old friend, Paul Allen. Microsoft's phenomenal success is rooted in a 1981 coup to supply operating systems for IBM's new line of personal desktop computers. They licensed a system known as QDOS (Quick and Dirty Operating System), adapted it to produce PC-DOS, and effectively created a stranglehold on the

nascent PC market. In 1986, Gates sold some of his stock at $21 a share; in 1999, he sold nearly 10 million shares at $86 a share. In its heyday, Gates' worth increased by an average of $1 million a second.

Much is made of Gates' and Allen's wealth, but scores of employees also made millions through stock options. In the 1990s, the neighborhoods around Microsoft's headquarters in Redmond were (and still are) lush with dotcom success stories.

Microsoft's power base is still the operating system, but as the internet gained momentum in the mid-1990s, Gates steered the company's focus towards the net. Fearing the browsers of Netscape and AOL could relieve users' dependence on Windows, Microsoft began the "browser war" by creating Explorer; allied with NBC to create the cable-TV and online news service MSNBC; and bought web businesses from WebTV to Hotmail.

IBM and Microsoft parted ways long ago, the former at one point partnering up with ex-opponents Apple and Motorola, while the latter has gone from strength to strength. The operating system that powers more than 90 percent of the world's PCs makes Microsoft formidable. Recently, the company took a step into the games-console market with the Xbox, and is tilting at Apple's iPod market with the unpromising Zune.

Such staggering success has not gone unopposed. Microsoft attracted massive antitrust suits from both the US Government and the European Union, and in recent years there have been battles over copyright theft in China; open-source movements in South America; and the open-source operating system, Linux. But as an individual company that is still wealthier than all but half-a-dozen of the countries in the world, Microsoft is unlikely to be in any danger. In June 2006, Gates announced he would step back from running the company full-time in order to administer the charitable foundation he established with his wife, Melinda. ❏

LEFT: exhibit in the Microsoft headquarters in Redmond showing co-founders and boyhood friends Bill Gates and Paul Allen.

grown to more than 1.2 million. Attempts were made to raze older sections of the city, but the growing population was fostering an interest in preservation and renovating what remained of old Seattle.

Fire Mountain explodes

On May 18, 1980, nature took a stab at containing the growth of Seattle and the Pacific Northwest itself when Mount St Helens, south of Seattle, lived up to its Native American name of Fire Mountain. After 200 years of being virtually dormant, 9,667-ft (2,949-meter) Mount St Helens erupted, sending much of the mountain's summit 60,000 ft (18,000 meters) into the air.

The eruption came after warnings from scientists and attempts to evacuate the area, but the flow of molten rock and clouds of ash still resulted in almost 70 deaths. Damage was estimated at $1 billion. Within three days, the ash cloud had crossed North America; within two weeks, it had traveled right around the globe. Mount St Helens itself became 1,300 ft (400 meters) shorter than it had been before the blast. Ash fell throughout the Northwest in heavy amounts, hindering transportation, industry, and – in the short term – agriculture. Ultimately, of course, the ash injected nutrients into the soil, as it has throughout the formation of the earth's lands.

Logging and protests

Seattle's very earliest commercial trade was a shipload of lumber, and logging has been a vital part of the economy ever since. That said, the environmental implications of commercial timber and forestry have become increasingly important locally.

Since the 1990s, environmentalists have had some cause for optimism. Activists began to see some success in halting the clear-cutting of ancient forests. The US Forest Service was becoming more environmentally sensitive and more responsive to public desires. Pressure groups forced the government of nearby British Columbia to cancel logging rights and to protect some magnificent, centuries-old,

first-growth, temperate rainforests, principally on southwest Vancouver Island. Last-minute decisions made by outgoing president Bill Clinton in 1999 included a moratorium on new forest road construction on nearly 60 million acres (24.3 million hectares) of national forests – used as access roads for timber companies – as well as a program to close many such roads and to restore them to a natural state.

But America under President George W. Bush saw a roll back on environmental protections. The Bush administration revised Clinton's plans, causing outrage among environmentalists and relief among lumber companies. A report presented by US Forest Service chief

Dale Bosworth in 2002 criticized specifically the Northwest Forest Plan – implemented by the Clinton administration – to balance timber harvests and wildlife preservation in the region.

During the 1990s Seattle became less economically dependent on logging. And on Boeing, too. This was fortunate, as in 2001 Boeing moved its corporate headquarters to Chicago, cutting 20,000 jobs in the process. Taking their economic places have been a number of companies iconic in the modern, high-tech, globalized world, their skyrocketing success igniting love-hate passions from people all over the world, as well as among Seattleites themselves. Though residents love

---

RIGHT: logging has been a prosperous industry for decades, but in the 1990s, protestors became alarmed at the loss of old-growth forests.

the convenience of their personal computers, online shopping and coffeehouses on almost every corner, it goes against the city's personality to see these desires turn to needs – and for them to be met by so few companies.

The explosive growth in high-tech industries produced scores of young millionaires, as well as changes in the local landscape. First came Microsoft, a little software company founded by a couple of former Lakeside high school classmates, Paul Allen and Bill Gates. Local boy Bill Gates became the richest man in the world in 1993 *(see page 30)*. Paul Allen, the other co-founder, stepped out of day-to-day operations in 1983 and spent huge amounts of money in

launched in the late 1990s; another was Benaroya Hall, the home of the Seattle Symphony, which has a 2,500-seat concert hall and highly enviable acoustics.

Coffee and big-name companies

Another company to change the local landscape was Starbucks. The first branch of the coffee empire was opened in 1971, by three caffeine lovers who named their little business after the first mate in Moby Dick. The small store at Pike Place Market (which can still be visited) sold dark-roasted whole-bean coffee, but had no tables and chairs. Howard Schulz was hired by the company in 1981 and led a group to pur-

civic projects around the Puget Sound area. He founded Seattle's Experience Music Project, a dynamic interactive music museum designed in high style by architect Frank Gehry *(see photo on page 110)*.

He bought the Seattle Seahawks football franchise, securing the team's future in the city, and constructed a world-class stadium and exhibition center on the site of the old Seattle Kingdome, adjacent to Safeco Field, the state-of-the-art baseball stadium that opened in 1999. Two years earlier, Allen purchased and began preservation work on Union Station, a century-old Seattle landmark. These are only two of many ambitious new projects the city

chase it in 1987. After an initial public offering in 1992, the first Starbucks outside North America opened in Tokyo in 1996; by 2006, nearly 11,000 stores sold coffee in more than 30 countries. And the company is still growing. Schulz endeared himself to Seattleites by leading a group to buy the city's basketball team, the SuperSonics, in 2001, but incurred their wrath by selling the franchise – including its women's team, the Seattle Storm – in 2006.

In the 1990s, Seattle became a high-tech mecca for companies such as Amazon.com and Nintendo of America. Even after the dotcom bubble burst, these companies stayed strong. In 1994, Pioneer Square-based Aldus Software, maker of popular software such as PageMaker and founded by Paul Brainerd, merged with Adobe Systems and set up shop in the Seattle neighborhood of Fremont.

Jeff Bezos launched his online bookstore, Amazon.com, in 1995 and soon added software, CDs, movies and video games. The company, headquartered in a former hospital on Beacon Hill, survived the "dot bomb," but remarkably didn't turn its first annual profit until 2003.

21st century and more

A magnitude-6.8 earthquake struck the Seattle area in February 2001, and caused property damage throughout the region, including to the

been at some cost, however. It has a dubious distinction as one of the nation's worst cities for traffic. The Interstate-5 corridor is particularly crowded, and the situation culminated in an incident that made international headlines. During a morning rush hour, a woman threatening to jump from the Ship Canal bridge held up traffic for hours. Impatient commuters yelled, "jump, bitch, jump!" Eventually she did (she survived). The riots at the 1999 World Trade Organization conference, and again at a 2001 Mardi Gras festival dented Seattle's image of politeness and courtesy. Neighborhoods changed. House prices kept rising.

But then, so did fantastic new buildings. The

Capitol building in Olympia. The epicenter of the quake was about 10 miles (16 km) northeast of Olympia, and 32½ miles (52 km) underground. Unlike many regions on the continent, the Pacific Northwest coastal area has constant reminders of its geological history and origins, the eruption of Mount St Helens being only one such example.

Seattle's latter-day phenomenal success has

FAR LEFT: riots following protests at 1999's World Trade Conference dented the city's polite image.
LEFT: installing Claes Oldenburg's *Typewriter Eraser* at the Olympic Sculpture Park, September 2006.
ABOVE: culture and commerce at the Central Library.

city's skyline has been complemented by a new home for the city's football team, Qwest Field (2002), and the Olympic Sculpture Park (2007).

The Washington State Ferries terminal, the Seattle Art Museum and the Seattle Aquarium have all been expanded or remodeled. The Rem Koolhaas-designed Seattle Public Library opened in 2004, with new branches in Ballard, Greenwood and Montlake. Better transportation links are planned, and the Metro bus system wins awards for efficiency and friendliness.

The scenery remains unrivaled in beauty, and resilience has become a desirable quality. So, despite setbacks, Seattle's reputation as a highly livable city remains intact. ❑

Decisive Dates

20,000 BC Small bands of Ice Age hunters cross the Bering Land Bridge from Asia.
7000–1000 BC Tribes of the Puget Sound region become dependent on fishing.
1592 Spanish ships visit the region.
1790 Chief Sealth – also known as Seattle – is born in the Puget Sound area.
1792 English navigator Capt. George Vancouver lands near present-day Everett, north of Seattle. His expedition explores Puget Sound, named for Peter Puget, a lieutenant on Vancouver's crew.
1820s The Hudson's Bay Company expands its

operations in the Pacific Northwest, based in Fort Vancouver, at the mouth of the Columbia River.
1833 The Hudson's Bay Company establishes Fort Nisqually in present-day Tacoma.
1851 David Denny and a group of settlers arrive at Alki Point, in what is now West Seattle. They name their settlement Alki-New York.
1852 Disappointed by Alki Point's severe weather and poor port potential, Denny and his crew shift north to Elliott Bay, near present-day Seattle.
1853 The relocated town is laid out and named for Chief Sealth (Seattle), a friend of the settlers.
1854 A treaty with the local tribes provides for the newcomers to "buy" Indian land.
1855 Chief Seattle – leader of the Duwamish,

Suquamish and other Puget Sound tribes – signs the Port Elliott treaty, giving away Indian land and establishing a reservation.
1856 Some Indians rebel against the treaty, but the rebellion is quickly quenched by the US Army.
1861 The well-regarded University of Washington is established.
1864 The transcontinental telegraph connects Seattle with the rest of the United States.
1866 Chief Seattle dies at the Port Madison Reservation, Washington.
1882 Flamed by the economic depression, animosity against Chinese immigrants increases.
1883 The city of Tacoma is incorporated.
1886 Racial violence breaks out against Chinese residents. Five men are shot and Chinese stores and homes are destroyed. Two hundred Chinese are forced onto a San Francisco-bound ship.
1889 A handyman pours water onto a flaming pot of glue in a paint store. The resulting explosion and fire destroys the entire 60-block downtown area of Seattle.
1890 The population of Seattle reaches 50,000; the city erects a monument to Chief Seattle.
1893 The Great Northern Railway arrives, making Seattle a major rail terminus.
1897 The SS *Portland* sails into the city, carrying hundreds of thousands of dollars worth of gold from the Yukon's Klondike. Seattle's mayor resigns and heads north for the gold.
Late 1890s Japanese laborers begin arriving.
1900 In Tacoma, Midwesterner Frederick Weyerhaeuser buys 900,000 acres (360,000 hectares) of Pacific Northwest timberland unwanted by the Northern Pacific Railroad.
Early 1900s Hills in the downtown area are removed by sluicing methods and the earth is used for harbor landfill. Ten surrounding cities and towns are annexed by Seattle.
1909 The Alaska-Yukon-Pacific Exposition is held.
1910 The city's population reaches 250,000.
1914 The Panama Canal opens, increasing Seattle's importance as a Pacific port.
1916 The Lake Washington Ship Canal opens. William Boeing, a prosperous lumberman, incorporates the Pacific Aero Products Company.
1917 Pacific Aero Products Company is renamed the Boeing Airplane Company.
1919 The country's first and longest general strike is held in Seattle; however, it becomes a tactical error as some of its supporters are targeted as Communists.

1928 Boeing becomes part of the United Aircraft & Transport Corporation, a merger of several aircraft manufacturers and airlines under the chairmanship of Boeing.

1934 Antitrust rules force United Aircraft & Transport to break up. Boeing emerges, as does United Airlines and United Aircraft.

1935 The B-17 *Flying Fortress* is first flown.

1941 The US entry into World War II invigorates Seattle's importance, both in shipbuilding and in aircraft manufacturing.

1942 6,000 Japanese-Americans are shipped from Seattle and placed in Idaho internment camps. James Marshall Hendrix, a.k.a. Jimi Hendrix, is born in Seattle.

1950 An economic recession is squelched by the Korean War; Seattle builds B-47 bombers.

1958 The Boeing 707 commercial passenger jet is introduced for regular service.

1960 Seattle's population exceeds 1 million.

1962 The Seattle World's Fair introduces the city – and the Space Needle – to the world.

1969 Boeing lays off 60 percent of its employees as the demand for commercial aircraft plummets. The city's economy heads into a tailspin.

1970 The Boeing 747 is put into service, with twice the carrying capacity of any previous passenger jet.

1971 The first Starbucks opens, situated in Pike Place Market.

1979 Seattle's SuperSonics win the National Basketball Association (NBA) championship.

1980 After being dormant for almost 200 years, the volcano of Mount St Helens explodes to the south of Seattle.

1982 The so-called Green River Killer begins a 49-person murder spree. He is never caught.

1992 Seattle becomes a music center as grunge music – Nirvana, Pearl Jam – sweeps the world.

1993 *Forbes* magazine rates Microsoft chairman Bill Gates as the richest man in the world.

1998 Adobe moves into an office park under the Fremont Bridge.

1999 Safeco Field replaces the Kingdome to host Major League baseball; Canada and the US sign a salmon-fishing treaty. Protesters shut down the World Trade Organization conference in high-profile clashes with the police; an antitrust trial involving Microsoft begins.

LEFT: tribal mask of Goomokwey, master of the deep.
RIGHT: multi-screening at Microsoft's headquarters.

2000 The controversial Frank Geary-designed building for the Experience Music Project opens; some people like it, but some think its architecture is too glossy for the city's laid-back image.

2001 The tech boom collapses and many people leave town. There's a nasty Mardi Gras riot. An earthquake measuring 6.8 on the Richter scale hits the area. Boeing moves its corporate headquarters to Chicago and many jobs are lost.

2002 Seahawks Stadium (now Qwest Field) opens for the NFL season; Seattle Central Community College is named College of the Year by *Time* magazine; Boeing's post-September 11 job losses hit 35,000; the US District Court conditionally approves a Microsoft antitrust settlement.

2003 Seattle-based Amazon.com turns its first profit after several years of trading.

2004 With women's national basketball, the city wins its first national sports title since 1979.

2005 Voters pass the strictest smoking ban in the US, prohibiting smoking in all workplaces, bars and restaurants and within 25 feet (7.6 meters) of doors and windows.

2006 Starbucks CEO Howard Schultz sells the Seattle SuperSonics basketball team to a group of Oklahoma City businessmen; the Seattle Seahawks (football) play their first Super Bowl; Seattle breaks a 73-year-old record for the most rain in one month (November).

2007 The Olympic Sculpture Park opens. ❏

Kindly Turn Off
Cell Phones & Pagers

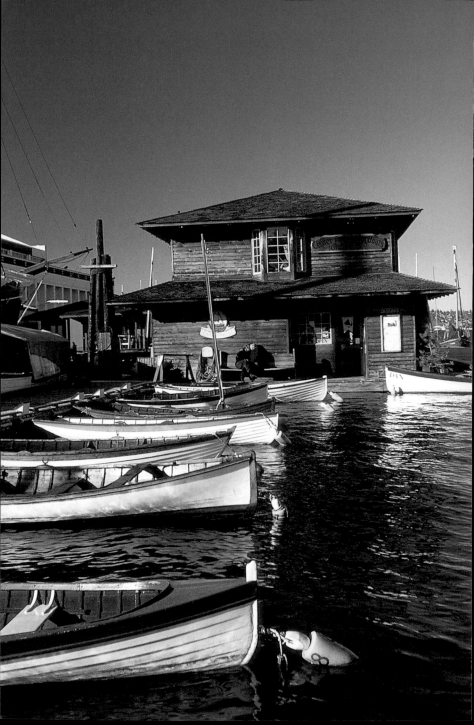

LIVING WITH WATER

Seattle is so close to the water it's an integral
part of the environment, and Seattleites
take full advantage of it

The water is more than a feature of the Northwestern landscape. The voluptuous shores and salt tides of Puget Sound, and the deep currents of the Columbia, Salmon and Snake rivers have carved the living environment. They are an integral part of it. The proverbial edge of the world is a Pacific coastline where the rain forests and rocky peninsulas are entwined with the sea.

It's water that keeps Washington green (a popular slogan on highway signs), and which also supports such a healthy fish, bird and sea-mammal population. It also provides plenty of opportunities for recreation; it's estimated that one in every six Seattleites owns a boat – whether it's a rowboat, a sailboat, a yacht or a kayak. With saltwater Puget Sound and a handful of in-city freshwater lakes, plus an 8-mile (13-km) ship canal linking the Sound to Lake Washington via another lake – Lake Union – Seattle has more than enough places to cruise, paddle and sail.

So, surrounded by water, people here don't expect to impose rhythm and tempo on nature in the way that southern Californians do or asphalt does across a Southwestern desert. This distinction – that Northwesterners are more changed by environment than it is by them – is crucial to understanding the local character. Seattleites and Pacific Northwesterners are a dreamy group, in a fine tradition of dreamers.

PRECEDING PAGES: waiting for the symphony at Benaroya Hall; posing and pouting at the Tractor Tavern.
LEFT: an afternoon by the Center for Wooden Boats.
RIGHT: fisherman at Seattle's Fishermen's Terminal.

Ferry first

For visitors who come to Seattle without a boat in tow, one of the easiest ways to get out onto the water is on a Washington State Ferry. Some of the best views of the Seattle skyline are from departing and arriving ferries, so it's worth timing in- and out-bound journeys at sunset or the evening to take full advantage. There are more ferries, carrying more passengers and vehicles, in Washington state than anywhere else in the US. Every year, 29 ferries transport at least 26 million passengers and more than 11 million cars. Popular routes link Seattle's Coleman Dock with the island town of Bremerton, and downtown Seattle to

Writing in the Rain

The *Seattle Times* in 1953 announced: "This January, Wettest Ever, Getting Wetter," proclaiming a 40-year-old record for January 27 broken that day. In June 1985, columnist Don Hannula asked, "Rainless Seattle: Will We Become Another Tucson?" "Drop In the Bucket: That Splatter Didn't Matter," was a later headline in the *Seattle Times*. In a city with only 50 totally clear days per year it is the lack of rain that provided the most stories. "How long, O Lord, How Long?" bemoaned columnist

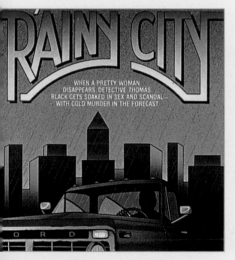

John Hinterberger in a year that clocked up only about half of the city's usual annual downpour. "What is giving us all this troublesome, lovely weather?"

Rainless summers can be troublesome indeed for Seattle, and that particular year lowered the Cedar River, where 300,000 salmon spawn, and slowed turbines which supply much of the city's power to half speed. The Fisheries Department worried, "There isn't enough water to cover all the gravel [in the river]."

Seattle's reputation as the rainiest city in America began to dry up. According to *The Best and Worst of Everything* by Les Krantz,

Seattle doesn't even make it into the top 10 list of US cities. The wettest ones – including Hilo, Hawaii; Pensacola, Florida; and New Orleans, Louisiana – actually get at least 10 inches more rain each year than the Emerald City does. Just as things were calming down, though, on November 30, 2006, the *Seattle Post-Intelligencer* (the city's other daily metro paper) reported, "It's Never Been This Wet," announcing a 73-year-old record for the rainiest month (previous record: 15.33 inches/38.9 cm in 1933).

Records to one side, what seems to make the difference here is the rain's ubiquity, a sheer, steady saturation slanting from what a 1902 columnist called "the humid vats of heaven." It rains so frequently yet so unobtrusively in Seattle that few people wear coats and fewer admit to owning umbrellas. In fact, one department store calculates it sells at least 13,000 brollies each year, while more than half that number are left on buses. A *Seattle Weekly* writer said, "drizzle and gray become the badge of pride for those who stay, and the curse that drives others away."

Local legend Craig Cappuccino, said to be Seattle's first outdoor espresso cart barista, waited week after week in the rain until customers came, building up a mystical connection between sipping and soaking that marks the espresso aficionado.

Walter Rue, author of *Weather of the Pacific Coast* said, "If the sun doesn't shine we don't consider the day lost. People here don't complain about a little rain." The *Weekly* quoted a visitor from Kansas: "People get nervous when it's sunny. They feel exposed. They like the gray days; they wrap up in them like a security blanket."

The late *Seattle Times* man Emmett Watson advocated The Lesser Seattle Movement, a disinformation program to promote the wet weather and discourage would-be Seattleites. Columnist Jean Godden helped his cause with "38 Things To Do In the Rain." High on the list was "Write letters to all your friends, and tell them how horrible the weather is. Tell them this isn't even a nice place to visit…" ❏

LEFT: how one writer sees Seattle.

Bainbridge Island. A passenger-only ferry takes commuters to Vashon Island. These are only a few of the many water routes that link Seattle to the rest of the Pacific Northwest.

Premonitions and belief

According to the Wasco Natives along the Columbia River, the tribe knew well before the white men came ashore at Alki Point in 1851 that a change was coming. As told in Ella Clark's classic *Indian Legends of the Pacific Northwest,* one of the Wasco elders dreamed that "white people with hair on their faces will come from the rising sun." The strangers were prophesied to bring with them "iron birds that

the movements of the shifting tides, how much more deeply might we be affected by the water's relationship with us?

Rain is a Northwest native and perhaps is all that shelters locals from the massive population and industrial exploitations of California to the south. The rain is so omnipresent, especially between October and June, that most Northwesterners disdain umbrellas.

Port Angeles poet Tess Gallagher explains it this way: "It is a faithful rain. You feel it has some allegiance to the trees and the people… It brings an ongoing thoughtfulness to their faces, a meditativeness that causes them to fall silent for long periods, to stand at their win-

fly" and "something – if you just point it at anything moving, that thing will fall down and die." These strangers also brought new tools and stoves to cook on. Along with new technology, these newcomers also brought the concept of land ownership.

The tribesmen felt that the land could not be owned, just as we may presently believe that the air or the clouds cannot be owned. Even now, Puget Sound property rights ebb and flow according to the tides, not by the boundaries set by legal land ownership. If even the ownership of Northwest land can be influenced by

ABOVE: love under the raindrops at the marketplace.

dows looking at nothing in particular. The people walk in the rain as within some spirit they wish not to offend with resistance."

Storytellers

The Northwest character is flexible, without the rigidness found on the East Coast. The Native Americans were known not as warriors but as fishermen. Although there were disputes over territory, there was also a diversity and abundance of food that was different from other tribes' struggles over scarce resources. With all this plenitude, traditions of Northwestern art flourished, and with it the richness of tribal storytelling.

In keeping with the landscape's watery changes, Native stories are full of legends in which animals change easily into people and back again. The Salmon People are an underwater tribe who also spend a season on land; the whales and seals can metamorphose into humans as easily as the ever-present mist, and clouds change into different shapes. Many Northwest coast tribes tell of merpeople – part human, part fish – who mediate between the worlds to keep a watery balance. One of the most respected Native gods was called Changer, a name perhaps explained by the local adage that if you don't like the weather, wait five minutes and it will change.

Many tribal mythologies have their roots in the water, the floods and the seas creating what we now know as, "the people." A Skagit creation story describes this beginning as happening when Changer decided to "make all the rivers flow only one way," and that "there should be bends in the rivers so that there would be eddies where the fish could stop and rest. They decided that beasts should be placed in the forests. Human beings would have to keep out of their way."

Take a step back

Here in the Northwest it is human beings who are urged to take a step back. People here tend

SEATTLE'S SOUND

Puget Sound, known by the native tribes as Whulge, was explored in 1792 by Captain George Vancouver. He named the sound for Peter Puget, a lieutenant in his expedition who probed the main channel. The southern terminus of the Inside Passage to Alaska, Puget Sound is a deep inlet stretching south for 100 miles (160 km) from Whidbey Island (north of which are the straits of Georgia and Juan de Fuca). Hood Canal, which defines the Olympic Peninsula, is an extension of the Sound. Rivers that enter the Sound include the Skagit, Snohomish and Duwamish. Puget Sound has several deep-water harbors, among them Seattle, Tacoma, Everett and Port Townsend.

to pride themselves, perhaps a little arrogantly, on living within nature's laws, on listening to the environment. It is here in the Northwest where the last nurturing old-growth forests stand in the lower 48 states – a topic of sharp, ongoing economic and social debate.

Oil spills have blackened the beaches, and species of salmon are endangered. Gray whales are found on their migrating courses belly-up from pollution in Puget Sound. There have been major closures of shellfish beds throughout the region because of toxic contaminations from industrial waste.

There is a growing movement among Pacific Northwest corporations to return some of their profits to protect the wilderness. Recreational Equipment Inc. (REI) and Eddie Bauer are two such businesses that believe in investing in local environmental resources. Boeing and the corporation's employees contribute to numerous charities, some of them environmental.

A former Microsoft manager created Social Venture Partners, a foundation to teach young tech millionaires about philanthropy, while in 2006, supremo Bill Gates announced that he would step down from the day-to-day running of the corporation to devote more attention to the foundation he has set up with his wife.

Just as Northwesterners claim closeness with their natural world, so too, they claim to be

WI-FI OVER THE WATER

So many people commute to and from Seattle by ferry, that in November 2006 – Seattle's wettest month for 73 years – representatives of Washington State Ferries announced onboard wireless internet access.

the spirit world." (Modern scientific thought seems to run along surprisingly similar lines.)

Human worries and foibles appear to carry less weight in this region surrounded by water. It is typically Northwestern that this "gone-fishing-while-the-world-falls-apart" attitude prevails, while in New York or Washington, DC, a population is transfixed by the TV

close to their history. The non-Native history here is less than 200 years compared with thousands of years of Skagit, Suquamish, Muckleshoot, Okanogan and other tribal roots. Some of the myths favored by Native Americans calmly predict that "the human beings will not live on this earth forever."

This prediction is an agreement between Raven, Mink, Coyote and what the Skagits call "Old Creator," concluding that human beings "will stay only for a short time. Then the body will go back to the earth and the spirit back to

LEFT AND ABOVE: it's said that Northwesterners are more changed by their environment than it is by them.

news. It's not that Northwesterners aren't involved, it's just that nature can be an antidote to such strong doses of conflict. Nature can also remind us that there are other mysteries at work in the world that just might hold more power than our own.

Water, water everywhere

The water grows the fruit and nourishes the cows that provide the meat. It gives a home to the salmon, and offers an endless playground for boats. What's more, it is believed to be one of the few things that keeps people from other parts from migrating here en masse. In a rainy, watery world, what's not to like? ❏

MUSIC, CULTURE AND THE ARTS

Go to an event and the audience will be dressed in
anything from Louis Vuitton to Levis. This glam-to-grunge
mix is a reflection of the Northwest's cultural style

From grunge legend Kurt Cobain to expatriate author Alice B. Toklas, Seattle's arts and culture scene is as varied as its inhabitants. With the discerning tastes of New Yorkers and the laid-back attitude of Midwesterners, Seattleites love both high- and low-brow entertainment any night of the week.

Ultra-sexy small clubs throughout the city host live music; local playwrights showcase their talents to packed houses in fringe theaters; and neighborhood galleries lure jeans-clad crowds to view local, national and international art. Seattle is a place where Louis Vuitton and Levi mingle – sometimes in the same outfit – and its arts and culture scene reflects this.

Live Music

Seattle is perpetually defined by its music scene, as the Paul Allen-funded Experience Music Project at Seattle Center attests (see pages 110–11). Love or hate the building's conspicuous Frank Gehry-designed exterior, the museum's interior is filled with attractions to appease all modern music fans, from Jimi Hendrix to Janis Joplin to a gallery devoted to the development of the "Northwest sound," as well as hands-on exhibits for aspiring musicians.

Long known as the birthplace of grunge rock (a la Kurt Cobain and Eddie Vedder), Seattle has a lively music scene beyond bass guitars and gritty vocals. From the highly regarded Seattle Symphony and Seattle Opera to concert series featuring star-studded line-ups and small

LEFT: the Chihuly Bridge of Glass in Tacoma.
RIGHT: Hendrix X 20 at the Experience Music Project.

venues hosting up-and-coming musicians – from jazz to indie rock – Seattle is a mecca for all musical tastes. Classical music aficionados head to Benaroya Hall, where Gerard Schwartz conducts the Seattle Symphony, which celebrated its centennial in 2003, and a distinguished roster of guest artists perform. Marion Oliver McCaw Hall is home to the Seattle Opera, with a commonly sold-out year-round schedule and the critically acclaimed Wagner's Ring Cycle performance every four years.

Beyond these first-class venues for the performing arts, the glory days of grunge still inspire a burgeoning music scene of innovative sounds for today's tastes. Those looking for live music find it at a variety of small venues – the Crocodile Café, Tractor Tavern, Jazz Alley, Showbox and Chop Suey, among others. The most complete gig listings can be found in the city's two free weekly publications, *Seattle Weekly* and *The Stranger.*

In summer, outdoor concerts feature a top-notch list of popular artists – plus opportunities to enjoy live music while picnicking. The Woodland Park Zoo hosts Zoo Tunes, drawing artists such as the Indigo Girls and indie-phenomenon The Decemberists. And Wood-inville's Chateau Ste. Michelle winery presents a blend of blues, jazz and rock, June through September, at its outdoor amphitheater. Con-

Dance

In the 1970s, a generation of aspiring choreographers moved to Seattle to perform and study with acclaimed modern-dance choreographer Bill Evans, whose dance company had just completed a national tour. Since then, dance – from classic to interpretive to modern – has found a sturdy foundation on Seattle stages, which have spawned choreographers such as Trisha Brown, Mark Morris, Pat Graney and Christian Swenson.

The state's largest professional contemporary dance company, Spectrum Dance Theater, has garnered national and international attention. When the company is not touring, it holds

certgoers bring their own dinners, buy a bottle of wine and dance in the grass to big-draw performers such as Pink Martini, Elvis Costello, Lyle Lovett and the Steve Miller Band.

Every Labor Day weekend Bumbershoot, one of the nation's largest urban arts festivals, floods the Seattle Center with writers, poets, craftspeople and performing artists. Though music is a primary draw, the nonstop showcase of musicians and rising stars on 30 different indoor and outdoor venues is complemented by crafts booths, fare from local restaurants and even an animated short-film festival.

In typical Seattle fashion, the shows go on, rain or shine.

most of its performances at the Moore Theatre.

And, recognized as one of the first institutions in the country to premiere experimental modern works by both national and international artists, On the Boards – nearly three decades old – is Seattle's premier contemporary performance organization. It showcases breakthrough performances by local artists in its spring Northwest New Works Festival and 12 Minutes Max, which highlights emerging artists, around six times a year.

Seattle's celebrated ballet company, the Pacific Northwest Ballet, draws the highest per-capita dance attendance in the country. Led by artistic director Peter Boal, the ballet's active repertoire includes classics such as *Swan Lake* and the popular annual performance of *Nutcracker*, choreographed by founding artistic director Kent Stowell, with sets designed by children's-book illustrator Maurice Sendak (*Where the Wild Things Are*).

On the screen

Far from the snowy peaks of Sundance or the sun-drenched beaches of Cannes, Seattle has its own film festival that draws close to 200,000 people to see more than 300 films each spring on Capitol Hill. From late May to mid-June, the Seattle International Film Festival premieres independent, documentary and foreign films

Jackson in January. Other local fests include the Seattle Jewish Film Festival (March); the Seattle Arab and Iranian Film Festival (March–April); the Langston Hughes African American Film Festival (April); Seattle's True Independent Film Festival (June); and the Seattle Lesbian & Gay Film Festival (October).

Visual Arts

As varied and distinctive as its inhabitants, Seattle's visual arts scene has a lot to offer – from paintings and photography to sculptures and video installations. At the center of it all, the Seattle Art Museum is internationally recognized for its extensive collection of African,

from many genres. Movies such as *Burning in the Wind* (2003) and *Nate Dogg* (2003) had their world premieres here, and many more, such as *Monster House* (2006) and Gus Van Sant's *Last Days* (2005) made North American debuts.

SIFF may be the city's largest film festival, but Seattle hosts several others throughout the year. Washington state's largest showcase for Asian American films, the Northwest Asian American Film Festival, is held at Theatre Off

Native American and Asian art, as well as modern art by Pacific Northwest artists. The permanent collection includes 21,000 pieces, and blockbuster exhibits visit the museum on an ongoing basis.

The museum's sister space, the Seattle Asian Art Museum, is housed in an Art-Deco structure on Capitol Hill and comprises an incomparable collection of Asian art and artifacts, from 4,000-year-old Japanese tomb art to 19th-century Chinese snuff bottles, as well as contemporary pieces. Thanks to its stately showcase of items, the museum ranks as one of the top collections outside Asia. In early 2007, SAM opened its Olympic Sculpture Park, a 9-acre (3.6-hectare)

FAR LEFT: sharp harp and shades in North Seattle.
LEFT: show time at the Repertory Theatre.
ABOVE LEFT: dance nite at the Tractor Tavern.
ABOVE RIGHT: Dale Chihuly at a Pilchuck fundraiser.

outdoor sculpture museum on the waterfront. The public space features visiting installations, as well as permanent works by celebrated artists like Louise Bourgeois, Roy McMakin and Richard Serra. And additionally, the park features one of the city's most celebrated visuals: dynamic views of the Olympic Mountains, Puget Sound and Seattle's cityscape. Not to mention the fact that it's all free.

On First Hill is the Frye Art Museum, where a modern façade hides a classical interior filled with representational landscape and portrait works as well as 19th-century German paintings from the collection of museum founders' Charles and Emma Frye. The Henry

fodder in Seattle's many galleries, some of which are located within walking distance of one another in Pioneer Square.

Literature

Year round, in cafés throughout the city, you'll find Seattleites lost in books – lattes in hand. But reading is not just a casual pastime for its literary-inclined residents, it's a *joie de vivre*.

Author events are held – and highly attended – throughout the area, from theater-packed lectures by famous authors to intimate readings at locally owned book stores. And writers such as Jonathan Raban *(Arabia: A Journey Through the Labrynth)*, Jon Krakauer *(Into Thin Air)* and

Art Gallery, on the University of Washington campus, is the Northwest's premier contemporary art space.

South of Seattle, in Tacoma, is the Museum of Glass, offering glass-blowing demonstrations as well as three galleries of contemporary glass-art exhibitions. The museum is linked to the Tacoma campus of the University of Washington by the Chihuly Bridge of Glass, a 500-ft (152-meter) pedestrian overpass filled with glass. Tacoma is the home town of world-renowned glass artist Dale Chihuly, who co-founded the Pilchuck Glass School in Stanwood, Washington, in 1971.

Art collectors and browsers find endless

David Guterson *(Snow Falling on Cedars)* have made the city their home, further raising Seattle's reputation as a creative mecca.

Seattle Arts & Lectures, founded in 1987, hosts an annual poetry series and its annual Literary Lecture Series, which has presented numerous literary giants including Stephen King, Frank Rich and Margaret Atwood. The quintessential Northwest bookstore, Elliott Bay Book Company – independent and family-owned since 1973 – offers a noteworthy line-up of speakers, paying equal attention to local and international writers. The store hosts author events ten times in an average week, and these are usually free.

Theater

Theater has well-established roots in Seattle. From fringe to top-notch traveling shows, the Seattle stage has a devoted audience. And as the city's reputation as the Broadway capital of the West Coast – with many Broadway-bound shows making their debuts in Seattle – shows, both large and small, will undoubtedly continue having successful runs.

Broadway-style shows can be found at the 5th Avenue Theatre, where *Hairspray*, which went on to win eight Tony Awards, and *The Wedding Singer* premiered for Seattleites before finding glory in New York. The Paramount Theatre, in a beautifully restored historic building,

WINTER OR SUMMER

Pioneer Square's First Thursday Gallery Walk draws an estimated 6,000–10,000 art lovers in the summer, and 1,000–2,000 in the winter.

But don't expect low-brow performances at these smaller venues. Intiman Theatre premiered *A Light in the Piazza,* which later garnered numerous Tony Awards in New York and toured the country.

One of America's premier nonprofit resident theatres, Seattle Repertory Theatre, founded in 1963, is an internationally recognized, Tony Award-winning regional theater with an audi-

draws large crowds for award-winning shows and traveling companies and performers, as well as top names in music and comedy. Another historic Seattle theater, the Moore Theatre (1907) hosts a rotating line-up of everything from off-Broadway shows to stand-up comics.

Professional performances can also be found in the more intimate settings of smaller theaters. Intiman Theatre, Book-It and Seattle Shakespeare Company, all at the Seattle Center, specialize respectively in revivals, adaptations of classic literature and productions of the Bard.

ence of 130,000 each season. The Rep produces high-caliber shows on two different stages, the Bagley Wright Theatre and Leo K. Theatre.

ACT Theatre is among the largest theaters in Seattle and presents innovative contemporary performances. From annual favorites like *A Christmas Carol* (first staged at ACT in 1976), to world premieres that have gone on to New York (like *Scent of the Roses* and *In the Penal Colony*), it's no wonder ACT's 10,000 subscribers continue coming back for more.

While many fringe and alternative theaters have come and gone, others have found a loyal audience in Seattle's discerning and culturally inclined crowd. ❏

LEFT: smooth sounds at the Seattle Asian Art Museum.
ABOVE: electrifying a captive Capitol Hill audience.

TRIBES OF THE NORTHWEST

There are more than 25,000 Native Americans in the Greater Seattle area

Evidence of the original band of Seattleites, the Duwamish, can be hard to find, but the city does have numerous resources for learning about native art and culture. The tribes that are the best documented are those of Southeast Alaska and British Columbia.

The Burke Museum of Natural History and Culture (tel: 206-543 5590), on Seattle's University of Washington campus, has one of the country's largest collections of Northwest coastal native art and artifacts. These include totem poles, model canoes, baskets, tools and a house front. It's a very interesting place to visit.

The Seattle Art Museum (tel: 206-654 3100) also has a valuable First Nations collection, with many fine pieces created by members of the Tlingit, Haida and Makah tribes.

The Daybreak Star Indian Cultural Center (tel: 206-285 4425) in Seattle's Discovery Park coordinates events and services for the city's native population. The center also has a collection of contemporary tribal art, and a small gallery where traveling shows are staged.

LEFT: This Haida wood carving represents the Thunderbird. Carved totem poles are found all over the Northwest, including in Seattle's Pioneer Square.

ABOVE: Tulalip tribe members drum during a "first fish" ceremony. Their reservation is at the mouth of the Snohomish River, north of Seattle, and is home for the Snohomish, Snoqualmie, Skagit, Samish and allied bands.

ABOVE: Tulalip tribesmen gather in their longhouse near Marysville to celebrate the first salmon ceremony.

LEFT: Museums and galleries in the Northwest have magnificent examples of Native American headdresses.

CHIEF JOSEPH OF THE NEZ PERCE

One of the most dramatic stories in Northwest Native American history is that of Chief Joseph, shown here in a photograph by Edward S. Curtis. He was a chief of the Nez Perce (Nimiipu).

In 1877, the US government enacted a new treaty with the Nez Perce, stripping the tribe of valuable lands. Violence erupted. Several chiefs, including Chief Joseph, refused to sign the treaty and a band which Joseph led fled on horseback and on foot toward Canada. The natives held off the US cavalry for 1,500 miles (2,400 km), surviving more than 20 battles along the way.

The Nez Perce eventually surrendered in northern Montana near the Canadian border, where Chief Joseph delivered his historic speech, with the conclusion, "I will fight no more forever."

Exiled to Oklahoma until 1885, Chief Joseph finally returned to the Pacific Northwest and lived on Washington state's Colville Reservation until his death in 1904.

ABOVE: Laws entitle Native American tribes to half of the annual salmon catch in Northwest waters.

RIGHT: *Bride of the Wishram Tribe*, photographed by Edward S. Curtis, depicts a young woman of the Chinook tribe of the Columbia River.

ABOVE: Edward S. Curtis documented Native American life in a massive photo essay, which included this picture of a daughter of a Skokomish chief.

SALMON AND SIMPLE INGREDIENTS

With one of the oldest produce markets in the country
and surrounded by nature that produces everything
from fresh fish to fabulous fruits, it's no wonder
Seattle's young chefs are winning accolades

Columnist Jeffrey Steingarten said of Seattle in *Vogue* magazine "I feasted for ten days on what is without doubt the finest fish and seafood in North America." He might also have mentioned the city's tomatoes, corn, root vegetables, peppers, apples, pears, shell beans... no wonder going to the farmers' market is a favorite local activity.

In the same essay, however, Steingarten referred to the city's food as "ingredients in search of a cuisine" – and it's a fair criticism. Individual ingredients are incomparable, but it's difficult to identify a "Pacific Northwest" cuisine the way someone might Cajun or Tex-Mex.

Local bounty

For most of the 20th century, Seattle's restaurant scene was dominated by upscale chophouses and seafood palaces, family restaurants and a few Japanese and Chinese places. The city also had elegant Scandinavian restaurants such as King Oscar's and the Norselander (which described itself as "matched only by restaurants in European travel capitals"). The spirit of northern Europe does live on, however, in the Ballard neighborhood, where there are Scandinavian food shops and an annual seafood festival, as well as one of Seattle's best farmers' markets (Sundays). The spirit of upscale chophouses prevails, too, in the form of Canlis, which opened in 1950 and is respected for its excellent service and wonderful waterside views, if not always for groundbreaking food.

LEFT: chef Thierry Rautureau of Rovers.
RIGHT: a pretty presentation from Wild Ginger.

Nowadays, Seattle has no dearth of chefs who know their way around the local bounty. One of the best is Jerry Traunfeld *(see page 157)*, whose dinners at The Herbfarm restaurant in Woodinville are legendary compilations of local products from small growers and producers. In the Madison Valley, Thierry Rautureau (the "Chef in the Hat") prepares French food for a loyal clientele; in Belltown, Christine Keff specializes in seafood at Flying Fish; and Downtown, Nathan Uy creates memorable Asian dishes at Wild Ginger. It may not add up to a "local cuisine" – but no one is complaining.

Seattle and salmon are near-synonyms. In the world's mind, Seattleites probably eat smoked salmon hash for breakfast, a blackened salmon sandwich for lunch, and grilled king salmon for dinner. This would not be a bad way to spend the day, but here's the dirty secret: Washington salmon populations are listed under the Endangered Species Act, and nearly all the salmon consumed in Seattle is from Alaska – or farmed from God knows where, the same stuff available in supermarkets nationwide *(see page 60)*.

The favorite fish

Wild Alaskan salmon is worth the search and the price. (The run lasts from May through late fall, so if you see "fresh" wild salmon for sale in the dead of winter, it was probably frozen

while fresh and now defrosted or mislabeled.) Five species of salmon are pulled from Pacific waters, but they are rechristened seemingly every season with an array of marketing names. Luckily, the two best species, sockeye and king, are always called sockeye and king. The others (coho, pink, and chum) may be sold under names such as keta, silver and "SilverBrite." If these are fresh and well-treated, they can be very good, but most of the lesser species end up smoked or in cans.

Like steak, salmon is best medium rare, and better restaurants serve it this way. Oh, and don't skip the skin: salmon skin is the most delicious of all fish skin; it tastes much like bacon.

Other Northwest fish of note include Columbia River sturgeon, Alaskan halibut and black cod. The latter is often marinated in *kasu* (a sweet byproduct of sake production) and grilled, a preparation that originated in Seattle and is still rarely found elsewhere.

Oysters are another specialty, with many species farmed locally. Unlike salmon, oyster farming is ecologically benign. Two of the best local varieties are Totten Virginicas, which *The New York Times* called "the best oysters in the world," and Olympias, a tiny oyster with a distinct cucumber flavor. Try them (preferably in a month with an "r" in its name) at Emmett Watson's Oyster Bar in Pike Place Market, which did as much as any place to put Washington oysters on the national radar.

With so much seafood to go around, it's no surprise that sushi is a major obsession. In downtown Seattle, Shiro's and Saito's are masterminded by serious artisans, while good sushi bars can be found in many neighborhoods.

To market we will go

Like the "festival markets" that have sprung up in other cities, Pike Place Market is a tourist haven, and you won't be disappointed if you go there seeking postcards and knick-knacks. Unlike other markets, however, Pike Place is 100 years old and still serves mainly local customers. Saved from the urban-renewal wrecking ball in 1972, it's the oldest continuously operating produce market in America. (Referring to it as "Pike's Market," however, is a sure way to make locals groan.)

Where to begin? Pike Place Fish, with its fish-throwing traders seen in the Visa commercial *(and on pages 12–13)* – is only one of four fishmongers. Sosio's produce is known for local "Holy Shit Peaches" in season. Delaurenti Specialty Food and Wine has the best (and most expensive) cheese counter in town.

A block away, you can watch the people at Beecher's Cheese make Flagship cheddar and buy their macaroni and cheese (lauded by MSNBC and the *Washington Post*) – frozen or ready to eat. Bavarian Meats offers every German meat you've heard of – and probably 20 you haven't – and the city's best bacon. Stillnovich Corner Produce is the place for rhubarb (the owners grow it on their farm).

No self-catering facilities? No problem. The

market has a variety of restaurants (including a number of good French ones such as Campagne and Le Pichet), as well as classic casual and takeout options such as Pike Place Chowder and the Market Grill, where you can, in fact, have a blackened salmon sandwich for lunch.

The Douglas Effect

The undisputed king salmon of Seattle dining is Tom Douglas. On the scene since 1984, Douglas's rise corresponds with an explosion in Seattle dining in general. His restaurant portfolio currently stands at five (including Palace Kitchen, Etta's Seafood and Lola), plus a bakery – a statistic that is likely to be out of

THE GRAPE ESCAPE

Washington wine is constantly winning accolades; syrah and riesling are among its successful grapes. For more on wine, *see page 154.*

Pacific winds

Probably the most popular dish in Seattle has nothing to do with local ingredients. It's pad Thai, the spicy noodle stir-fry made in every one of Seattle's hundred-plus Thai restaurants. Even more Vietnamese people than Thai live in Seattle, and upscale Vietnamese in particular is flourishing, both in Little Saigon (around 12th and Jackson) and outside it. Try Green Leaf,

date by the time you read this, since Douglas is a restless expansionist. He also recently defeated famous Japanese chef Morimoto on the popular TV show *Iron Chef America*, although the ingredient *was* wild king salmon, giving Douglas a major home-court advantage.

He's a talented guy whose freewheeling style incorporates frequent Asian touches, plus whatever influences strike his fancy. All of his restaurants are within a few blocks of his epicenter, Dahlia Lounge, at 4th Avenue and Virginia.

LEFT: buying from a local supplier is a favorite activity.
ABOVE: the nine-course dinners at The Herbfarm are legendary; book far in advance for the adventure.

Tamarind Tree, Bambuza and Green Papaya.

Seattle's suburbs have sizable Korean populations. In Federal Way, especially, enormous Korean supermarkets sell dozens of varieties of handmade *kimchi*. But you don't need to leave Seattle for this: Uwajimaya, in the International District, sells ingredients from all over Asia, with a special emphasis on Japan and Hawaii. And the store's food court features every east Asian cuisine you can think of – plus burgers.

While visitors may not leave with an easy definition of a "typical Seattle meal," chances are everyone will discover quintessentially Seattle flavors. ❑

● *Restaurants are listed in the Places chapters.*

NATURE IN THE NORTHWEST

Bald eagles nest in Seward Park and harbor seals follow ferries within sight of downtown Seattle. Even wilder life is only a couple of hours' drive away

Around Seattle and Puget Sound, nature is never far away. The blaze of foods and produce that bedeck the markets attest to Seattle's coexistance with the natural world. Always in view, the snowcaps and tree lines of the great Cascade Mountains and the verdant foliage covering the region are colorful reminders of the blanket of ancient wilderness within which the city snuggles.

The combination of fresh- and saltwater, marshes, and forested hills gives Seattle abundant bird habitats, right in the city center. Double-crested cormorants are seen from fall to spring, perched with their wings outstretched on buoys or on bridge pilings. Glaucous-winged gulls are regularly spotted in fresh- and saltwater settings. Mallards and coots nest all year round in the freshwater lakes punctuating Seattle, along with great blue herons and pied-billed grebes. Migratory waterfowl as diverse as buffleheads, western grebes, and surf scooters are common in winter.

Wings aloft

Two native birds – crows and Canada geese – have thrived so well in this urban environment that they have come to be seen as pests. During the day, crows scavenge for food in shrubbery, garbage cans, around park benches or even in cars with open windows. At night, they return to communal roosts; the largest is on Foster Island in the Washington Park Arboretum, where up to 10,000 birds congregate.

LEFT: Seattle seen from Beacon Hill.
RIGHT: Northwesterners are passionate about nature.

In the early 1960s, Seattle's goose population was down to about 100, and geese were brought from the Columbia River. Unfortunately, they were a non-migratory type, and the abundant grassy fields and a predator-free shoreline formed the perfect habitat. The present population is about 5,000 geese. They have crashed into a jet landing in Renton; set off alarms at the Bangor nuclear submarine base north of the city; and forced the closure of beaches on Lake Washington because of fouling. Attempts to hunt them, roust them with dogs or return them to eastern Washington have had little effect.

The peregrine falcon has made a spectacular comeback after being endangered – they were not introduced but returned to the area naturally. Peregrines dive at speeds of up to 200 mph (320 kph) to feed on pigeons, sparrows and wrens in the urban corridor; there was once even a pair of peregrine falcons nesting on the 56th floor of the Washington Mutual Tower, right Downtown.

Nesting pairs of bald eagles can be spotted at Seattle's Seward, Discovery, and Green Lake parks. They live in the parks year-round, feeding on fish and waterfowl from the nearby waters. Several pairs have successfully raised their young in this urban environment.

The bald eagle population grows in winter with the arrival of northern migrants. Several hundred eagles descend on the Skagit River valley along Highway 2, about two hours north of Seattle, for the nearly perfect combinaion of flora and fauna. The river teems with spawned-out and dying salmon, and Douglas firs along the riverbanks offer ideal perches.

The simple life

"Once seen, never forgotten" could describe the state's only marine bivalve honored in song. The clam's most laudable attribute is also celebrated by the motto of Evergreen State College in Olympia, *Omni Extaris*, which translates as "let it all hang out." This is the geoduck (pronounced *gooey-duck*). Unlike most clams, the geoduck is not contained within its shell. The grey, tubular, wrinkled neck can grow to 3 ft (1 meter) in length. Geoducks spend most of their lives buried in the sand, static save for the contraction and extension of their necks.

Described by one ecologist as "a cruelly destructive pest, if there ever was one," slugs seem to be almost universally detested. Slugs are champion herbivores, using a tongue-like organ, the radula, to rasp plants into edible nuggets. Their vegetable consumption is the root of their unpopularity with gardeners.

The Northwest area has 23 species of native slugs. The best known is the banana slug, yellow-green forest dwellers that grow to 12 inches (30 cm) in length. Like all slugs, they are hermaphroditic, having both male and female organs.

THE SALMON'S ENDLESS CYCLE

One biologist wrote that salmon "reduce life to its simplest, most heroic terms." During its life, a local salmon may travel up to 10,000 miles (16,000 km), swimming from a small freshwater stream in the Seattle area to Alaska, and eventually back again, to spawn and die. Other salmon start from 2,000 miles (3,200 km) inland up the Columbia and Snake rivers.

Five species of salmon – coho (silver), chum (dog), king, sockeye and pink – inhabit the waters of the Puget Sound region. Salmon range in size from 3 lbs (1.4 kg) to more than 100 lbs (45 kg), and in color from mottled grey with tinges of red to brilliant red.

The salmon's life ends where it began, in its birth stream. Before they die, the salmon release eggs and milt (sperm), which settle into the gravelly stream bed. After hatching, the young remain nearby for up to two years before migrating to saltwater, returning to where they were born up to seven years later, to complete the cycle. Overfishing, dams, logging (which allows sediments to wash into streams, smothering the eggs), and suburban sprawl have all driven down the population.

Many of the Puget Sound species are now listed under the Endangered Species Act, preserving the hope that their numbers will rise again.

Marine mammals

The most commonly sighted marine mammals are the harbor seals, year-round residents of Puget Sound and coastal Washington. The mottled adults can reach more than 6 ft (2 meters) in length. In summer, mothers are seen tending young pups. Like most marine mammals, harbor seals are wary of human contact. When surprised by walkers along the beach, they scramble en masse into the water.

Often confused with seals, the Northwest's two sea lion species are distinguished by their ears. California and Steller sea lions both have small, rolled-up ear flaps; harbor seals don't. Other differences are apparent underwater. Sea

FLYING DINERS

Outdoor tables at waterfront restaurants regularly attract flocks of seagulls, cawing and clamoring for scraps. Residents have a love-hate relationship with these marine scavangers.

Killer whales – orcas – are a primary consumer of salmon, and their common name is from the hunting ability that makes them them the top marine predator (they do not eat people). They are efficient hunters and form cooperative groups to kill larger prey, such as gray or baleen whales. Roughly 90 individuals in three pods – extended family units – spend

lions employ their broad, flat front flippers to propel themselves, often with show-off acrobatics. Harbor seals scull conservatively with their hind flippers.

Male sea lions grow to more than 6 ft (2 meters) long and can weigh 600 lbs (270 kg). Females are smaller, and usually weigh around 200 lbs (90 kg). Steller sea lions migrate from breeding grounds in California and British Columbia and are easily recognized by size alone. Bull males approach 10 ft (3 meters) in length and 2,000 lbs (900 kg).

LEFT: serene settings are common in Seattle.
AVOVE: a tulip field in the Skagit Valley.

late spring to early autumn in waters around the San Juan Islands. Orcas are the largest of the dolphin family and grow to 25 ft (7.5 meters) in length, weighing up to 6 tons (5,500 kg). Females typically live for 50 years, while a male's lifespan averages around 25 years. Orcas have a highly evolved social structure and communicate with a repertoire of whoops, whistles and chirps. Each pod has its own dialect.

Look for the whale's back fin, 5–6 ft (1.5–1.8 meters) tall, slicing through the water. The distinctive black-and-white whales may also be seen breaching the water. The Whale Museum, at Friday Harbor in the San Juans (see page 196), offers whale-watching tours throughout the summer. Gray whales, minke whales, harbor and Dall's porpoises also make excursions into the waters of Puget Sound.

The harbor porpoise, seen around Puget Sound and the San Juan Islands, is the smallest oceanic cetacean. Unlike the bottle-nose dolphin, harbor porpoises are not gregarious. Dall's porpoises can swim at up to 30 knots in front of ships' bows. Pacific white-sided dolphins travel in schools of more than 50 members and turn somersaults up to 20 ft (6 meters) in the air.

Gray whales are seen along the ocean coast on their 12,000-mile (19,000-km) annual migration. Once endangered with just a few

hundred remaining, protection has increased their numbers to 20,000 or more. Distinguishing it from other whales are the 10–14 "knuckles" along the ridge of its 40–50-ft (12–15-meter) back.

Douglas-firs and flowers

Douglas-firs were key in the economic development of Seattle and the Puget Sound area. Within a month of the city's founding, the first boatload of Douglas-fir trees was booked for exportation to San Francisco, and they are still the most important timber in the Northwest. Unfortunately, the high value has led to extensive clear-cutting throughout the region.

Only a handful of monumental Douglas-firs remain standing in Seattle – in Seward, Carkeek and Schmitz parks. These reserves pale by the Northwest's old-growth forests, mostly in the national parks, with some remnants in national forests, and on state lands. Alongside the western red cedar and western hemlock, the fir was the primary conifer of the old-growth ecosystem. Cedars have always been the most important tree for the Native peoples, who cut the wood for canoes and houses, and used the bark in clothing.

The common name of the firs honors David Douglas, a Scottish botanist who took the first seeds back to Britain. Douglas introduced more than 200 plants to Britain, describing his namesake tree as "one of the most striking and truly graceful in Nature."

Neighborhood namesake

Three neighborhoods in Seattle – Laurelhurst, Magnolia and Madrona – were all named after one of the area's most beautiful native trees, the madrona, which comes from the same family as the laurel. Capt. George Davidson of the US Coast Survey named Magnolia in 1856, thinking he saw magnolias on the bluffs. A better botanist would have recognized the distinctive red-barked trees, which produce white flowers in the spring and orange fruit in late summer.

Rhododendrons are a common relative of the madrona. In the Cascade foothills, they favor the shady understory of Douglas firs and western hemlocks. Native varieties produce spectacular pink blooms in spring and, along with azaleas, are almost ubiquitous in yards, parks, and gardens around Puget Sound. The western rhododendron became the Washington state flower in 1892.

The Northwest has a reputation for edible, juicy berries of all kinds, including cranberries, several varieties of huckleberry, blueberries, strawberries, blackberries, squashberries, snowberries, salmonberries, thimbleberries, dewberries and elderberries. But berry-loving hikers might have to contend for their fruit with bears, who may live on little else during late summer, when the berries are at their ripest. ❏

LEFT: starfish on the shore.
RIGHT: Snoqualmie Falls, overlooked by Salish Lodge, is less than an hour's drive east of Seattle.

PLACES

A detailed guide to the city with the principal sites
clearly cross-referenced by number to the maps

eattle is known for its water; most people associate the city with rain, although several US cities have much more annual rainfall. Water in larger bodies, though, is integral to life around Puget Sound and all part of the Seattle experience. Even a short ferry ride, just to skim the waves, is a good way to begin an acquaintance with the town. The outdoors is another Seattle specialty – fjord-like waters in Puget Sound, rainforests on the Olympic Peninsula, volcanoes in the Cascade Mountains to the east, and a convenient foreign country – Canada – just a couple of hours north.

Seattle's distinct neighborhoods are defined not by ethnic clusters, but more by social groups and aspirations. As such, they evolve over time as Seattleites progress and migrate. The young, free and single, for instance, head for the renovations and lofts in Belltown and, more recently, Downtown. When they're ready to settle, many like to nest in the tidy single-home plots of West Seattle or latterly, South Seattle. Wealthy folks with a bit of style and money move into leafy mansions on Capitol Hill, near Volunteer Park and the Conservatory, and the Asian Art Museum. A location overlooking the lake, bristling with sailboats, is among the enticements for Bellevue and Redmond, along with the smart, Eastside shopping. Views of Downtown and the Space Needle are important in Wallingford and Queen Anne Hill, while Magnolia and West Seattle look out over the harbor, the city, Puget Sound and the Olympic Mountains to the west.

For visitors, the views of the boats on the water from the terraces in Pike Place Market are hard to beat. And they're free. For a long while, Fremont has been more upscale than funky, but the nickname of "Funky Fremont" persists for software giant Adobe's area. The University District, surrounding the University of Washington, is clearly student-oriented, while Woodinville has fine dining and wineries, and attractive Ballard, long the city's Scandinavian center, is home to several cool bars and clubs.

The city that gave birth to Microsoft, Starbucks, Boeing and Nirvana offers a wide variety of lively neighborhoods to explore, not to mention the dramatic landscape on its doorstep. ❏

PRECEDING PAGES: Seattle overview at dusk; the games people play at Microsoft.
LEFT: Le Panier Bakery, Pike Place Market.

Seattle

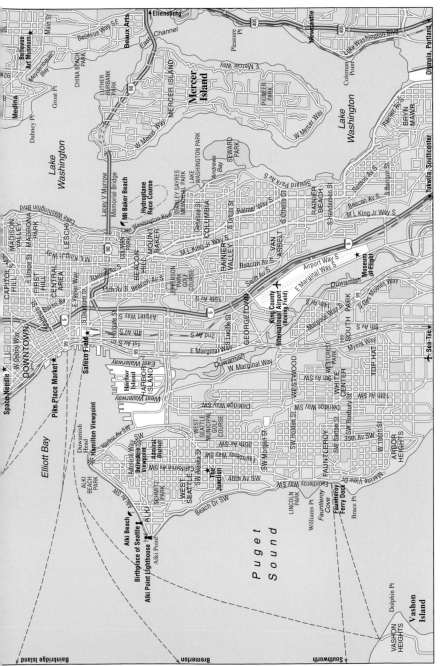

PIONEER SQUARE AND THE INTERNATIONAL DISTRICT

This oldest part of Seattle has an architectural ambience that lends itself to tall tales, real ales and long, tall totem poles

Modern Seattle was established in 1852 when Arthur and David Denny, along with other pioneers, moved up from Alki Point, on which they had first landed only a few months earlier. They named their home after a Native American – Chief Sealth (or Seattle), of the Duwamish and Suquamish tribes – who was among the settlement's first visitors.

The businessmen who came later were less respectful to the locals, however. A group representing the Seattle Chamber of Commerce visited Alaska's Fort Tongass in 1899 and stole a tribal totem pole while the men of the village were out on a fishing expedition. For nearly 40 years this totem stood at 1st Avenue and Yesler Way until it was set on fire by an arsonist. Shamelessly, the city asked for a replacement. An unsubstantiated but amusing story follows: when the tribe said it would cost $5,000, the city sent a check. The reply came back: thanks for finally paying for the first one – and the second one will cost another $5,000. The city duly paid up.

Pioneer Square

The 60-ft (18-meter) replacement totem pole today stands on a brick plaza where 1st, James and Yesler intersect in front of the Pioneer Building. This plaza is commonly known as **Pioneer Square** , although the name actually refers to the entire 20-square-block neighborhood, which is now a designated historical park. The official name of this popular triangular park is Pioneer Park Place.

As well as being low-rise and walkable, Pioneer Square is a great place for nightlife. In funky old bars and restaurants, music can be heard almost any night of the week, from rock to blues and jazz.

Map on page 74

LEFT: the Elliott Bay Book Company in the 1890 Globe Building.
BELOW: Uwajimaya is a huge store in the International District.

The totem pole in Pioneer Square belonged to the Tlingit tribe.

Pioneer Square became the center for the settlers when they left Alki Point for the superior harbor at Elliott Bay. The **totem pole** is near to James A. Wehn's **bust of Chief Sealth**. Wehn arrived in Seattle soon after the 1889 fire and remained in Seattle until he died in 1953. He also designed the city's seal, which bears Chief Sealth's profile. When Chief Sealth died in 1866, he was buried on the Kitsap Peninsula, northwest of Seattle overlooking Puget Sound.

Underground Seattle

At 1st Avenue and Yesler Way, the street is still surfaced with the original cobblestones. Pioneer Park Place has long been dominated by a **Victorian iron-and-glass pergola** built in 1905 and which once sheltered the patrons of the 1.3-mile (2.1-km) cable-car route which, until 1940, ran between Yesler and Lake Union, north of Downtown. The pergola was destroyed by a

truck in January 2001, but was so popular with the townsfolk that a new cast- and wrought-iron pergola – with a safer and stronger steel structure – was unveiled 19 months later. Behind the pergola is the Merchant's Cafe, the city's oldest restaurant and which in Gold Rush times served 5-cent beers to miners, as they waited for their turn in the brothel upstairs. Seattle's Great Fire of 1889 *(see page 27)* wiped out almost all of the bar's neighbors in the Pioneer Square area.

Architect Elmer Fisher, who was responsible for at least 50 of the new structures, set the dominant style. A characteristic example of his work is the elegant **Pioneer Building ❷** on James Street opposite the plaza. Its tenants included several dozen mining companies above a saloon which was once operated by Dr "Doc" David Swinton Maynard, who was among the area's first and pre-eminent settlers.

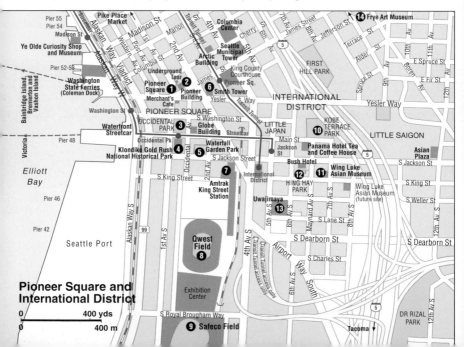

Pioneer Square and International District

Doc Maynard's saloon is now a bar called **Doc's Lounge** (610 1st Avenue, tel: 206-682 4646; Fri–Sat 8pm–1am), and is a stop on the popular **Underground Tour**, an inspection of the shops and rooms that were abandoned when this part of town was rebuilt. To eliminate what had been persistent flooding, some of the buildings were raised by as much as 18 ft (5 meters) and the remaining subterranean city was sealed off, until Bill Speidel, an enterprising newspaper columnist, began the conducted tours.

The tour takes in a warren of the musty, debris-lined passageways and rooms that had been at ground level. Passing under the glass-paneled sidewalk at 1st and Yesler, the tour ends at the Rogue's Gallery, where old photos, magazines, artifacts and scale models depict the area as it was before the fire, when Yesler Way was three times as steep as it is today. On sale are books written by Bill Speidel.

Some of the guides in charge of the Underground Tour provide a refreshingly irreverent journey through Seattle's history. "Henry Yesler had no moral or ethical values whatsoever," one guide announced. "Naturally he became our first mayor." On another occasion the guide said: "That's the true Seattle spirit – even if it's a lousy deal, we'll stick with it."

Occidental Park

Occidental Avenue gives way to a brick pedestrian mall-park between South Washington and Jackson streets. Enticing aromas drift out of a bakery near the Grand Central Building into **Occidental Park** ❸ (also sometimes referred to as Occidental Mall).

In 2006, the park was revamped to help revitalize Seattle's urban areas. Improvements included upgraded lighting for increased safety, bocce courts and chess tables, enhanced settings for the **four cedar totem poles** and more. The totems were carved over a 10-year period by Duane Pasco, a Washington State master carver with an international reputation, and are positioned following the tradition of having their

Map on page 74

There are at least three tours every day; call 206-682 4646 for details. True fans can even get married underground.

BELOW: Pioneer Square's compact size makes it perfect for an afternoon stroll.

faces to the sea and hollowed backs to the forest, though the forest is now the skyscrapers of the city. The tallest totem in Occidental Park – *Sun and Raven* – depicts the Raven bringing light to the world. Farther down the 35-ft (11-meter) pole is the Chief of the Sky's daughter giving birth to the Raven, and the Chief himself holding the sun in his hands, and the box that holds "light."

The second totem, *Tsonoqua,* is a human figure with outstretched arms; the other two totems are *Bear* and *Man Riding on Tail of Whale.*

Skid Row

Also in Occidental Park is a memorial to Seattle firefighters who have died in the line of duty since 1889, when the city's Fire Department was formed after the Great Fire. The bronzed sculpture features four life-size firefighters in action.

On Main Street, across from Occidental Square, is the confusingly named **Klondike Gold Rush National Historical Park ❹** (daily 9am–5pm; free; tel: 206-220 4240). The museum has exhibits and

photographs recounting the saga of the hectic 1890s, when half of Seattle caught Gold Rush fever. As well as this store-front museum, the National Park Service administers units in southeast Alaska in the town of Skagway and the Chilkoot Trail.

Thousands, including the mayor, left jobs and homes to follow the call of gold. The rigorous journey 1,500 miles (2,400 km) north to Alaska was over forbidding mountains and up treacherous rivers. Few of the spur-of-the-moment adventurers struck it rich, however, since most of the valuable claims had already been staked long before the newcomers' arrival.

Many of those who stayed behind in Seattle did better. To ensure that prospectors could withstand the northern wastes, Canadian authorities insisted that they brought with them a year's supply of goods and provisions (400 lbs/180 kg of flour and 25 cans of butter, for example), and many of the city's early merchants did very brisk trade.

Dating from 1890 is the **Globe**

Pioneer Square has a bust of Chief Sealth, for whom the city is named. It was created by James A. Wehn.

BELOW: great sounds nightly at the New Orleans Creole Restaurant.

Building, at Main and 1st Avenue, the site now occupied by the **Elliott Bay Book Company**.

One year earlier, when the Great Fire destroyed hundreds of buildings, it burned deep into the commercial heart of the city. Because it was here, in 1853, that Doc Maynard and other settlers had donated land to Seattle's very first industry: a steam-powered lumbermill built by German-born Henry Yesler *(see page 25)*. The sawmill was installed at the top of what is now **Yesler Way** which began as Skid Road, the steep ramp down which the lumber was slid to the sawmill. In Yesler's day, the mill ran day and night, employing almost half the working population.

According to Arthur Denny's account, Doc Maynard showed up drunk for a meeting to plan the street grid of Pioneer Square. Maynard insisted on orienting his streets to the compass points, but Denny and Carson Boren disagreed, which explains the strange turns at Yesler.

After World War II, Skid Road was a wasteland of cheap hotels and homeless winos. For at least a couple of generations, 1st Avenue was renowned for low-rent stores, prostitutes, X-rated bookstores and taverns. Local pawnbrokers' stock ranged from jewelry and watches near Pike Place to guns, radios and typewriters at establishments nearer to Pioneer Square.

In the 1960s, artists began to establish studios in the low-rent lofts. Prevented from rebuilding by the city's rejection of wholesale urban renewal, property owners remodeled building interiors in wood and brass, setting the tone for the gentrification and regeneration that would follow later.

Waterfall Garden Park

A great place for a picnic is just a block east, up Main Street at the enclosed **Waterfall Garden Park** ❺, surely one of the prettiest miniature parks in the country. It was built in gratitude to the employees of the United Parcel Service (UPS), founded in Seattle in 1907 by 19-year old local resident James Casey. The park's tables are set around

Map on page 74

The term "skid row" originated in Pioneer Square. Wooden skids built to transport logs from Yesler to the waterfront became a divider that separated the "distasteful" south from the respectable downtown area.

BELOW:
Smith Tower peeks out over a Pioneer Square red-brick building.

Smith Tower

When L.C. Smith's tower went up in downtown Seattle in 1914, it was touted as the tallest building in the West. Picture postcards depicting the 500-ft (150-meter) structure claimed that from "the world-famous catwalk surrounding the Chinese temple may be seen mountain ranges 380 miles (600 km) in the distance." Well, not quite. The mountain ranges in view – the Olympics and the Cascades – are about 60 miles (100 km) away. But 4,400 people flocked to the opening anyway, paying 25 cents each to whizz past local government agency offices and to admire the view from the observation deck.

"A work of art worthy of the builders of the awe-inspiring cathedrals of the Middle Ages," boasted the tower's historian, Arthur F. Wakefield, who revealed that New York's American Bridge Company had taken 20 weeks to make the building's steel, transported cross-country from their Pittsburgh, Pennsylvania, plant in 164 railcars.

Smith spared no expense. The $1.5 million building's 600 rooms had steel doors, teak ceilings, walls of Alaskan white marble or tinted Mexican onyx, elevator doors of

glass and bronze and, on the 35th floor, an expensive Chinese Room decorated with bronze lanterns, oriental furniture and 776 semi-porcelain discs. A throne-like Chinese chair, reputed to have been a gift from the Empress of China, was actually obtained from a waterfront curio shop but did spawn its own legend. One year after Smith's daughter posed sitting in the chair, she got married, convincing other would-be brides that to sit in the "Wishing Chair" would bring them a husband. Even today, couples still occasionally choose the room to host their wedding reception.

One year after the tower's opening, some of the office tenants saw a one-armed parachutist floating down past their windows, and a year or two later watched Harry – The Human Fly – scale the building. "I gave him a little help by hanging ropes over the cornices," recalled William K. Jackson, just before his retirement as building superintendent in 1944. Jackson, then 72, had worked in the tower since it opened, during which time Seattle had changed from "a friendly, clean little city to a town of strangers going so fast you can feel the tempo of wartime even in your own building." Recording the city's changes by what he'd seen in the harbor – first lumber barges and fishing boats, then liners, freighters and navy ships and now "mostly smoke" – he observed that the city "sort of grew up under me." The tower was still getting 300 visitors a day, was still the tallest building in the West, and on most days still offered a clear view of Mount Rainier.

Stunts at the tower abounded. In 1938, two high-school students ran upstairs to the 36th floor in less than 10 minutes (and down again in four); four years later, a proud grandfather announced his new domestic status by running up a flag on the flagpole reading, "It's a girl."

The Smith Tower was bought in 1985 by a San Francisco firm, whose partners remodeled it with respect, even acquiring parts and equipment to retain the original (1914) copper, brass-and-glass elevators. ❏

LEFT: Smith Tower: the Observation Deck wraps around all four sides and is worth visiting.

flowers and trees in front of a glorious waterfall designed by Masao Kinoshita, which drops 22 ft (6.7 meters) onto huge boulders and recycles 5,000 gallons (20,000 liters) of water every minute.

At the end of the 19th century, Lyman Cornelius Smith arrived in Seattle after his wife fell in love with the town. Smith, already wealthy from the sale of his gun company (later Smith & Wesson) and then his revolutionary new typewriter (later to be Smith Corona), promptly bought several blocks around Main Street and 1st Avenue.

In 1901, he built the L.C. Smith Building. Goaded by the plans of a business rival, he then plotted the 42-story **Smith Tower ❻** (daily 10am–sunset in summer; weekends only 9am–4pm in winter; admission charge).

When it was completed in 1914, this was the tallest building outside New York. The distinction was gradually diluted until in 1962, its last remaining title – that of the tallest building in Seattle – was taken by the Space Needle. Smith

Tower remains a sentimental favorite, however, and the view from the **Observation Deck** is extensive, taking in all four directions – north, south, east and west.

Sports stadiums

There are some fine structures in Pioneer Square, but few are more striking and noteworthy than the **Arctic Building**, at 3rd Avenue and Cherry, with its row of sculpted walruses adorning the upper levels. Believing the original terracotta tusks to be a potential danger to pedestrians walking below, the building's owners removed them some years ago and replaced them with epoxy versions.

Apart from a scattering of people, who hardly seem enough to keep the espresso stands in business outside rush hours, the once handsome **Amtrak King Street Station ❼** (2nd Avenue and King) is often deserted. Architecture enthusiasts and other observant visitors will spot the tower's resemblance to St Mark's campanile in Venice, after which it was modeled.

Map on page 74

The Arctic Building (1916) at 206 Cherry Street was constructed to house a social club for people who had struck it rich in the Klondike Gold Rush.

BELOW:
Waterfall Garden Park.

Qwest Field is said to be the loudest stadium in the National Football League. Its distinctive, curved roof is designed to direct the noise of the crowd back onto the field, which is a huge distraction for out-of-town teams.

BELOW: during certain hours, Downtown's buses are free.

It is, however, the departure point for the fabulous 3½-hour journey to Vancouver, British Columbia, where the train hugs the coastline most of the way.

Much of the terrain around the station and Safeco Field is reclaimed land from what was once the bay. As much as 60 million cubic ft (1.7 million cubic meters) of earth was used for landfill and to raise the level of the city.

White, curvy **Qwest Field** ❽ (corner of S King Street and Occidental Avenue, tel: 206-381 7555) was completed in 2002, and is a venue for pop concerts as well as boat and motorcycle shows. But it is most famous as the home of the city's football team, the Seahawks. Ninety-minute tours of the state-of-the-art Qwest Field take place twice daily, all year round: reservations are not required.

For 22 years before Qwest and Safeco fields were built, the creaky and gloomy Kingdome on the same site was Seattle's sports venue, a skyline landmark since 1976.

The Kingdome was demolished the year after **Safeco Field** ❾ (corner of 1st Avenue S and Edgar Martinez Drive, tel: 206-346 4001), home to the Mariners, hosted its first baseball game. Safeco Field is a retractable-roofed stadium, which opened at a final cost of just over half a billion dollars in 1999. With views of Puget Sound, cedar-lined dugouts, picnic areas and a real field of Kentucky bluegrass and ryegrass, Safeco became one of baseball's most expensive stadium projects.

The International District

Known for more than a century as the city's Chinatown (Chinese were among the earliest residents), the **International District** has grown both geographically and culturally to include residents representing numerous Asian groups, especially Chinese, Japanese, Vietnamese, Filipino, Korean and Southeast Asian.

In 1871, a man named Wa Chong built the third brick structure in the city and was also responsible for the first building to go up after the 1889 fire. The Wa Chung Tea Store, at the corner of Washington and 3rd,

An Artful Bus Line

Seattle's Metro buses are free in the daytime around the downtown area, as well as being ecologically efficient. Another Metro claim is its sponsorship of public art. Scores of works are shown in the stations of the bus tunnel, which has now been upgraded and retrofitted for buses and light-rail trains to use. The tunnels pass beneath midtown Seattle. Granite stairs are colored white for north, black for south, green for east, and red for west.

Art is chosen specifically for the station in which it is shown, and for what is above it, overground. Under Pioneer Square, engineers have sited a relic from the cable-car system that ran along Yesler Way: a huge, cast-iron flywheel more than 11 ft (3.5 meters) in diameter. This has been supplemented with contemporary artwork, including a ceramic mural incorporating Indian baskets and a dugout canoe. The quotations here are from Chief Sealth (Seattle) and Seattle pioneers Arthur Denny and Doc Maynard.

The station at the International District has tiles created from designs by children of the neighborhood and an enormous origami work of painted aluminum. The open plaza above is tiled with symbols of the Chinese zodiac.

advertised in 1877 that contractors, mill owners and others requiring Chinese labor "will be furnished at short notice." And, as an afterthought, the store offered "the highest price paid for live hogs." A front-page announcement in that same paper by Tong Wa Shing & Co., dealers in Chinese Fancy Goods, offered Asian specialties including tea, rice and opium.

Japan Town

The area around **Kobe Terrace Park** ⑩ (221 6th Avenue S; daily 6am–11.30pm) at the top of the hill to the northern edge of the International District is what began as Nihon-machi, or **Japan Town**.

This area lost most of its population to the US Government's internment policies of World War II, when Japanese-Americans were removed to camps in Idaho or eastern Washington. Presidential Order 9066, forcibly relocating Japanese-Americans on the mainland (most in Hawaii were left alone) to these internment camps, was signed by President Franklin D. Roosevelt in

February of 1942. It was revoked in December of 1944. Of the Japanese interned during that period, about 7,000 were Seattle residents.

This area was later decimated by the construction of the Interstate 5 freeway. Kobe Terrace Park, from which there's a panoramic view, contains tiny gardens tended by low-income neighborhood residents. There's also a stone lantern donated by Seattle's sister city of Kobe, Japan.

Just outside the southwestern end of the park is the **Panama Hotel Tea and Coffee House** (607 S Main Street, tel: 206-515 4000). This building, where rooms are still rented out to travelers, dates from 1910 and served as a meeting place for generations of immigrants.

During World War II, the residents of the hotel stashed belongings in the basement before going to the internment camps. These unreclaimed relics are displayed in the hotel's café, and in the basement. Tours are also available of the old Japan Town bathhouse, which is preserved at the base of the hotel.

Map on page 74

Mariners fans can walk all the way around Safeco Field and still see the game.

BELOW: in 1999, Safeco Field replaced the old Kingdome.

TIP

When you're in China-town, take the chance to sample Bubble Tea. This "smoothie" comes in a range of 28 fruit flavors, and is characterized by the giant tapioca balls at the bottom of the cup. It's an acquired taste popular with Seattle's young Asian set.

BELOW: festival time in Chinatown.
RIGHT: Bubble Tea and happy fan.

Chinatown

By the turn of the 20th century, Seattle's **Chinatown** had become a city within the city, riddled with secret passages and tunnels. Few white faces were seen, except for furtive opium smokers. Violent *tong* or gang wars were fairly common features. A 1902 story in the *Seattle Post-Intelligencer* described well-guarded Chinese gambling houses from which whites were barred.

But long before World War II, the community began to stabilize, largely under the influence of civic bodies like the Chung Wa Association, of which all prominent Chinese were members. The riotous and notorious gambling dens, though, survived until at least 1942.

The **Wing Luke Asian Museum** ⓫ (407 7th Avenue S, tel: 206-623 5124; Tues–Fri 11am–4.30pm, weekends noon–4pm; admission charge) is named after the first Asian-American official elected in the Northwest, who joined Seattle's city council in 1962. The museum has many exhibits, from Balinese masks to Persian miniatures.

The museum's permanent collection includes historical photographs and artifacts such as a 50-ft (15-meter) dragon boat, used for festival races in China, and a mock-up of a Chinese apothecary. A few years ago, the museum purchased the historic East Kong Yick Building, on the southwest corner of 8th Avenue S and S King Street. Construction is underway to renovate and preserve the building, which the Wing Luke Asian Museum expects to make its home by spring 2008.

Hing Hay Park ⓬ (423 Maynard Avenue S) has an ornamental arch dating from 1973 and designed in Taiwan by architect David Lin. The dragon mural is a larger-than-life depiction of local Asian events. The park is also the setting for occasional martial-arts exhibitions and Chinese folk dancing, and even a little early-morning *taiqi*.

As a young Chinese immigrant, Bruce Lee washed dishes in Chinatown to pay the rent while he developed his street-fighting skills. The martial arts star is buried in Capitol Hill (*see page 114*).

A common sight in stores around here are rows of jars displaying herbs, flowers and roots – peony, honeysuckle, chrysanthemum, ginger, ginseng and especially licorice, which have been used for centuries to build strength and "balance the body's energy."

On 6th and Jackson, brightly colored figures from legends cover the wall of **Washington Federal** (formerly United Savings and Loan Bank), one of many banks that safekeep funds. In earlier eras, money might have been stuffed under floorboards or in private safes. Once preferred over banks, safes were shared by up to 10 people, each with a key that would work only with all the other partners.

A block away, at the corner of 6th and Weller, is the large department store, **Uwajimaya** ⓭, which stocks everything from cookware to fruit and exotic vegetables. The food court is a truly international district. Cuisines from Korea, Vietnam, China, Japan and more are on offer, as well as desserts like ice cream and strange Bubble Tea.

Little Saigon

East of the freeway, the streets around the Japanese-owned Asian Plaza shopping mall at Jackson and 12th are sometimes known as **Little Saigon**, where many of the hundreds of Vietnamese-owned businesses in Seattle operate.

Unlike the center of Chinatown, which houses mostly restaurants, gift shops andjust a few food shops, Little Saigon consists mainly of large grocery stores, jewelry shops and just a few dining establishments. The district is still expanding to the north.

Several blocks northeast of the International District in the **First Hill** neighborhood, the **Frye Art Museum** ⓮ (704 Terry Avenue, tel: 206-622 9250; open daily; free) hosts frequently changing exhibits as well as poetry readings, chamber music and other kinds of performance. The museum first showcased 19th-century German paintings from the late Charles and Emma Frye's collection. Exhibits are more diverse now, and include excellent salon paintings. ❑

Map on page 74

For information on the merchants and businesses in the International Distict, visit www.cidbia.org

BELOW: taking a break in Chinatown.

RESTAURANTS, BARS & CAFES

Restaurants

China Gate
516 7th Avenue S
Tel: 206-624 1730
Open: L and D daily. $$
Perfect for large gatherings, this airy restaurant is dependable for good Chinese food. Free parking is available weekends.

Fado Irish Pub
801 lst Avenue
Tel: 206-264 2700
www.fadoirishpub.com
Open: B Sat–Sun, L and D daily. $
A Pioneer Square pub filled with Irish memorabilia. Relax with a "perfect pint" (a 20-ounce glass shaped to fit the palm) and traditional fare such as shepherd's pie, bangers 'n' mash, as well as American

favorites. Irish bands and dancing are also a draw, but there's no set schedule for these events.

Green Village
516 6th Avenue S
Tel: 206-624 3634
Open: L and D Mon–Sun. $
It doesn't get any quicker or cheaper for authentic Chinese cuisine than at Green Village. Ordering is from the counter, fast-food style. Servings are large and meals hearty.

Jade Garden
424 7th Avenue S
Tel: 206-622 8181
Open: L and D daily. $$
The long line of diners waiting to get in snakes out the door and around the corner. The dim sum is hands down the best in all of Seattle, and the price is decent, too. Reg-

ular menu items are also tasty and fresh – seafood is so fresh it's likely swimming in the restaurant's tanks until an order comes in.

Il Terrazzo Carmine
411 1st Avenue S
Tel: 206-467 7797
www.ilterrazzocarmine.com
Open: L Mon–Fri, D Mon–Sat. $$$$
This romantic Italian restaurant in a Pioneer Square office building has been a consistent customer pleaser for more than 20 years, and has a loyal regular clientele. In the light, white-tableclothed dining room, patrons enjoy professional service and classic Italian specialties like gnocchi Sorrentina, *cioppino* and osso bucco. The alley patio is surprisingly intimate.

Malay Satay Hut
212 12th Avenue S
Tel: 206-324 4091
www.malaysatayhut.com
Open: L and D daily. $$
This cozy little strip-mall restaurant serves delicious Malaysian cuisine in an exotic tropical atmosphere. But the décor most often passes unnoticed as the delicious roti *canai* dips into the curry, or the scent of the mango tofu wafts across the table. The food is quite simply spectacular, and vegetarian diners also find plenty to please their palates.

Maneki
304 6th Avenue S
Tel: 206-622 2631
Open: D Tues–Sun. $$
Locals have long raved about Maneki's divine sushi, as well they might. With over 100 years of service, this is the oldest sushi restaurant in town, and the large menu has reasonably priced treats.

New Orleans Creole Restaurant
114 1st Avenue S
Tel: 206-622 2563
neworleanscreolerestaurant.com
Open: L and D daily. $$
In Pioneer Square's historic Lombardy building, this restaurant is the spot for live music and good Louisiana cooking. Local and national musicians play jazz, Dixieland, blues and more as patrons enjoy Creole and Cajun favorites like jambalaya and gumbo.

Saigon Bistro
1032 S Jackson #202
Tel: 206-329 4939
Open: B, L, D daily. $
Above the Viet Wah Asian market, this place is a little light on ambiance, but the wonderful, well-prepared food more than makes up for the plain-Jane décor. The duck and cabbage soup is a favorite delicacy.

Salumi
309 3rd Avenue S
Tel: 206-621 8772
Open: L Tues–Fri. $
Lines at lunch time are long at this Pioneer

Square eatery, and meat lovers swear by Armandino Batali's house-cured cuts.

Sea Garden
509 7th Avenue S
Tel: 206-623 2100
Open: L and D daily. **$$–$$$**
This is Seattle Chinese seafood at its best. Some find the flavors are a tad Americanized, but they're close enough to the real deal to draw plenty of Asian diners. Standout dishes include salt and pepper-seasoned deep-fried calamari and crab in black-bean sauce.

Seven Stars Pepper
1207 S. Jackson Street, Suite 211
Tel: 206-568 6446
Open: L and D daily. **$$**
The restaurant is not an esthetic masterpiece, but the food is guaranteed to please the palate. Seven Stars Pepper features cuisine from the Szechuan province of China, which is known for spicy cooking. Don't miss the hand-shaven noodles, green-onion pancakes and the excellent twice-cooked pork.

Shanghai Garden
524 6th Avenue S
Tel: 206-625 1689
Open: L and D daily. **$$**
This spot offers dishes that are common in China, but are harder to find in the States. Hog's maw and black fungus are among the authentic Chinese offerings. The less adventurous need

not shy away; tasty and healthy dishes like the hand-shaven barley green noodles and pea vines are also available.

Sichuanese Cuisine Restaurant
1048 S Jackson Street
Tel: 206-720 1690
www.sichuan.cwok.com
Open: L and D daily. **$**
Look past the physical detractions (small, not spotless) of this hole-in-the-wall restaurant and you'll find the best and most affordable Szechuanese cuisine in the whole Seattle area. The special hot beef chow mein, dried-cooked string beans and Szechuanese-style chicken are all must haves. But be forewarned that if you order the spicy dishes, the spice quotient is up to truly authentic levels, so be prepared.

Tamarind Tree
1036 S Jackson St, Suite A
Tel: 206-860 1404
www.tamarindtreerestaurant.com
Open: L and D daily. **$$**
Vietnamese dining in Seattle rarely gets as fancy as this. The interior radiates with a contemporary warmth and style, and the patio transports diners to a luscious bamboo forest, complete with a twinkling waterfall. The food itself is very pretty, always tasty and affordable, but, unless the party includes a fluent Vietnamese speaker, service can be something of a challenge.

Uwajimaya Village
600 5th Avenue S
Tel: 206-624 6248
www.uwajimaya.com
Open: L and D daily. **$**
Kill two birds with one stone at this Asian grocery store – shop for exotic items, then head over to the food court. There, you'll find a variety of Asian fast-food cuisine ranging from Chinese to Korean to Vietnamese.

Bars and Cafés

Bush Garden, 614 Maynard Ave S, is a perfect spot for a stiff drink to unwind for some karaoke.
Caffe Umbria, 320 Occidental Ave S, offers an authentic Italian bar experience with pulled espresso, pastries, wines and more.
Café Paloma, 93 Yesler Way, serves light Mediterranean fare in an

eatery that feels more like a hideaway from the bustling city life.
Central Saloon, 207 First Ave S, is Seattle's oldest saloon, with more than 115 years of history to dwell on at the bar.
Sluggers, 539 Occidental Ave S, is a dream for Mariners and Seahawks fans. The place is plastered with the sports teams' memorabilia.
Zeitgeist, 171 S Jackson St, is not your average Seattle coffee house. View artwork that challenges you to think as you sip your hot drink.

PRICE CATEGORIES

Prices for a three-course dinner per person with half a bottle of wine:
$ = under $20
$$ = $20–45
$$$ = $45–60
$$$$ = more than $60

LEFT: Salumi's sausages are worth waiting in line for.
RIGHT: Seattleites eat well in the International District.

SHOPPING IN SEATTLE

Everything from couture clothes to kitschy knick-knacks can be found in the birthplace of Nordstrom and Starbucks

ABOVE: Nordstrom began in Seattle as a shoe store in 1901; now there's at least one in every American state. Seattle's flagship store is situated at 500 Pine Street. Tel: 206-628 2111.

The Emerald City is a wear-whatever-you-want kind of place, where people turn up at the symphony in anything from jeans to John Galliano. Nevertheless, the Seattle area has shopping opportunities galore, from miniature Space Needles (and Space Noodles) in waterfront souvenir shops, to high-end boutiques Downtown and in the upscale suburbs of the Eastside. The city's climate and outdoor life contributed to the success of Eddie Bauer (now a national chain of stores); REI (a local co-operative with stores opening across the country; the North Face and Patagonia. Many Seattle traditionalists look as if they've just stepped out of one of these sporty shops.

RIGHT: REI (Recreational Equipment Inc) has this 65-foot (19.8-meter) high free-standing indoor climbing wall called The Pinnacle. The store is at 222 Yale Avenue N. Tel: 206-223 1944.

Pike Place Market has crafts by local artisans, from jewelry to home décor, as well as eclectic gifts from all over the world and the freshest produce in the city. Archie McPhee *(above)* in Ballard has a fascinating selection of weird, kitschy stuff; in fact, Ballard, Fremont and the University District are the areas to head for when looking for one-of-a-kind selections. Outlet malls have also come to Washington, the most prominent being in North Bend (east) and Tulalip (north). Retail realists should note that an 8.8 percent sales tax is added to any purchase price.

LEFT: a huge range of Native American arts and crafts, from masks and ceramics to carvings and jewelry, is available from stores all over Seattle, including several around Pike Place Market.

ABOVE: Made in Washington is exactly what it says. Shop for upscale souvenirs like jewelry, or sockeye salmon and local cherries in chocolate. Various locations, including the airport.

LEFT: Luly Yang is a Seattle-based couture designer with a big reputation. Her store is at 1218 4th Avenue (at the Fairmont Olympic Hotel). Tel: 206-623 8200.

ABOVE: Starbucks came up with the perfect pick-me-up solution in the pursuit of fantastic purchases. Themselves a worldwide retail phenomenon, the first Starbucks store began selling roasted coffee beans in Pike Place Market in 1971. There are now 99 branches in the Seattle area and more than 10,800 worldwide. The Starbucks headquarters *(above)* is at 2401 Utah Avenue.

DOWNTOWN SEATTLE AND PIKE PLACE MARKET

Seattle's pleasant downtown area has hills, refined architecture, public sculpture, lapping waves and one of the oldest public markets in the US

N orth of Pioneer Square and the International District is Downtown, lined steep with skyscrapers, and unexpectedly pleasant with hills, sculptures and peek-a-boo views of sparkling water at the bottom of streets.

Until recently, when the workers who occupied the skyscapers vacated each evening, few people ventured out at night, and visitors in the hotels around 5th and 6th avenues were left isolated, dependent on taxis to take them out to livelier neighborhoods. Lately, though, urban pioneers have moved in to occupy stylish lofts and apartment buildings, and restaurants, stores and signature buildings have followed in their wake.

Skyscraper city

Seattle's tallest building – one of the highest in the West, in fact – is the 76-story **Columbia Center ❶** (701 5th Avenue), which rises 954 ft (291 meters) and is served by 46 elevators. Below street level at the center are carpeted, picture-lined corridors. One leads to the **Seattle Municipal Tower** (700 5th Avenue) next door, and an attractive mall lined with shops, classy snack bars and tables. The Starbucks on the fourth floor is said to serve 500 customers an hour during its morning rush, and claims

to be the world's busiest espresso bar, though a number of other Seattle espresso counters must surely be in contention.

Enormous skyscrapers began to rise in downtown Seattle in the 1960s and early 1970s, but the really big boom didn't get underway until the following decade. Opinions about the esthetics of these newcomers vary, but the buildings have been a boon for sculptures under the city's "one-percent-for-art" ordinance, which requires that 1 percent

Map on page 90

LEFT: Seattle's Central Library.
BELOW: the Harbor Steps connect Downtown with the waterfront area.

Kerry View Point Park
Fremont
Maritime Heritage Center, Center for Wooden Boats
SOUTH LAKE UNION PARK
Shurgard Building
Roy Street Marketplace at Queen Anne
Roy Street
Valley Street
Mercer Street
CASCADE
Seattle Repertory Theatre
Intiman Theatre
Marion Oliver McCaw Hall
Mercer Arena
KCTS-TV Studios
Exhibition Hall
Republican Street
Republican Street
Northwest Rooms
International Fountain
Memorial Stadium
King's Studios (NBC)
CASCADE PLAYGROUND
SEATTLE CENTER
Harrison Street
Harrison Street
Key Arena
Fisher Pavilion
Seattle Center House
Experience Music Project
Science Fiction Museum
Thomas Street
Seattle Times Building
Seattle Center Pavilion
Thomas St
Children's Theatre
Muyral Amphitheatre
Fun Forest Amusements
Space Needle
John Street
John Street
Myrtle Edwards Park
Pacific Science Center
IMAX
Sculpture Gardens
KOMO Studios (ABC)
DENNY PARK
DENNY PLAYFIELD
Denny Way
Denny Way
TILIKUM PLACE
KIRO Studios (CBS)
OLYMPIC SCULPTURE PARK
Pavilion
BELLTOWN (DENNY REGRADE)
UA Theater
King Cat Theatre
Broad St Station
REGRADE PARK
Cinerama
Plaza 600 Bldg
Greyhound Bus Terminal
Convention Center Station
Seattle Trade Center
Victoria Clipper
Port of Seattle Headquarters
Pier 70
Pier 69
Pier 68
Pier 67
The Edgewater
Art Institute of Seattle
World Trade Center
Westin Hotel
1600 Bell Plaza
Pacific Place
Nordstrom
Westlake Center
WA Convention and Trade Center
Pier 66 (Bell Street Pier)
Bell Harbor International Conference Center
Odyssey Maritime Discovery Center
Bell Street Pier
VICTOR STEINBRUECK PARK
Soames Dunn Building
The First Starbucks
Pike Place Market
Securities Building
Moore Theatre
Bon Marche
Westlake
Sheraton
Union Square
US Bank Centre
5th Av Theater
Inn at the Market
Olympic Tower
Century Square
Puget Sound Plaza
Rainier Square
FREEWAY PARK
PIKE PLACE MARKET HISTORIC DIST.
Benaroya Hall
University St
US Courthouse
Seattle Aquarium
Pier 59
WATERFRONT PARK
University St
Gray Line Tours
Bay Pavilion
Seattle Art Museum
Washington Mutual Tower
HARBOR STEPS
Second & Seneca
Central Library
Puget Sound
Pier 63
Pier 62
Piers 60&61
WATERFRONT
Pier 57
Pier 56
1001 Fourth Av. Plaza
Columbia Center
FINANCIAL DISTRICT
Seattle Municipal Tower
Pier 55
Pier 54
Ye Olde Curiosity Shop & Museum
Madison St
Waterfront Place
Federal Office Building
Maritime Building
Norton Bldg
Pioneer Building
Port of Seattle
Pier 53
Pier 52
Washington State Ferries (Coleman Dock)
Victoria, Winston & Bremerton
Joshua Green Fountain
Washington St
Pier 51
Smith Tower
PIONEER SQUARE

Downtown to Seattle Center

0 — 500 yds
0 — 500 m

of funds appropriated for municipal construction projects be set aside for art in public places.

On 5th Avenue, for instance, is the *Fountain of Wisdom* by George Tsutakawa, a 9-ft (2.7-meter) tall sculpture which integrates water and bronze. Tsutakawa is a local artist whose works grace many of the city's public areas *(see page 99)*.

Another skyscraper with world-class art on its grounds is **1001 Fourth Avenue Plaza** ❷. The art is Henry Moore's haunting *Three Piece Sculpture: Vertebrae*, which now belongs to the Seattle Art Museum. During its construction, 1001 Fourth Avenue Plaza was nicknamed "the box the Space Needle came in." From the 46th-floor foyer, there's a great view of the skyline, the busy harbor and the boats on Puget Sound.

Read all about it

Directly behind 1001 Fourth Avenue Plaza is Seattle's state-of-the-art **Central Library** ❸ (4000 4th Avenue, tel: 206-386 4636; Mon–Thur 10am–8pm, Fri–Sat 10am–

6pm, Sun noon–6pm). Designed by Pritzker Prize-winning architect Rem Koolhaas, the 11-story exterior has a dazzling skin of glass and steel; the weight in steel alone is said to be enough to have made the Statue of Liberty 20 times over.

The brightly colored interior is filled with light and open spaces. The carpets are woven in patterns of green that are designed to replicate the vegetation that grows on the other side of the glass *(see photo on page 88)*, and art is integrated throughout the space.

For a while, it's possible to forget that you're in a library – until you realize that the spiral feature is actually presenting the entire non-fiction collection in one continuous run. Central Library is a place that all Seattleites – young, old, trendy, poor – seem to use, and not just for the free internet access. General and architectural tours are available.

Constructed years earlier and so less whizzy, the **Washington State Convention and Trade Center** ❹ (at the corner of 7th and Pike), also makes a feature of glass, looking as

Posh pooch and owner; there are about 1,500 pet dogs in Seattle.

LEFT: *Three Piece Sculpture: Vertebrae*, by Henry Moore.
BELOW: the dazzling Central Library.

though it's built from green glass cubes. The center's ground-floor **Tourist Office** (daily 9am–5pm; tel: 206-461 5840) is a good place for maps and brochures.

Hanging above a sterile walkway to Pike Street on the building's second level are bells from schools, churches and other landmarks in each of Washington's 39 counties. Controlled by an intricate computer system, the bells are played on the hour each day, with special performances twice daily.

In the walkway park adjoining the convention center itself is the aluminum sculpture – *Seattle George* – by the local artist Buster Simpson, combining silhouetted heads of George Washington and Chief Seattle. The latter silhouette is destined to become a memory, as ivy grows over it.

Freeway Park

The convention center – airy, spacious, busy and spotless – segues into **Freeway Park** ❺ (700 Seneca Street; daily 6am–11:30pm), an oasis of greenery and waterfalls straddling busy Interstate 5. Both projects span the freeway in an imaginative use of air rights.

Tree-shaded paths wind past a multi-level "canyon" in which invigorating cascades of water pour down sheer walls into pools, swirling, gurgling and endlessly recycling. Freeway Park is one of the most restful oases Downtown.

Near the park, **Two Union Square** is a pleasant office building that forms part of **Union Square** ❻. There are stores on the main level, and higher up, huge 56th-floor windows look out over the freeway and an outdoor plaza with another waterfall. Across the street, the **Pacific West Center** has comfortable chairs in an airy atrium.

An underground walkway runs from Union Square to **Rainier Square** ❼ (1301 5th Avenue), two blocks west. The most accessible collection of photographs of old Seattle is found along the carpeted walkway running under the **Skinner Building** (1326 5th Avenue), which forms part of the Rainier Square complex. The collection includes

Hammering Man by Jonathan Borofsky, the sculpture in front of the Seattle Art Museum, hammers four times a minute from 7am to 10pm. He rests his arm each evening, and all day on Labor Day.

BELOW:
the hard-working *Hammering Man* sculpture stands by the Seattle Art Museum.

Nearly Ageless Stone

Walking through downtown Seattle is a tour along a geological time line, beginning with 1.6 billion-year-old Finnish granite at 1000 2nd Avenue to the Seattle Art Museum and its young, 300-million-year-old limestone walls. Farther along fossils, some up to 4 inches (10 cm) long, are embedded in grey limestone at the Gap store on 5th Avenue. And this is just the beginning.

Around the corner and underground in the Westlake Center bus station is the burned oatmeal-colored travertine, deposited less than 2 million years ago near the Rio Grande River in New Mexico.

Seattle's switch to stone instead of wood for building began after the 1889 fire that destroyed much of the city's downtown business district. Initially, local rock was used, quarried from the Puget Sound region, especially near Tacoma and Bellingham and it was soon in favor for streets, walls and foundations.

As the city grew wealthier, builders sought out stone from Vermont and Indiana. Later still, with more economical transport and stone-cutting technology, local and regional geology became almost obsolete as contractors ordered stone from South Africa, Brazil and Italy.

pictures of the Moran Brothers' shipyard in 1906, prospectors of the Alaska Gold Rush, and some that celebrate the history of Boeing.

A major hotel area is half a dozen blocks northeast. Two of the biggest are the Westin Hotel (1900 5th Avenue, tel: 206-728 1000), whose distinctive twin towers double as a geographical landmark, and the 840-room Sheraton Hotel (1400 6th Avenue, tel: 206-621 9000). These are handily placed near to two shopping malls, **Westlake Center ❽** (between Pine Street and Olive Way, and 4th and 5th avenues; tel: 206-467 3044), and Pacific Place.

The southern terminus of the city's **Monorail** is on the top floor of the Westlake Center, from where it powers north 1.3 miles (2.1 km) to the Space Needle and Experience Music Project. Like the Space Needle, the Monorail dates from the 1962 World's Fair.

Since then, the Monorail has had its share of problems. In late 2005, two trains sideswiped each other and became entangled. A year later, trains stalled on the tracks, making

residents wonder whether this historic attraction wasn't approaching the end of its lifespan. Nevertheless, in late 2006, the Monorail was back in action again.

Pacific Place ❾ (6th Avenue and Pine Street, tel: 206-405 2655) is an upscale retail center with restaurants, a multi-screen movie theater and high-end stores like Tiffany & Co. and MaxMara keeping company with well-known chain stores. The overhead Skybridge connects the mall with the flagship branch of **Nordstrom**, the department store that was founded in Seattle at the beginning of the 20th century and has since opened in cities throughout the US *(see pages 86–87).*

Music and art

A few blocks west towards the waterfront is **Benaroya Hall ❿** (200 University Street, tel: 206-215 4747), home of the Seattle Symphony. The building is an architectural delight. Inside, the cylindrical lobby gives wonderful views of the Seattle Art Museum and Puget Sound, while outside, as the website

Map on page 90

In 2004, Pearl Jam released a double-disc album called Live at Benaroya Hall. *It became an instant cult classic.*

BELOW: Benaroya Hall at night "gives the effect of a giant lantern."

TIP

For a great map of Pike Place Market, *see page 248*. Market news: from June to September there are free cooking demonstrations on Sundays. During the same months, plus October, the produce is organic on Wednesdays.

BELOW: Pike Place Market is the oldest continuously operating public market in the United States.

says, "at night, its surfaces of clear and frosted glass give the effect of a giant lantern illuminating the streetscape." Classical music is piped onto the sidewalk outside during the day, lending a cultural air to the Downtown bustle.

Almost next door is the **Seattle Art Museum** ⑪ (daily 9am–5pm; admission charge; tel: 206-654 3100), at University and 1st Avenue. It was designed by Robert Venturi, winner of architecture's highest award, the Pritzker Prize, and credited with the wry observation that "less is a bore."

The museum's home here allows its former premises in Volunteer Park to display its collection of Asian art as the Seattle Asian Art Museum *(see page 114)*. About the Seattle Art Museum building, its exterior inlaid with richly hued terracotta, Venturi said: "We think civic architecture should be popular; it should be liked by a range of people. It should not be esoteric."

Galleries in the museum are devoted to collections that include Japanese art, African art, and Pacific Northwest tribal art, plus special exhibitions from around the world. In early 2006, the museum closed for a one-year expansion project. It reopened in early May with 70 percent more gallery space, a new restaurant and store, and two floors of public space.

Pike Place Market

Seattle's anchor and primary visitor destination began in 1907 with half a dozen farmers bringing produce to Seattle, to space that the city set aside for a commercial market, responding to a public demand for lower prices. Over the years, the number of farmers has varied from a high of several hundred in the 1930s to a low of 30 in 1976. Developers wanted to demolish the market, but locals got the issue placed on the ballot and voted overwhelmingly to retain it.

Since then, the number of visiting farmers has stabilized at around 100, but **Pike Place Market** ⑫ (1501 Pike Place, tel: 206-682 7453) has become so famous for its other attractions – including charming,

eccentric and individually owned stalls – that its role as the country's oldest continuously operated public market can almost be overlooked.

A number of interlinking buildings on several floors, all with knock-out views of Puget Sound, Pike Place Market runs between Virginia and Lenora streets and envelops Pike Place, a short avenue sandwiched between First and Western avenues. Pike Place and Pike Street intersect at the main entrance to Pike Street Market. No need to worry – everyone here always confuses all the different Pikes.

Market forces

Most of the fruit and vegetable stalls, as well as those stacked with gleaming ice banks of fish, are in the semi-open arcade along Pike Place. They center around Georgia Gerber's life-size bronze piggybank *Rachel the Pig* (under the market sign at Pike Street and Pike Place) and on whose back there is nearly always a child posing for a photograph. Rachel, who gets sackloads of fan mail, arrived at the market in

1986 and annually collects between $6,000 and $9,000 for charities through the slot in her back.

Also near the entrance to the market is Metsker Maps (1511 1st Avenue, tel: 206-623 8747). This is the best place in the city to buy travel books, atlases and maps. Among Metsker's many globes and maps is the Geochron, a map/clock that shows real time all over the world, with day and night indicated by a lighting and shading panel.

Not everybody comes to the market at the front entrance. Many approach from the waterfront, either via **Victor Steinbrueck Park** on Western Avenue at Virginia and named for the architect who revived the market in the 1970s, or else up the **Hillclimb** steps from the foot of Pike Street (not to be confused with Pike Place).

Musicians gather at this spot, perhaps because of the good acoustics. There are half a dozen other places where musicians with permits (around 50 are issued each year), are authorized to perform. Many of the regulars – among them a classical-

Map on page 90

Scenes from the Tom Hanks and Meg Ryan hit movie Sleepless in Seattle *were filmed in the market.*

BELOW: some visitors find the local produce so irresistible they opt for self-catering accommodation.

music trio, a gospel singer and a man who wheels around his own piano – can be found somewhere near the **neon billboard clock** at the market's main entrance, at Pike Street and Pike Place.

Just north of the entrance clock, around the uncovered stalls, crafts-people gather each morning to be allocated a place for the day. Some of them have been attending the market for years and seniority plays a role; there are hundreds of people on the waiting list who move up only if existing craftspeople turn up less than two days a week.

Eating, shopping and fish

Eating at the market is a joy because there are so many choices: home-style diner cooking, fine dining with views of the bay, French cuisine, Bolivian fare, fresh-baked pastries, raw oysters at a casual bar, over-stuffed sandwiches at a deli counter. The public buildings called **Corner Market**, **Post Alley Market** and **Sanitary Market** (the latter so-named because no horses were allowed) are joined by walkways

Seattle has two boat shows – one indoors and one on the water.

BELOW: the deck at the Inn at the Market is a perfect place to watch the ever-changing scene on Puget Sound.

with eating spots on all levels. Don't overlook the **Soames Dunn Building** on the city side of Pike Place, between Stewart and Virginia, which also houses restaurants, as well as the planet's first **Starbucks** (1912 Pike Place).

You might find it useful to obtain a map of the market, which you can get at the voluntarily manned **information booth** by the main entrance at 1st and Pike. This is where the major fish stalls are located. At **Pike Place Fish** – home of the "flying fish" *(see photograph on pages 12–13)* – visitors with cameras can outnumber the customers.

Some visitors find it so frustrating to be unable to take the market's luscious fresh produce home to cook that one local magazine recently ran a listing of Seattle accommodations with cooking facilities. If you want to take some of the Northwest's fresh fish back home (within the US), stop at the market en route to the airport and arrange to have your salmon packed in ice for the trip.

Everyone's an individualist

Under the Pike Street Market's main arcade (on the water side of Pike Place) is a labyrinth of corners, corridors, cubbyholes, shops, stalls, stairs and empty spaces. Magic tricks, old posters, talking birds, Australian opals, Turkish pastries, books, funky clothes… these are but a few of the thousands of items for sale. No chain stores or franchises are allowed, so everyone's an individualist, and there's no shortage of characters.

Even some of the tiles on the floor are eccentric. Locals were invited to pay $35 for their own design some years ago, and a mathematician's wife listed all of the prime numbers under 100.

According to merchants, the market is also home to a few ghostly inhabitants. The Market Ghost

Tours (tel: 206-322 1218) go under and around this popular attraction, retelling stories of hauntings and sightings told by workers and residents. The tour ends – appropriately – at Seattle's first mortuary.

In the six-block market area is virtually anything that you might need. Everything except for a parking space. Leave the car behind and come by the (free) Downtown bus. In case you can't bear to leave at all, the popular 70-room **Inn at the Market** (corner of 1st Avenue and Pine Street, tel: 206-443 3600) has pretty rooms (some with waterfront views), and an outdoor deck, perfect for watching the sun set over the islands. Be sure to book in advance.

Along the waterfront

The **Seattle Aquarium** ⑬ (1483 Alaskan Way, tel: 206-386 4300; 9.30am–7.30pm in summer, 10am–5pm at other times; admission charge) is a visitor-friendly attraction on Pier 59 just west of Pike Place and features 200 varieties of fish native to Puget Sound, plus environments simulating the region's rocky reefs, sandy sea floor, eelgrass beds and tide pools. A working fish ladder illustrates the salmon life cycle and other exhibits show the paths that water travels on its way to Puget Sound.

Vividly striped lion fish, lethal electric eels, chameleon-like flatfish, octopus, dogfish and salmon dart by, side by side with irresistibly entertaining otters and seals. The twice-daily oceanic tides flood Puget Sound and mix with ample fresh water from rainfall to nurture "an unequaled estuarine haven for plants, animals and humans," as one of the educational captions says.

The Aquarium completed an expansion project in 2007, which gave it an extra 18,000 sq ft (1,670 sq meters) that includes a three-story great hall with educational kiosks and conservation exhibits. The main attraction in the new hall is the enormous tank filled with fish, sea anemones and other marine life.

What was once Pier 57 is now **Waterfront Park** ⑭ (1301 Alaskan Way; daily 6am–11:30pm), a relax-

Map on page 90

The Port of Seattle is one of the most important in the US for the delivery of goods from Asia. Some of the cargo is tech toys that are then shipped to other parts of the country.

BELOW: the Seattle Aquarium's 2007 expansion includes a three-story great hall.

ing place to sit, or to watch the sun set. Green and white Foss tugs – a local icon, as almost all tugboats on the Sound belong to the Foss company – ply the waters of the Sound, hauling timber, sand and gravel as they have for a century. Norwegian immigrant Thea Foss started the company with her husband by renting boats to fishermen. Foss was thought to be the model for Norman Reilly Raine's *Tugboat Annie* in a series of 1930s movies.

Mummie's the word

On Pier 54 is **Ye Olde Curiosity Shop and Museum ⓰** (1001 Alaskan Way, tel: 206-682 5844; daily 9am–9:30pm during summer, call for off-season hours; free), with bizarre carnival attractions like Siamese twin calves, mummies, shrunken heads, shark jaws and pins engraved with the Lord's Prayer. The shop-museum is owned by descendants of Joe Standley, who opened it in 1899, later selling his ethnological collection to New York's Museum of the American Indian. Sharing Pier 54

Ivar Feeding the Gulls, *on Pier 54, is a tribute to the late restaurateur Ivar Haglund.*

BELOW: on a clear day you can see Mount Rainier from here.

is a bronze statue by Richard Beyer, *Ivar Feeding the Gulls*, of late restaurateur Ivar Haglund, feeding seagulls.

A lovably irascible character who opened the city's first aquarium in 1906, Seattle-born Haglund began his career playing guitar and singing on local radio and TV. He later made a fortune with his seafood restaurants, Ivar's, including the one here on the waterfront, which collectively sell a quarter of a million clams each year. The tramcar stop across the street from Ivar's is called Clam Central Station.

The **Washington State Ferries Terminal ⓰** (Pier 52) at the waterfront end of Yesler Way may be the US's busiest water-bound commuter route. Renovated in 2004, the well-lit, modernized facility provides visitors access to restaurants and stores, and generates additional revenue for the ferry system.

The 29 ocean-going boats of the Washington Transportation Department's Maritime Division each year carry more than 26 million passengers and more than 11 million cars.

Sound Ferries to Everywhere

Commuters, squinting in the early-morning light, hustle onto the ferry at the Bainbridge Island terminal, some incompletely kempt. Ferry commuters are a breed with a gentle outlook. The Washington State Ferry System is a vital link for both Puget Sound and Seattle residents and travelers. Among the thousands of islands and inlets that wrinkle the coastlines of the Sound, sea travel is often the quickest means, and the least costly.

Washington State Ferries range from small boats to jumbo ferries. The Bainbridge Island and Bremerton ferries carry over 200 cars and 2,000 people each, and have large, comfortable lounges and food services. Major ferry routes have hourly departures during daylight hours, with fewer boats at night. On most routes, frequency is greater during the summer months; in winter, check schedules before making plans if time is tight. The Victoria Clipper, for instance, which travels between Seattle and Victoria, BC, has a greatly abbreviated timetable in winter.

If you plan to use the ferries to island hop around Puget Sound *(see page 181)*, make sure that you reserve accommodations on the smaller islands in advance, as these tend to get booked up.

About half of them cross Puget Sound to or from island homes, often in less than 35 minutes. Fares collected cover only 60 percent of the operating costs.

The **Joshua Green Fountain** outside the ferry terminal at Pier 52, on Alaskan Way, is named after the late centenarian Joshua Green. Arriving in Seattle in 1886, Green operated steamboats on Puget Sound and helped establish one of the city's first banks. The fountain is by local sculptor George Tsutakawa, who is also responsible for the fountain outside the *Seattle Post-Intelligencer* building about a mile farther north along Elliott Avenue.

Heading north

Pier 66, also known as the **Bell Street Pier** , is an $84-million development including a large plaza on the water, a lively promenade, the excellent, family-oriented **Odyssey Maritime Discovery Center** (2205 Alaskan Way, tel: 206-374 4000; Wed–Thur 10am–3pm, Fri 10am– 4pm, Sat–Sun 11am–5pm; admission charge) and, on clear days,

a glimpse of Mount Rainier 60 miles (100 km) away through binoculars (which are free).

A couple of blocks north of Downtown and Pike Place, along 1st through 5th avenues, is the trendy **Belltown** area, once better known as the Denny Regrade. Denny Hill was removed to provide much of the landfill to raise Downtown's muddy streets. The Regrade is now covered with stylish condos, office buildings and cool media offices, like those of TV stations and the makers of tech computer games.

In recent years, as hipsters move into the neighborhood, Belltown has become a nightlife hub. It has fine restaurants, a couple of hotels, interesting shops and popular bars and clubs. With the influx of residents, the area, once known for illicit activities, has been cleaned up. There is a small, dog- and family-friendly park, **Regrade Park**, at the corner of 3rd and Bell. Belltown also gave birth to "grunge" music. It was in tiny, sweaty, hotspots here that bands like Nirvana, Pearl Jam and Soundgarden got their starts. ❑

The mummies at Ye Olde Curiosity Shop, Sylvester and Sylvia, are for real. A CT scan revealed that Sylvester is extremely well preserved, which contradicts the story that he was found buried in a desert.

BELOW: sailing Puget Sound from Seattle, cellphone at the ready.

RESTAURANTS, BARS & CAFES

Anthony's Fish Bar
2201 Alaskan Way.
Tel: 206-448 6688
www.anthonys.com
Open: L and D daily. **$**
This outdoor fast-food spot on the waterfront serves seafood classics such as fish 'n' chips and fish tacos. Outdoor seating is available in spring and summer.

BOKA Kitchen + Bar
1010 1st Avenue
Tel: 206-357 9000
www.bokaseattle.com
Open: L and D daily. **$$$**
Lovely presentation of creative preparations. Local ingredients include salmon, steak and pastas. In Seattle's upscale Hotel 1000, also a place to see and be seen.

Café Campagne
1600 Post Alley
Tel: 206-728 2233
www.campagnerestaurant.com
Open: B Sat–Sun, L and D daily. **$$**
The "little brother" of Campagne restaurant, and in no way inferior to its pricier sibling, just a little less complicated.

Campagne
Inn at the Market
86 Pike Street
Tel: 206-728 2800
www.campagnerestaurant.com
Open: D daily. **$$$$**
Campagne does the right things right. The service is impeccable, the appetizers – especially the soups – are exquisite, and the wine list is comprehensive without being overwhelming. A wine steward friend confides that their red and white burgundy list is the best in the city. Anyone who appreciates food will enjoy Campagne.

Crab Pot Restaurant and Bar
1301 Alaskan Way
Tel: 206-624 1890
www.pier57seattle.com/restaurants.html
Open: L and D daily. **$$$**
Centrally located on the waterfront piers, the Crab Pot is a great place for tasty, fresh seafood. In the summer, sit at one of the patio tables and enjoy the fresh breeze from the Sound as you dine.

Elliott's Oyster House
1201 Alaskan Way, Pier 56
Tel: 206-623 4340
www.elliottsoysterhouse.com
Open: L and D daily. **$$$**
A waterfront restaurant that has been satisfying locals and visitors for more than 30 years. Oysters are a house specialty, but all kinds of seafood reign supreme.

Emmett Watson's Oyster Bar
1916 Pike Place, Suite 16
Tel: 206-448 7721
Open: L and D daily. **$**
The late *Seattle Times* journalist Emmett Watson gave Seattle its first oyster bar. Fish and chips and soups are also quite tasty.

Etta's Seafood
2020 Western Avenue
Tel: 206-443 6000
www.tomdouglas.com
Open: B Sat–Sun, L and D daily. **$$$**
It's not all seafood at Etta's, but fish is the highlight. Don't skimp on the side dishes, either; the servers give excellent advice on what best complements what.

Le Pichet
1933 1st Avenue
Tel: 206-256 1499
www.lepichetseattle.com
Open: B Sun–Thur, L and D daily. **$$**
This cute French café is regularly acclaimed by locals as one of the best French restaurants in town. The fare is simple and delicious, as are the espresso and pastries.

Matt's in the Market
94 Pike Street, Ste 32
Tel: 206-467 7909
www.mattsinthemarket.com
Open: L Mon–Sat, D Tues–Sat. **$$$**
The tiny second-floor dining room overlooks Pike Place Market, and is one of the best places for watching the bustling scene below. Lunch brings catfish and oyster po'boy sandwiches, and favorite dinner entrées feature fresh fish.

McCormick & Schmick's
1103 1st Avenue
Tel: 206-623 5500
Open: L and D daily. **$$$**
Northwest cuisine and seafood make this restaurant a very popular hangout with the local workforce, particularly as a venue for power lunching, and at the cocktail hour.

Metropolitan Grill
820 2nd Avenue
Tel: 206-624 3287
www.themetropolitangrill.com
Open: L Mon–Fri, D daily.
$$$$
With the number of awards the Metropolitan has received as "Seattle's Best Steakhouse," you might expect complacency. Not a bit of it. The steaks are done within a degree of your preferred temperature and break the scales with their girth, but the service with an elegant flourish really makes this place.

Palace Kitchen
2030 5th Avenue
Tel: 206-448 2001
www.tomdouglas.com
Open: D daily. **$$$**
The appetizers here are great value and surprisingly generous. The place can get pretty boisterous later in the evening hours, and the kitchen stays open until 1am.

Pan Africa
1521 1st Avenue
Tel: 206-652 2461
Open: B, L, D daily. **$**
Native Ethiopian Mulugeta Abeta opened his Pike Place Market restaurant in 2003, and is still one of only a few restaurants in the city serving African cuisine. About half of the menu is Ethiopian, the other half changes monthly, with specialties from other African countries. One of the more popular Seattle dining destinations for vegans.

Pink Door
1919 Post Alley
Tel: 206-443 3241
www.thepinkdoor.net
Open: L Tues–Sat, D Tues–Sun. **$$$**
The lack of signage hasn't kept folks from finding this Pike Place Market favorite. Unpretentious Italian food and regular shows in the adjacent bar, but best of all are the views of Puget Sound from the sheltered deck.

Red Fin
620 Stewart Street
Tel: 206-441 4340
www.hotelmaxseattle.com
Open: B, L and D daily. **$$$**
Sleek and sylish sushi restaurant adjoining the equally stylish Hotel Max, with helpful and knowledgable wait staff.

Six Seven
2411 Alaskan Way
Tel: 206-269 4575
www.edgewaterhotel.com/dining.cfm
Open: B, L and D daily, Br Sun. **$$$–$$$$**
Dining at Six Seven is like eating in a forest lodge that floats on a lake. Large tree trunks serve as architectural support while the floor-to-ceiling windows display views of Elliott Bay and the Olympic Mountains. Upscale Pan-Asian and American cuisine.

Tulio
1100 5th Avenue
Tel: 206-624 5500
www.tulio.com
Open: B and D daily, L Mon–Fri. **$$$**

Located in the Hotel Vintage Park, Tulio is more than just a hotel restaurant. Authentically Italian delicacies include house-cured meats, fresh pastas and baked focaccia. Save enough space for the *gelato*.

Wild Ginger Asian Restaurant
1401 3rd Avenue
Tel: 206-623 4450
www.wildginger.ne
Open: D daily, L Mon–Sat. **$$$**
Although the dishes draw inspiration from sources as diverse as Singapore, Bangkok, Saigon and Djakarta, this restaurant doesn't suffer from any lack of focus. Favorites include the coconut laksa (a Malaysian seafood soup) and the fragrant duck. The mahogany satay bar offers scallops, eggplant or wild-boar skewers.

Bars and Cafés

Commuter Comforts Café and Wine Bar, 801 Alaskan Way. A cozy spot for a drink and a quick bite if you miss your ferry.

Dahlia Bakery, 2001 4th Ave. Renowned chef Tom Douglas' delicious pastries are baked on the premises. Fantastic soups and salads, too.

Nite Lite Lounge, 1926 2nd Ave. A bar for pool and people-watching.

Suite 410, 410 Stewart St. A stylish and intimate bar serving cocktails with panache.

PRICE CATEGORIES

Prices for a three-course dinner per person with half a bottle of wine:
$ = under $20
$$ = $20–45
$$$ = $45–60
$$$$ = more than $60

LEFT: Le Pichet serves simple, elegant dishes.
RIGHT: Matt's in the Market.

SPACE NEEDLE AND SEATTLE CENTER

The Space Needle was built to showcase the 1962
World's Fair, but Seattle Center's museums
and theaters are definitely 21st century

Just north of Downtown is the ever-popular **Seattle Center**. Only one World's Fair was the set for an Elvis Presley movie *(It Happened at the World's Fair)* and that was the one held in Seattle in 1962. Most Seattle residents are proud of the fair's lasting legacy: the internationally recognized Space Needle, and one of the only Monorail systems in America.

The Monorail travels on its 1.3-mile (2.1-km) single-rail elevated track between Westlake Center Downtown (at 5th Avenue and Pine Street) and the station next to the Space Needle. The trains depart every 10 minutes, can carry up to 450 passengers each trip and pass through – yes, through – the Experience Music Project.

Eye of the Needle

Built in 1962, the 605-ft (184-meter) **Space Needle** (daily 9am–11pm, Fri and Sat to midnight; admission charge; tel: 206-905 2100) was a marvel of design and engineering. It cost $4.5 million. The centerpiece of the fair, the flying-saucer shape (an idea, according to local lore, first sketched on a placemat in 1959) was chosen from many designs. Construction was speedy, but the three elevators that transport visitors from the ground to the Needle's restau-

rant and observation deck were last to arrive; the final one got to Seattle just a day before the fair opened.

In 1993, two of the elevators were replaced with computerized versions that travel at 10 mph (16 kmph); the third, which is mostly used to transport freight, moves at 5 mph (8 kmph). Almost as big an attraction as the elevators is elevator operator Jenny Dibley, who celebrated 30 years on the job in 2006. She has traveled about 30,000 miles (48,280 km) vertically.

Map on page 90

LEFT: the Space Needle was built in 1962.
BELOW: scary entrance to the Science Fiction Museum.

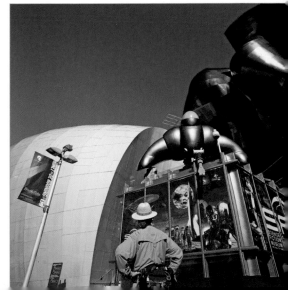

With a restaurant 500 ft (152 meters) above ground and an observation deck just above, the Space Needle offers some of the city's best views: to the east are Lake Union, the immensely larger Lake Washington and the distant Cascade Range; westward, Elliott Bay opens into Puget Sound in front of the Olympic Mountains; and southeast is the snowcapped peak of 14,411-ft (4,392-meter) Mount Rainier 60 miles (100 km) away. The revolving restaurant, **SkyCity**, provides a 360-degree view. As diners enjoy tasty – if expensive – Northwest cuisine, the restaurant completes a rotation every hour with the aid of a 1.5 horsepower motor.

One floor up, the **Observation Deck** level has free Swarovski telescopes on the outside deck, and a variety of graphic displays inside to help visitors to orient. Also inside is a coffee counter and bar to help warm up in cold weather.

Back on the ground, directly east of the Space Needle is the Seattle Center's **Sculpture Garden**, which has four distinctive artworks by dif-

ferent artists. Perhaps the best known of the four is *Olympic Iliad*, a huge red-and-orange sculpture made of gigantic industrial tubes, designed by Alexander Lieberman, former editorial director of Conde Nast Publications.

Northwest of the Needle is the **Seattle Center House** ⑳. Originally built as an armory in 1939, the building housed half-ton tanks and the 146th Field Artillery. It was remodeled into a vertical mall for the World's Fair, and now contains shops, an international food court (including chain restaurants such as Subway and Kabab Korner), and a public performance area.

Kids come here

Of particular interest to families is the **Children's Museum** (Mon–Fri 10am–5pm, Sat–Sun 10am–6pm; admission charge; tel: 206-441 1768) on the first floor of the Center House. The 22,000-sq-ft (2,043-sq-meter) space features hands-on, interactive and child-size exhibits on world culture, art, technology and the humanities. East of the

During the summer, lines to get into the Space Needle's elevators are long. If you can bear to miss the spectacular sunsets, midnight has the fewest crowds.

In 1966, Bill Gates won a free dinner at the Needle by reciting the Sermon on the Mount from memory. He was 11 years old.

RIGHT: view of Mount Rainier from the Space Needle on a rare sunny day in Seattle.

Center House is the **Fun Forest**, an amusement park with carnival rides like a roller coaster and Ferris wheel, games and a snack bar.

The **Entertainment Pavilion** has more than 60 video games, laser tag, mini golf and more. Tickets for the rides can be pricey, but visitors can buy a wristband for the cost of about 25 tickets, which will gain a family an unlimited number of rides.

EMP and SFM

Downtown may have an architectural marvel in the form of a library designed by renowned Dutch architect Rem Koolhaas, but Microsoft co-founder Paul Allen brought the artistic eye of California-based architect Frank O. Gehry to Seattle Center with the **Experience Music Project ㉑** (daily 10am–8pm in summer; call for off-season hours; admission charge; tel: 206-367 5483). No one can ignore the structure clad in psychedelic shades of aluminum and stainless steel *(see pages 110–111)*. The rock 'n' roll building houses an interactive music museum that combines state-of-the-

art technology with a world-class collection of artifacts from Jimi Hendrix, Nirvana, KISS, Usher and many more.

For a small additional fee, MEGs (Museum Exhibit Guides) play recordings and narration synchronized to the exhibits through wireless headphones. For music fans, it's easy to spend hours here looking around.

For something out of this world, visit the spooky **Science Fiction Museum** (daily 10am–8pm in summer, call for off-season hours; admission charge; tel: 206-724 3428), the first museum dedicated to the genre. It's situated in a part of the Experience Museum Project building, but its separate entrance and outer walls are electric blue, unlike the dazzling red, purple and silver of the music museum.

Like the EMP, the SFM houses a collection compiled by Paul Allen. Here, the focus is on sci-fi memorabilia, with pieces on loan from private collections and movie studios. The museum covers everything from novels (gigantic stacks of

Map on page 90

In sky-high SkyCity, the restaurant rotates, but the windows don't. Avoid propping belongings on the rim next to the table, as it will be an hour before they come around again (if at all).

hand-written pages from one author) to television series (Captain Kirk's chair from *Star Trek*) to blockbuster movies (the alien queen prop from *Aliens*).

As you exit the EMP and head north, stop to admire *The Reeds*, an art installation by John Fleming. The 110 laminated orange and yellow steel rods stand 30 ft (9 meters) tall and sway gently with the breeze.

Center for the arts

Performance halls line Mercer Street between 4th Avenue and Warren. The $127 million **Marion Oliver McCaw Hall** 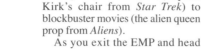 covers 295,000 sq ft (27,406 sq meters) which includes a 2,900-seat auditorium, a glass lobby, a public plaza and more. Home to the Seattle Opera and Pacific Northwest Ballet, it often hosts concerts, festivals, conventions and other events.

At Mercer and 2nd is the aptly named **Intiman Theatre**, whose name in Swedish means "the Intimate." It seats 446 people around a 3,110-sq-ft (289-sq-meter) stage.

One of the state's oldest and largest theater institutions, Intiman is recognized nationally for its programs and its fresh approach to classics as well as new productions.

A little farther west on Mercer are the three theaters of the **Seattle Repertory Theatre**, known locally as "The Rep." The non-profit group is internationally recognized for its productions and also delivers workshops and educational programs. The best-known and largest of the Rep's three stages, the **Bagley Wright Theatre**, seats 856; the Leo K and the tiny PONCHO Forum seat 286 and 100, respectively.

The sprawling, park-like campus of Seattle Center, with its numerous venues, is a perfect host for arts and cultural festivals that bring Seatleites and visitors together to celebrate the city's diversity. Some of the largest and most popular events held here include Bumbershoot (September), the Bite of Seattle (July) and Folklife (May), which draw several hundred thousand attendees every year. (For more information, *see pages 222–3*.)

TIP

Skateboarders and music fans will want to check out the skate park at Seattle Center. Designed by skateboarders themselves, it was developed with the help of a $50,000 gift from Pearl Jam.

BELOW: kid and kids' stuff at the Children's Museum.

Fountains and theaters

Originally built in 1961 for the World's Fair, the **International Fountain** is in an open area near the center of the park. Rebuilt in 1995, the fountain features a bowl with a diameter of 220 ft (67 meters), a 10-ft (3-meter) tall dome and 274 nozzles spraying mist and shooting jets of water (the highest reaches 120 ft, or 37 meters). The nozzles are also set to play 12-minute water shows, choreographed to different pieces of music. On sunny days, families picnic on the grassy area around the fountain, and children flock to the fountain bowl to dart among the jets, while daredevils climb the smooth dome (with three types of water treatments, the fountain water is quite clean).

The **Key Arena ㉓** (1st Avenue between Thomas and Republican) is a 17,000-seat arena which hosts big rock concerts as well as family shows and is also the home stadium for the city's hockey team, the Seattle Thunderbirds.

The playfully designed **Seattle Children's Theatre** produces fam-ily-friendly performances on two stages, the Charlotte Martin and Eve Alvord theatres. Performances have included classics such as *Goodnight Moon* and *The Diary of Anne Frank*. The theater company also develops and teaches educational programs in theater arts, including drama courses, residencies and workshops.

Just east of the SCT is the **Mural Amphitheatre**, another great spot for a picnic. Often during festivals, the amphitheatre features live musical acts. Its mural backdrop by Japanese artist Paul Horiuchi provides a lovely background. In summer, the amphitheatre hosts "Movies at the Mural," a well-attended free event.

Pacific Science Center

Under five white arches at the corner of 2nd and Denny is the non-profit **Pacific Science Center ㉔** (daily 10am–6pm in summer, call for off-season hours and laser show and IMAX show times; admission charge; tel: 206-443 2001), the first US museum founded as a science and technology center. With the goal

Map on page 90

The Science Fiction Museum is dimly lit. Be sure to look over your shoulder.

BELOW: SFM: close encounters of the museum kind.

Map
on page
90

In the town of a thousand coffeehouses now comes – Space Coffee!

BELOW: the arches of the Pacific Science Center.

of advancing public knowledge and interest in science, the PSC provides five buildings of interactive exhibits, two **IMAX theaters**, the **Butterfly House**, an excellent **planetarium** and laser shows.

Hands-on math and basic science exhibits offer delights to school-age children, and other exhibits excite the inquiring mind with demonstrations of virtual reality, computer science and robotics. Two exciting permanent exhibits are "Dinosaurs: A Journey Through Time," which features eight full- and half-size robotic dinosaurs that roar, a beehive and the Insect Village, inhabited by live and robotic insects.

Waterfront parks

About three blocks southwest of the Pacific Science Center is the Seattle Art Museum's third venue, the **Olympic Sculpture Park** ㉕ (between Broad and Bay streets; free). The Z-shaped 9-acre (3.6-hectare) park opened in early 2007, and added green space, 574 trees and 900 ft (274 hectares) of restored beach to Seattle.

In the process, it restored what had been the contaminated soil of an industrial area into an open park and recreation zone with a salmon-friendly sea wall, where visitors can enjoy strolling among works of art. The park's 22 sculptures include Richard Serra's *Wake*, Claes Oldenburg's *Typewriter Eraser (see photo on page 32)* and Alexander Calder's 39-ft (12-meter) *Eagle*; a glass pavilion that displays the beauty of the Olympic Mountains and Puget Sound and provides a space for performances and events. The amphitheater serves as a venue for movie screenings, as well as an outdoor play area for children.

Myrtle Edwards Park ㉖ (3130 Alaskan Way) is adjacent to the Olympic Sculpture Park. Rippling along the waterfront, the park offers another spot with lovely views of the Olympic Mountains, Mount Rainier and Puget Sound. There is also a winding cycle and walking trail that runs along Elliott Bay. Picnic tables are sited in perfect positions for dining alfresco and enjoying the stunning views. ❑

RESTAURANTS

Bamboo Garden
364 Roy Street
Tel: 206-281 6616
www.bamboogarden.net
Open: L and D daily. **$**
Though the menu includes familiar dishes such as *kun pao* chicken, everything is vegetarian; all of the "meat" is made from vegetable protein – some of which tastes remarkably meaty. Often crowded, but the wait isn't long.

Crow
823 5th Avenue N
Tel: 206-283 8800
Open: D daily. **$$–$$$**
A restaurant in a converted warehouse near the Seattle Center featuring shared plates. Fish-of-the-day specials, good cured meats and the house lasagna make the wait worthwhile for those without reservations.

Daniel's Broiler
809 Fairview Place N
Tel: 206-621 8262
www.schwartzbros.com
Open: L Mon–Fri, D daily.
$$$$
One of three steakhouses under the same name in the Seattle area (the others are in Bellevue and the Leschi neighborhood), this restaurant is known for the consistently reliable steaks.

Five Point
415 Cedar Street
Tel: 206-441 4777
Open: B, L, D daily. **$**
A local legend, the Five Point has been serving cheap, tasty diner food since 1928. It really comes to life after the bars close at 2am.

Mecca Café
526 Queen Anne Avenue N
Tel: 206-285 9728
Open: B, L and D daily. **$**
For a true dive bar in Seattle, try the Mecca. It's popular with the late-night crowd for its stiff pours and 'round-the-clock classic American fare.

Mediterranean Kitchen
366 Roy Street
Tel: 206-285 6713
Open: L Mon–Sat, D daily. **$$**
Atmosphere is not what draws people to this restaurant – it's the rich aroma of garlic, and dishes like *schwarma*, *shish tawook* and couscous. Platters come with hummus and rice, and as spicy as you want them.

The Melting Pot
14 Mercer Street
Tel: 206-378 1208
www.meltingpot.com
Open: D daily. **$$$**
The Melting Pot is fun with fondue. Cozy into a booth with your own table-top fondue pot, start with cheese, and end with chocolate. Featured entrées include lobster tail and filet mignon, as well as simpler fare like ravioli and chicken. Valet parking is available, with a charge.

SkyCity
400 Broad City
Tel: 206-950 2100
www.spaceneedle.com
Open: B and Br Sat–Sun; L and D daily. **$$$$**
It takes an hour for your seat to rotate around the restaurant, but you'll want to linger at least that long for the view. Prices are high, but the cuisine is better than locals claim.

Sushi Land
803 5th Avenue N
Tel: 206-267 7621
www.sushilandusa.com
Open: L and D daily. **$**
Sit at the counter and grab what you want as it glides by. This is conveyor-belt sushi at its best – fun, delicious and cheap. Sure, it's not top-notch sushi, but considering the price, it's darn good. Seasonal specials like Copper River salmon.

Waterfront Seafood Grill
2815 Alaskan Way, Pier 70
Tel: 206-956 9171
waterfrontpier70.com
Open: D daily. **$$$$**
On the waterfront side of the Olympic Sculpture Park, the views are the main attraction here, but the well-prepared seafood is a close second. There's also steaks as well as desserts worth saving room for.

PRICE CATEGORIES

Prices for a three-course dinner per person with half a bottle of wine:
$ = under $20
$$ = $20–45
$$$ = $45–60
$$$$ = more than $60

RIGHT: SkyCity: the food is better than you think.

EXPERIENCE MUSIC PROJECT

With undulating steel ribs and a rippling, multi-colored skin, it's pretty hard to miss EMP

EMP was the brainchild of Microsoft co-founder Paul Allen. The project draws a good deal of its inspiration, including the "Experience" part of its name, from Seattle-born guitar virtuoso, Jimi Hendrix. A sizeable exhibit is dedicated to the rock legend, and his concerts are screened daily.

Allen commissioned Frank Gehry as the architect of the distinctive, sinuous structure, all 180,000-sq feet (16,722 sq meters) of it. The skin was designed on an aerospace computer system made in France for jet planes and assembled from more than 21,000 shingles of aluminium and stainless steel. The materials were milled in Germany, and the colors of the stainless steel were applied with an "interference coating," by a specialist company in England. The panels were shipped to Kansas City to be cut and fabricated, before being taken to Seattle and attached to the 280 steel ribs that shape the construction. No two panels are the same shape.

The finished structure, in billowing folds of red, blue, purple, silver and gold houses a Sound Lab for musical and audio exploration, and the Sky Church (another Hendrix-inspired name), a massive 70-foot (21.3 meter) high performance and gathering area, which includes the world's largest indoor LED screen.

325 5th Avenue N; tel: 206-367 5483; www.emplive.org. Open daily 10am–8pm in summer; call for winter hours. Also see page 105.

ABOVE: Toronto-born architect Frank Gehry said, "I wanted to evoke the rock 'n' roll experience without being too literal about it." He also said, "we did a building by computer for a computer guy."

LEFT: legend Jimi Hendrix (1942–1970) had mixed feelings about his birthplace. After being drafted, he returned to Seattle only four times before his death.

ABOVE: *Roots and Branches* is an interactive musical sculpture. From Scottish melodies that preceded American folk, to Chicago blues, live music is provided by instruments in the sculpture itself.

SEATTLE ROCKS

Washington state has certainly played its part in the development of contemporary music, but the birthplace of crooners Bing Crosby and Nat King Cole never glimmered with such resonance as it did in the 1990s. In addition to the feminist girl-punk mini-quake that was Riot Grrl, exemplified by the band Bikini Kill, there was a sound called grunge.

A meld of punk and heavy metal, with a penchant for lyrics that made the Doors sound like light entertainment, Soundgarden, Alice in Chains, Mudhoney and Mother Love Bone (later Pearl Jam) made the Belltown club sound of the 1980s and 1990s, along with their compatriots, Nirvana.

Nirvana achieved worldwide success with their record *Nevermind*, but had a difficult relationship with MTV and the growing trend towards censorship in US chain stores like K-Mart. The tragic death of songwriter Kurt Cobain *(above)* in 1994 brought Nirvana to an end, but drummer Dave Grohl went on to form Foo-Fighters, and producer Butch Vig teamed up with Scottish singer Shirley Manson to form Garbage who, among many achievements, performed the theme song for the James Bond movie *The World is Not Enough*. Soundgarden singer Chris Cornell also sang a Bond theme, *You Know My Name*, for *Casino Royale*.

Cobain's widow, Courtney Love, also keeps the Seattle banner on record shelves, first with her band, Hole, and later by working with excellent producers.

RIGHT: the Sound Lab shows off musical and recording technology. Instruments, mixing desks and effects are available for visitors to record their own CD to take away. Sampling and scratching exhibits are included to engage the dance generation.

BELOW: On Stage is part of the interactive Sound Lab exhibit. It enables visitors to sing or play on a virtual stage, with lights, smoke machines and – of course – screaming virtual fans.

RIGHT: as well as exhibits on Hendrix and Pacific Northwest music, EMP promotes numerous educational and outreach projects, by taking musical workshops into schools and communities with a year-round concert program, and by hosting Experience Arts Camp, an arts summer camp for children. Electric Bus is an 18-wheel mobile unit that carries the musical mission even farther afield.

SEATTLE NEIGHBORHOODS

Neighborhoods like Capitol Hill, Queen Anne Hill, Madison Park and Magnolia have traditional names, but still showcase Seattle's spirited, sophisticated personality

N orth of the International District, and east of Downtown, **Capitol Hill** gets its name not from any seat of government, but from Denver, Colorado. Real-estate promoter James A. Moore, whose wife was from that city, gave it the name – after the Capitol Hill in Denver – in 1901.

The area is culturally, economically and racially mixed, and the hill is home to a big gay and lesbian population. A concentration of condos does little to detract from the charm of the mansions of Millionaires' Row (14th Avenue E, between Mercer and Prospect streets).

The end result is a refreshing mix of tree-lined streets with elegant homes and excellent museums, alongside a vibrant street scene. Great clubs, coffeehouses and restaurants complete the scene. With two colleges and a university nearby, Capitol Hill stays up later than most "early to bed" neighborhoods.

On Broadway

Broadway (Pine Street to E Roy Street) is the hill's main thoroughfare and commercial district; it is also one of the few places in town where casual strollers are seen on the street at midnight, even on weeknights. The **Egyptian** on E. Pine Street and the **Harvard Exit** on E. Roy Street are handsome reminders of earlier cinema eras. Both specialize in first-rate foreign-film presentations and host shows during the annual Seattle International Film Festival (May and June).

Another neighborhood movie theater, the Broadway, gave way years ago to a local discount store, although its theater marquee remains. Now, the sign which beckoned passers-by with promises of first-run films, instead entices with rock-bottom prices on lawn chairs.

Map on page 114

LEFT: autumn on Capitol Hill.
BELOW: Espresso Vivace Roasteria on Capitol Hill; note the "latte art" on the wall.

Lake View Cemetery, north of Volunteer Park, is the final resting place of Bruce Lee and his son, Brandon, as well as figures significant from Seattle's earlier history.

Traffic is heavy on Broadway at almost any time of day and parking is nearly impossible, but the ever-changing street scene of shops and restaurants makes this a good place for walking. Walkers can even learn some traditional dances from artist Jack Mackie's **bronze footsteps** embedded in the sidewalk, part of the city's public-art program.

Several blocks east, **15th Avenue East** is another Capitol Hill shopping district, one that's less congested and less flamboyant than Broadway, with a handful of good restaurants representing varied cuisines, several interesting shops, and the uniquitous espresso stands.

Volunteer Park

A few blocks north of the retail district on 15th Avenue is one of Seattle's largest and loveliest parks, 45-acre (18-hectare) **Volunteer Park ❷**. Originally a cemetery for the city's early pioneers, the land became Lake View Park when it was decided in 1887 to site a reservoir at the southern part of the property. The graves were moved north to what is now **Lake View Cemetery**, the final resting place of Seattle notables such as Doc Maynard and his wife Catherine, Henry Yesler, Hiram M Chittenden and John Nordstrom. In 1901, the park was renamed Volunteer Park in honor of Seattle men who served in the 1898 Spanish-American War.

With an elevation of 445 ft (135 meters), the park has magnificent views of the Space Needle, Puget Sound and the Olympic Mountains. The park's attractions are the **Volunteer Park Conservatory** (daily 10am–7pm summer, 10am–4pm winter; free; tel: 206-654 4743) with its five lush greenhouses, and the **Seattle Asian Art Museum** (Tues–Sun 10am–5pm, Thur to 9pm; admission charge; tel: 206-654 3100). When the Seattle Art Museum

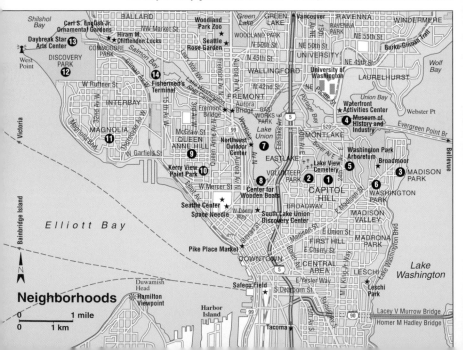

Neighborhoods

0 — 1 mile

0 — 1 km

moved Downtown in 1991, the Art Deco (1932) building in Volunteer Park was renamed and renovated to display the museum's extensive Asian art collections, including 14th–16th-century ceramics from Thailand and netsuke from Japan.

Madison Park

East of Capitol Hill is Madison Valley. The area west from Lake Washington Boulevard to 23rd Avenue E along both sides of Madison Street underwent a transformation in the 1980s and 1990s, and two-story retail complexes now anchor the intersection of Madison and Lake Washington Boulevard. A few consistently top-rated restaurants, an expansive gardening store and a number of pleasant delis and cafés, along with numerous new condominiums lining the hill side, signal the resurgence of this formerly overlooked neighborhood.

At the eastern foot of **Madison Street** – Seattle's only waterfront-to-waterfront street, running east to west from Elliott Bay to Lake Washington – is the unmistakably affluent community of **Madison Park** ❸, once the western terminus of a passenger-boat line connecting Seattle to the east side of Lake Washington. Here are restaurants that range from trendy to a local-favorite bakery, as well as a village of shops. The park itself has floodlit all-weather tennis courts and a beach, thronged on hot summer days by a lively urban mix from surrounding neighborhoods.

Northwest of Madison Park is the intriguing **Museum of History and Industry** ❹ (MOHAI; daily 10am–5pm; admission charge; tel: 206-324 1126). The museum contains thousands of items related to the development of Seattle and the Puget Sound area, and is much more interesting than its dry-sounding name might suggest. There are also exhibits which kids enjoy.

Adjacent to Madison Park is the **Washington Park Arboretum** ❺ (daily dawn to dusk; free; tel: 206-684 4725), a 200-acre (80-hectare) public park and botanical research facility for the University of Washington. One of the highlights is **Azalea Way**, a wide, grassy strip

Map on page 114

The collections at the Museum of History and Industry include 1.5 million photos, and cultural exhibits like this one.

BELOW: the Art Deco Seattle Asian Art Museum is as lovely as its exhibits.

The conservatory has five greenhouses, including one devoted to palms, and another to ferns.

winding through the park and lined by azaleas, dogwoods and flowering cherry trees. It was developed by the Public Works Administration in the 1930s, the federally funded "right to work" scheme begun during the Great Depression.

Another of the arboretum's highlights, the 3½-acre (1.4-hectare) formal **Japanese Garden** (daily 10am–8pm in summer, closes earlier and on Mondays in spring and fall, closed winter; admission charge), has tea-ceremony demonstrations in summer and guided tours April through October.

Just up the hill from Madison Park is the wealthy neighborhood of **Washington Park** ❻. A showcase for this residential area of stately homes and doted-upon lawns is the majestic thoroughfare on **36th Avenue E**, extending south between Madison and E. Mercer streets. Towering trees arch toward each other high above the street from both sides of 36th Avenue to form Seattle's most magnificent natural cathedral. Here too is the handsome brick mansion of the president of the University of Washington, at 808 36th E, with (one hears) a lovely rose garden, although you will need to be invited to see it.

Opposite 36th Avenue on the north side of Madison Street is the residential community of **Broadmoor** (private), complete with a fine golf course. Behind gatehouses and armed guards at both entrances, bank presidents, corporate lawyers, financiers, city fathers and others of the upper crust take refuge from the urban clash and clatter.

A sparkling waterfront neighborhood south of Madison Park along the western shore of Lake Washington, **Leschi** is named after the Native American leader who enjoyed camping here. Leschi was said to have been among those who planned an attack in 1856 on the city of Seattle, during the so-called Indian Wars. Conflict broke out after some local tribes signed treaties and were moved to reservations. The first automobile ferry, the *Leschi*, named after him, started regular service from here to the east side of Seattle in 1913.

At one time considered a social hot spot, Leschi is today a quiet neighborhood of waterfront homes, condominiums and apartment buildings, with a public beach, small-sailboat marina and the lushly green **Leschi Park** – once an amusement park at the terminus of the Yesler Street cable-car line. There are a couple of attractive restaurants that offer waterfront dining.

Eastlake and Lake Union

Cut off from Capitol Hill by Interstate 5 and north of Downtown along the east side of Lake Union, the district of **Eastlake** is a lively mix of large historic homes, multifamily dwellings and a thriving houseboat community. The residential neighborhood shares space, uneasily at times, with ever-chang-

ing commercial and industrial properties. The Boeing Company got its start here in 1915, when William Boeing began building seaplanes that he tested on Lake Union, in a hangar at the foot of Roanoke Street. Boeing moved the company to the south end of the city two years later, but the hangar remained here until 1971. It was demolished to make way for an abortive condominium project, which was defeated after a fierce 13-year legal battle fought by determined neighborhood groups.

The south end of **Lake Union ❼**, once an exclusively industrial area, has seen an explosion of developments and residents in recent years, which doesn't please all. The **South Lake Union Discovery Center** (101 Westlake Avenue N; tel: 206-342 5900; daily 11am–6pm; free; www.discoverslu.com) serves as a community center for this neighborhood-in-the-making, as well as a sales center for the many condominium and commercial projects springing up, most financed by Vulcan Real Estate, devised by Microsoft co-founder Paul Allen.

A small group of restaurants rings the south end of the lake, most with outdoor decks overlooking the water and docking facilities. More are planned for the future. The **Center for Wooden Boats ❽** (daily 10am–8pm in summer, 10am–6pm fall–spring; free; tel: 206 382 2628) is a nostalgically charming maritime museum with some 100 sailboats and rowboats, many of which are available for rent. Rowing or paddling is the most enjoyable way to appreciate the lake, and is the only chance to get close to the **houseboats and floating homes** that bob along the northeast and northwest shorelines.

Lake Union is also the home of a number of commercial seaplane services, including Kenmore Air (950 Westlake Avenue N; tel: 425-486 1257; www.kenmoreair.com), which

offers flights around the city, to the San Juan Islands, and to the Canadian cities of Vancouver, Victoria and other places on Vancouver Island.

On the west side of the lake, the **Northwest Outdoor Center** (NWOC; 2100 Westlake Avenue N; tel: 206-281 9694; Apr–Sept Mon–Fri 10am–8pm, Sat–Sun and hols 9am–6pm; hours vary during other months; www.nwoc.com) has kayak rentals by the hour.

Queen Anne Hill

Northwest of Downtown, behind the Seattle Center and west of Lake Union is the area known as **Lower Queen Anne**. It is mainly made up of condos and apartments, and marks the tail end of the more graceful **Queen Anne Hill ❾**. An interesting array of shops, coffeehouses and restaurants occupy Roy and Mercer streets, as well as Queen Anne Avenue just south of Mercer.

Queen Anne Hill, in the words of Seattle photo-historian Paul Dorpat, "is cleansed by winds, girdled by greenbelts, and topped by towers and mansions." The hill rises

Map on page 114

TIP

Harbor cruises of Lake Washington and Lake Union are available from Argosy Cruises, tel: 206-623 1445. Ask the narrator to point out Tom Hanks' Lake Union floating home from the movie *Sleepless in Seattle.*

BELOW: rowboats and kayaks can be rented on Lake Union.

Call me Fishmail: "floating homes" is a better description than houseboats for many of the Eastlake residences; some are two storys tall with gardens, porches and underwater compartments for storage.

BELOW: floating homes line the northern shores of Lake Union.

sharply on all four sides to a summit of 457 ft (139 meters), the second-highest elevation in the city (35th Avenue SW in West Seattle reaches 514 ft/157 meters). Seattle pioneer Thomas Mercer, who arrived in 1853, filed the first claim on Queen Anne Hill and had to cut through a forest in order to build a home.

The hill got its name from Rev. Daniel Bagley, who referred to it as "Queen Anne Town," a jocular reference to the lavish mansions some of the city's prominent citizens built on the hill in the 1880s in an American variation of the Queen Anne architectural style in England.

Queenly views

Bounded by Mercer Street on the south, Lake Union on the east, Lake Washington Ship Canal on the north, and Elliott Avenue on the west, the Queen Anne district is home to around 50,000 residents. Because of its height, the hill has spectacular views of Puget Sound, the Olympic Mountains, and dramatic sunsets to the west; Lake Union, Capitol Hill and the Cascade

Range to the east; Elliott Bay, Downtown and Mount Rainier to the south; and the Ship Canal and Mount Baker to the north.

Getting to the best viewpoint requires a drive through some of the loveliest residential streets in the city. Head west on Highland Drive from Queen Anne Avenue, about halfway up the hill. Gracious apartment buildings line both sides of the street. **Kerry View Point Park** ⑩ is a narrow stretch of green with wide-open views of the Space Needle, downtown office towers, the Elliott Bay harbor, and, weather permitting, Mount Rainier. The views from here are spectacular at more or less any time of day or night *(see photo below and on pages 10–11).*

West of Kerry View Point Park, stately mansions line both sides of Highland Drive, which ends in tiny, secluded **Parsons Garden**, a beautiful public park.

Magnolia

In 1856, a captain in the US Coast Survey named the southern bluff overlooking Puget Sound for the

magnolia trees growing along it. But the trees turned out to be madrona trees. The community liked the name Magnolia better than Madrona and decided to keep it.

Northwest of Downtown, affluent **Magnolia** ⓫ is a well-ordered, conservative neighborhood of mostly single-family homes nestling on expansive lots. Magnificent waterfront properties along the western edge, south of Discovery Park, are protected from view by vegetation and long driveways. the main shopping area, **Magnolia Village** (W. McGraw Street between 32nd and 35th avenues), has fashionable stores and watering holes.

At 527 acres (213 hectares), **Discovery Park** ⓬ is Seattle's largest green open area. The park was named for the ship of the English explorer Captain George Vancouver, who, during his 1792 exploration of Puget Sound, spent several days with the HMS *Discovery* at anchor within sight of this land.

A 2½-mile (4-km) loop trail around the park winds through thick forests and crosses broad meadows and high, windswept bluffs with spectacular views of Puget Sound and the Olympic Mountains. Wildlife is abundant here, with bald eagles occasionally seen in the treetops, as well as regular sightings of falcons, herons, beavers and foxes. In 1982, a mountain lion was encountered in Discovery Park.

The **Daybreak Star Arts Center** ⓭ (Mon–Fri 9am–5pm; free; tel: 206-285 4425) is a local attraction sponsoring Native American events, and exhibiting contemporary Indian art. Discovery Park also has picnic areas, playgrounds, tennis and basketball courts.

Fishermen's Terminal ⓮, on W. Thurman Street on Magnolia's northern side, provides an opportunity to admire the boats of a major fishing fleet. This is home port for more than 700 commercial fishing vessels, many of which fish for salmon, halibut or crab in Alaskan waters. The craft range in size from 30 ft (9 meters) to 300 ft (90 meters). Visitors can sample the day's catch at the restaurants, or by purchasing from the fish market. ❑

The view of the city and the Space Needle seen in the hit TV show Frasier *is from Queen Anne Hill. But to enjoy such a sweeping panorama, the balcony of Frasier's apartment would need to have been half way up one of the radio towers on top of the hill.*

BELOW: Seattle and Mount Rainier from Kerry View Point Park, Queen Anne Hill.

RESTAURANTS

Cactus
4220 E Madison Street
Tel: 206-324 4140
www.cactusrestaurants.com
Open: L Mon–Sat, D daily. **$$**
This Madison Park hot
spot was one of the city's
first tapas restaurants,
serving inventive Mexi-
can, Southwestern and
Spanish-inspired fare.

Café Flora
2901 E Madison Street
Tel: 206-325 9100
www.cafeflora.com
Open: Br Sat–Sun, L Mon–Fri,
D daily. **$$–$$$**
A vegetarian restaurant,
where carnivores don't
miss the meat. The food
is fantastically flavorful
and beautifully plated,
and service is excellent.
Don't miss the Oaxaca
tacos or the portabella
mushroom wellington.

Café Septieme
214 Broadway Avenue E
Tel: 206-860 8858
Open: B, L, D daily. **$$**
Capitol Hill cool spot on
Broadway. Inexpensive
but inventive bistro menu
and strong drinks. The
staff range from charming
to coldly indifferent. It's
darkly lit with blood-red
walls, deep, cozy booths
and a particularly fine
selection of desserts.

Chinook's at Salmon Bay
1900 W. Nickerson Street
Tel: 206-283 4665
www.anthonys.com
Open: B Sat–Sun, L Mon–
Sat, D daily. **$$**
Part of the local
Anthony's chain, the
strongest recommenda-
tion for this seafood
restaurant at Fisher-
men's Terminal probably

comes from the number
of fishermen who travel
to Magnolia to dine here.

Coastal Kitchen
429 15th Avenue E
Tel: 206-321 1145
www.chowfoods.com
Open: B, L, D daily. **$$**
This hip Capitol Hill hang-
out keeps diners guess-
ing with its regularly
changing menu. How the
cooks do so well at so
many different ethnic
styles is a mystery, but
they do. There's never any
doubt, though, about their
weekend brunches, espe-
cially the pork-chop plate.

Crave
1621 12th Avenue
Tel: 206-388 0526
www.cravefood.com
Open: B, L, D daily. **$–$$**
Crave bills itself as serving "honest food," and
the menu and friendly
service live up to the
billing. Food changes by
the season, but favorites
include curried lamb,
goat's cheese gnocchi,
and shiitake macaroni
and cheese.

Deluxe Bar & Grill
625 Broadway E
Tel: 206-324 9697
Open: L and D daily. **$$**
Relax with a meal of
American classics in this
casual restaurant at the
north end of Broadway.
A diverse selection of
local microbrew beers
makes a great comple-
ment to the half-price
burger specials offered
every Wednesday.

Dilettante Chocolate Café
416 Broadway E
Tel: 206-329 6463
www.dilettante.com
Open: L and D daily. **$**
Indulge a sweet tooth at
this café, which is known
for sugary treats. The
menu is dominated by
chocolate – from rich,
chocolatey mochas to
decadent cakes – but
lighter fare like salads
and sandwiches are also
available. It's the perfect
place for a pick-me-up
after a long day.

Elysian Brewing Co
1221 E Pike Street
Tel: 206-860 1920
www.elysianbrewing.com
Open: L and D daily. **$**
A wide selection of micro-
brew beers is the biggest
draw here. Some are
brewed on the premises
and others imported,
and the pub food is not
too bad, either.

5 Spot
1502 Queen Anne Avenue N
Tel: 206-285-SPOT
www.chowfoods.com
Open: B, L, D daily. **$–$$**
A terrific spot for break-
fasts, on top of Queen
Anne Hill. The regularly
changing menu is
another attraction.

Frites
925 East Pike
www.belgianfrites.com
Open: D daily. **$**
This little hole in the wall
specializes in Belgian
fries (and serves a few
varieties of bratwurst).

The tasty potato morsels – best in all of Seattle – are fried twice to ensure extra crispiness on the outside and perfect moistness on the inside. Fun with a group of friends, sample the variety of sauces for dipping.

Galerias
611 Broadway Avenue E
Tel: 206-321 5757
Open: L and D daily. **$$**
Each dish at this Mexican restaurant is a work of art, as are the huge margaritas. Delicious, affordable, and also has people-watching seating right on Broadway.

Green Papaya
600 E Pine Street
Tel: 206-323 1923
www.papayaonpine.com
Open: L and D Tues–Sun. **$**
This Capitol Hill Vietnamese restaurant features food from three different regions of Vietnam.

The Hunt Club
900 Madison Street
Tel: 206-343 6156
www.hotelsorrento.com/dining-hunt-club.php
Open: B, L D daily. **$$$$**
Top-notch Northwest cuisine, including game and seafood, is matched by the posh, clubby atmosphere in the Sorrento Hotel near First Hill.

Kingfish Cafe
602 19th Avenue E
Tel: 206-320 8757
Open: L Sun–Mon, Wed–Fri, D Wed–Mon. **$$**
Southern soul food, served up with style,

sauce and smiles. The grits go well with everything and the catfish is pretty miraculous, as is the fried chicken. Long lines attest to the café's popularity, particularly for weekend brunch.

Lark
926 12th Avenue
Tel: 206-323 5275
www.larkseattle.com
Open: D Tues–Sun.
$$$–$$$$
Shareable platters, an oft-changing menu and knowledgeable servers add to the appeal of this charming Capitol Hill bistro. Flickering candlelight and the buzz of the food-savvy beautiful people complement dishes, which range from seared Sonoma foie gras to carpaccio of yellowtail.

Mamounia Moroccan Restaurant
1530 Bellevue Avenue
Tel: 206-329 5388
www.mamouniarestaurant.com
Open: D daily. **$$**
Step out of the Pacific Northwest and into exotic Morocco when you visit Mamounia. Top-notch service as you recline on embroidered pillows. Flavorful and modestly priced Moroccan dishes.

Nishino
3130 E Madison Street
Tel: 206-321 5800
www.nishinorestaurant.com
Open: D daily. **$$$**
Chef/owner Tatsu Nishino serves exquisite sushi in the Madison Valley. Sitting at the bar is the most fun.

Palisade
2601 W Marina Place
Tel: 206-285 1000
www.palisaderestaurant.com
Open: Br Sun, L Mon–Fri, D daily. **$$$–$$$$**
Just across the Magnolia bridge, at the Elliott Bay Marina, sits this tourist magnet with sweeping views of the Seattle skyline and Puget Sound. Seafood is the specialty.

Rover's
2808 E Madison Street
Tel: 206-325 7442
www.rovers-seattle.com
Open: L Fri, D Tues–Sat. **$$$$**
A Madison Valley French restaurant, presided over by the "Chef in the Hat," Thierry Rautureau, serves beautiful multi-course tasting menus (options for vegetarians), as well as à la carte selections.

Szmania's
3321 W McGraw Street
Tel: 206-284 7305
www.szmanias.com

Open: L Tues–Fri, D Tues–Sun. **$$$**
Ludger Szmania's fine-dining restaurant in Magnolia has a loyal local following, and is worth the trip for his seafood, steak and German-inspired fare.

Via Tribunali
913 E Pike Street
Tel: 206-321 9234
Open: D Wed–Sat. **$$**
Be prepared to wait for a table at this dark, sexy Capitol Hill hot spot. This sophisticated Italian pizzeria has been out-the-door popular since the day it opened. Many ingredients come from Italy.

PRICE CATEGORIES

Prices for a three-course dinner per person with half a bottle of wine:
$ = under $20
$$ = $20–45
$$$ = $45–60
$$$$ = more than $60

LEFT: the 5 Spot is a good spot for breakfast.
RIGHT: the Kingfish Cafe does soul food with style.

NORTH SEATTLE

From the pleasant University of Washington
campus to the cageless Woodland Park Zoo,
North Seattle blends lovely outdoor scenery
with cool neighborhoods like
Fremont and Ballard

The 8-mile (13-km) long **Lake Washington Ship Canal ❶** separates the northern neighborhoods of Seattle from the city center. Completed in 1917, the canal winds through the Ballard, Fremont, Wallingford, University and Montlake districts linking salty Puget Sound with the fresh waters of Lakes Union and Washington. A series of locks *(see page 132)* raise and lower ships making the transit. Six bridges cross the canal, leading into a cluster of neighborhoods that make up North Seattle. These districts, born as independent townships in the 19th century, retain distinctly individual characteristics.

The University District

The **Burke-Gilman Trail** is a 12-mile (19-km) biking and walking route, begining in Ballard, swinging along Lake Union past Gas Works Park, winding through the University of Washington campus before coursing north on the left bank of Lake Washington. The innovative and scenic track follows the course of the lakeshore railroad, which connected these communities in the 19th century, an imaginative "recycling" that is part of a national "rails-to-trails" movement.

The **University District** is an eclectic commercial center thriving

on the cultural, educational and athletic amenities afforded by the University of Washington. **University Way Northeast**, affectionately called "**the Ave**" by locals, is a busy strip of shops, theaters, newsstands, book stores, pubs and eateries. Some Seattleites treat this animated district with caution, as an increasing number of panhandlers, rebellious young people and homeless bring with them a sometimes shadowy subculture. But the diversityof the community, made up of students, businesspeople,

Map on page 124

LEFT: mascot at the University of Washington's Husky Stadium.
BELOW: Adobe headquarters in Fremont.

The Quad at the University of Washington was designed by the Olmsteds, who were responsible for New York's Central Park.

academics and vagrants certainly has a verve and vitality. The **University Bookstore** (4326 University Way NE; tel: 206-634 3400), a stalwart of the Ave since 1925, has a huge selection of contemporary fiction as well as textbooks, school and art supplies and T-shirts. Along the street are used-book stores, import shops, new- and used-clothing stores, jewelry stores, music stores and an array of specialty stores.

Six blocks west of the Ave, on NE 45th Street, is the venerable **Blue Moon Tavern** (712 NE 45th Street; tel: 206-545 9775), opened in 1934 and which apartment developers almost managed to demolish several years ago. This seedy, once-smoky den of glory – denizens have included the late poet Theodore Roethke and novelist Tom Robbins – fought back against development and won, not only with new historical landmark status but also a cast-iron 40-year lease. They couldn't, however, win against Washington's 2005 state-wide ban on smoking in all bars and restaurants.

University of Washington

A few blocks to the east is the 640-acre (260-hectare) **University of Washington** ❷ campus itself. Started on a 10-acre (4-hectare) plot that it acquired – and still owns (and which generates massive rents) – in downtown Seattle on University Street in 1861, the university moved to its present site in 1895.

Almost 40,000 students and more than 20,000 staff come here to the state's finest public university, best known for its medical and law schools, and for fine research facilities. Pick up a self-guided walking tour brochure from the **Visitors' Information Center** (4014 University Way; tel: 206-543 9198).

Much of the original campus was designed by the Olmsted family, famous for New York's Central

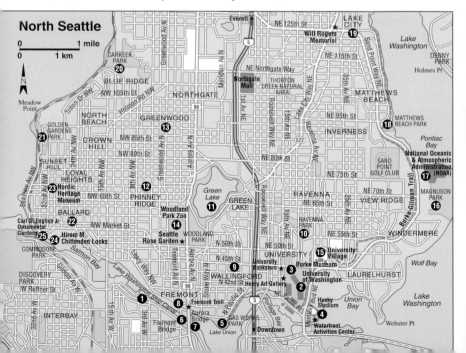

North Seattle

0 ____ 1 mile
0 ____ 1 km

Park. **Drumheller Fountain** sits at the top of the Rainier Vista Mall, the gateway to the Gothic-style Quad, where in April rows of cherry trees burst into pink or white blossoms.

The addition of the **Allen Library** expanded by 40 percent the capacity of **Suzzallo Library**, a Gothic-style cathedral-like hall that was opened in 1927 and dubbed the soul of the university by then-president Henry Suzzallo.

This modern addition was built with a $10-million donation from Paul Allen, co-founder of Microsoft, who bought the city's football team and created the Experience Music Project (*see page 110–11*). The red-tiled plaza adjoining Suzzallo was added in 1969 and dubbed Red Square. On summer evenings at the **Theodor Jacobsen Observatory** (open first and third Wed evenings, variable hours; free; tel: 206-685 7856), near the north campus entrance, visitors can gaze at the heavens through one of the observatory's telescopes.

The **Burke Museum ❸** (daily 10am–5pm, first Thur of each month to 8pm; admission charge; tel: 206-543 5590) is the Northwest's premier museum of natural and cultural history. It has the only dinosaur skeletons in the Pacific Northwest, as well as the region's most comprehensive collection of Native art from the Northwest Coastal tribes.

The impressive anthropology, geology and zoology collections when combined total more than 3 million specimens and artifacts. The museum underwent a remodeling in the late 1990s and now has a "walk-through" volcano, in addition to two permanent exhibits. One illustrates 500 million years of regional history, while the other highlights Pacific Rim cultures.

Art and recreation

Not far from the Burke is the **Henry Art Gallery** (15th Avenue NE and NE 41st Street; tel: 206-543 2280; Tues–Sun 11am–5pm, Thur to 8pm; admission charge). Expanded and renovated in 1997, the gallery has 46,000 sq ft (4,300 sq meters) of exhibit space to show its 19,000 pieces of 19th- and 20th-century

Map on page 124

Coastal tribal art is well represented at the Burke Museum.

BELOW: the Burke Museum is the Northwest's best natural history museum.

MacUser awards, in Adobe's headquarters in Fremont. The offices are not open to the public.

art, including Japanese ceramics and the American and European painting collection of Horace C. Henry, a real-estate and railroad magnate for whom the museum was named in 1927.

Husky Stadium 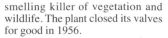 is just to the southeast. It is one of the largest in the Pacific Northwest, with a capacity for 72,000 spectators to watch its extremely popular football games. Just below the stadium, on Union Bay, weekend water warriors rent rowboats or canoes at the lake's **Waterfront Activities Center** (open daily 10am–6pm; tel: 206-543 9433), while others bring their own beer and boats.

Gas Works Park

Hulking specters of a bygone age dominate **Gas Works Park** ❺, on a southerly knob of land jutting into Lake Union and the front door to North Seattle. The Seattle Gas Light Company began to produce heating and lighting gas in this refinery on the 20-acre (8-hectare) knoll in 1906, fueling a rapidly growing city while earning a reputation as a filthy, foul-

smelling killer of vegetation and wildlife. The plant closed its valves for good in 1956.

When the site was proposed as a park in the early 1960s, the city council hired landscape architect Richard Haag to create a lush, arboretum-type park. Instead, Haag submitted a plan incorporating much of the old gas plant. His design – with the rusting hulks of the gas works in the middle of an undulating lawn – triumphed after a storm of controversy from those wishing for a more traditional park.

The industrial-site conversion park was opened in 1975. Although concerns are still occasionally raised about contaminants in the soil under the park's green layer of grass, the city hasn't closed or restricted its use.

Kites fly high over the park's **Grand Mound**, a grassy hill built west of the park's core from abandoned industrial waste. Picnickers and joggers share the space along an incline, and at the crown, visitors admire a mosaic sun and moon dial. The crest offers a great panorama of inner Seattle – Downtown, Queen Anne Hill, the Aurora Bridge (where Highway 99 crosses the Lake Washington Ship Canal) to the west, and Capitol Hill to the east. To the north, the park gives way to the University of Washington and the pretty residential houses of Wallingford and Fremont.

Fremont

No bridge in the state opens more often than the **Fremont Bridge** ❻, which was completed in 1917 over the Lake Washington Ship Canal. You can watch boats go under the blue and orange drawbridge from a peaceful overlook at the **Fremont Canal Park**, a walkway on the north side of the waterway that features outdoor public art. Just east of the bridge on the north side is the headquarters of **Adobe Software**.

Fremont, strategically located at the northwest corner of Lake Union, was once a busy stop on the 1880s Burke-Gilman's SLS&E Railway, which carried lumber, coal and passengers between Downtown and Ballard *(see pages 131–2)*.

During Prohibition, Fremont's thriving taverns and hotel salons were closed, though the basement speakeasies flourished in spite of the frequent police raids. The **Aurora Bridge** ❼ opened in 1932, bypassing Fremont.

By the 1960s, hippies and unemployed drifters had taken over the Fremont and Triangle hotels, but the 1970s brought a long-awaited local renaissance. Artists moved into the cheap brick studios in lower Fremont, setting up the kind of eclectic galleries, shops and cafés that define the neighborhood today. Fremont got funky. In fact, nary a tale is told of **Fremont** ❽ without the alliterative description "funky."

Funky vintage collectibles are sold in the neighborhood's second-hand stores, funky crafts are available at specialty shops, and funky musical instruments can be found at stores which specialize in drums and hand-crafted acoustic instruments. Longtime Seattleites, however, view the current "Fremont funkiness" as a little forced. Countless condo projects, which followed the offices of companies like Adobe and Getty Images, pushed Fremont property values up, and pushed out many of the artists and other folks who gave the neighborhood its charm.

These days, its stores are likely to be chic boutiques rather than hippie havens, but they *are* invididually owned and fun to visit.

Good nightlife

Fremont's tavern life has survived during these changes, and options have even expanded. Choices now range from a biker atmosphere, to young adults on the prowl, to pubs serving microbrews and almost-nightly live music. Good restaurants serve cuisine ranging from vegetarian fare, to Asian, to Greek, to upscale fine dining.

On 34th Street just north of the Aurora Bridge, the Fremont statue

Map on page 124

Hunkering under the Aurora Bridge is the enormous, concrete one-eyed Fremont Troll. *He's clutching a Volkswagen.*

BELOW: two landmarks everyone in Fremont knows, although few know why they are here.

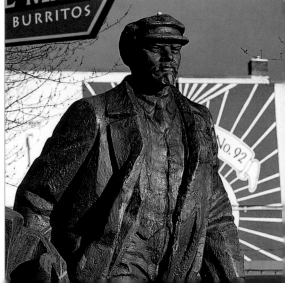

that has come to represent this area is ***Waiting for the Interurban***, artist Rich Beyer's sculpture of five life-size adults, a baby in arms and a dog (said to have the face of a former mayor), all supposedly waiting for the electric trolley, which until the 1930s ran north to the town of Everett. Although some art critics are appalled by this sculpture, it is loved by the public, who regularly decorate the people, and the pergola above them, with T-shirts, balloons and streamers wishing friends happy birthday or good luck.

East of Fremont, **Wallingford** N has a residential history steeped in memories of the sounds and stench that arose from the gasworks at the bottom of the neighborhood.

The district attracted working-class people who took a special pride in their schools. The earliest school in the area, Latona, was founded in 1889. The Home of the Good Shepherd, a girls' orphanage started in 1906 by the Sisters of Our Lady of Charity, is now a cultural and community center. Many of the neighborhood's old houses are now

elegant showpieces. The historic 1904 Interlake Public School at the corner of 45th and Wallingford was converted into a mixed-use complex in 1983. Now **Wallingford Center**, it has restaurants and shops, with apartments above. Shops and cafés line **45th Avenue** for several blocks, and you can find bakeries, bars, coffee- and teashops, as well as little specialty stores. The street even has two small movie theaters.

A park, a lake and a zoo

Seattle is young enough that residents still wistfully imagine the land as it was a century ago – a wilderness of virgin forests and crystal waterways. Just north of the University of Washington is lush **Ravenna Park** N, an unspoiled, deep and wooded gorge far from the cosmopolitan life. Standing in silence next to a towering tree or a spill of green fern, it is not hard to envision early settlers meeting a grizzly bear on the track or gathering herbs for healing. Both the town and the park were named Ravenna after the Italian city on Italy's north-

BELOW LEFT AND RIGHT: on and around the water, Green Lake.

ern coast, which also stood on the edge of an ancient forest. The shimmering waters of **Green Lake** ripple against grassy shores in the high-density neighborhood of the same name.

It's a lake in a city surrounded by water, an algae-tinged reservoir born of glacial gougings 15,000 years ago. Runners and inline-skaters zip along the busy 2.8-mile (5-km) perimeter path in all weather. Rent a pair of blades or admire the occasionally aggressive ducks at the **Waldo Waterfowl Sanctuary**. Also keep a look out for great blue herons and an eagle.

A community center and its environs offer facilities including football fields, tennis courts, a swimming pool, gym, rowboat and canoe rentals and a beach. Restaurants around the lake range from trendy watering holes to fine Italian dining, to fish and chips.

The neighborhoods of **Phinney Ridge** ⓬ and **Greenwood** ⓭ blend easily together. Greenwood Avenue, once touted as Seattle's Antiques Row, mixes traditional antiques and second-hand stores with modern merchants and specialty-food stores. There are galleries with contemporary Northwest art, home-style cafés and several popular drinking establishments.

Wilderness estate

Almost 300 animal species inhabit the hills that tuck between Phinney Ridge and Green Lake at the **Woodland Park Zoo** ⓮ (5500 Phinney Avenue N; tel: 206-684 4800; daily 9.30am–6pm, to 4pm in winter; admission charge; www.zoo.org). The former wilderness estate of Guy Phinney, a leading Seattle real-estate developer in the 1880s, this 92-acre (37-hectare) park pioneered the concept of creating naturalistic habitats for animals.

The zoo demonstrates a true commitment to cageless animal care. Eight bioclimactic zones provide comfort for the animals and encourage natural behavior. The Asian Elephant Forest and African Savannah have earned international recognition, and the Northern Trail area is a visitors' favorite. Near the southeast exit,

Map on page 124

Seattle's zoo was among the first to create natural habitats for animals.

BELOW: wise eyes and bird, Woodland Park Zoo.

take time to smell the roses in the magnificent **Seattle Rose Garden** (free), originally laid out in the 1890s by old man Phinney himself.

Upscale shopping

Northwest of the University of Washington is **University Village**  shopping complex. Large chain stores such as Crate and Barrel, Restoration Hardware and Pottery Barn cater to the area's comfortably off homeowners, and high-end shops act as magnets for wealthy housewives. They come from the neighborhoods bordering Lake Washington to the east, where spacious contemporary homes on landscaped hill sides capture sweeping views of the Cascade Mountains and Mount Rainier.

Ballard has fun, individually owned stores and independently minded people.

On the southern stretch of the **Sand Point** peninsula, which juts out into Lake Washington north of the university, at least 87 species of birds and innumerable kinds of wildlife frequent the re-contoured terrain of **Magnuson Park** ⓰, once a naval air station and now adorned with bluffs, sports fields, trails and

BELOW: Halloween house in Ballard.

long, serene stretches of beach. On the same delta extending into Lake Washington, Bill Boeing flew his first airplane in 1916. In 1921, the first around-the-world flight began and ended here – four Navy aircraft left on April 6 and three arrived back on September 28.

In 1974, the city of Seattle granted the **National Oceanic and Atmospheric Administration** ⓱ (NOAA) the northern 114 acres (46 hectares) of what had been the naval air station for NOAA's Western Regional Center. It is now the largest federal center for atmospheric and oceanic research in the United States. Many of the facilities are open to the public through tours, but arrangements should be made first: National Weather Service, tel: 206-526 6087, and the Pacific Marine Environmental Lab, tel: 206-526 6810.

Walkers are invited to saunter along the **Shoreline Walk** to where five publicly funded environmental artworks have been so successful that the project has attracted national attention for public art. The artists combined earth, wind and water among their media: a concrete spiraling dome gives views in every direction; a viewpoint over the lake with chairs and sofas is cut from boulders; a bridge is lettered with excerpts from Moby Dick; and a "sound garden" of lacy towers and tuned organ pipes makes music from the wind.

About a mile to the north of Magnuson Park is Seattle's largest freshwater bathing beach (a lifeguard is on duty) at **Matthews Beach Park** ⓲, just off the Burke-Gilman Trail. At the south end, cross the footbridge above Thornton Creek to reach the tiny, charming **Thornton Creek Natural Area**, where wildlife finds a convenient retreat from the noisy, urban meleé.

In the tiny hamlet of Pontiac, a railroad worker once hung a sign

saying just "Lake" on a shed near the tracks of Northern Pacific Railroad. The name stuck, and **Lake City** ⓳ was annexed by Seattle in 1954. Here, the blur of car lots, gas stations and supermarkets lining Lake City Way may not make a huge impression, but the region has a few spots of distinction. A flagpole dedicated to World War II veterans sits in the smallest official city park, and a **Will Rogers Memorial** (12501 28th Ave. NE) honors the Oklahoma-born wit and philosopher, who spent one of his last days playing polo here. He then left Seattle for Alaska, and he was killed in a plane crash.

Heading west

If access to the jeweled shores of Puget Sound means prosperity, then Seattleites are rich indeed, for 216-acre (87-hectare) **Carkeek Park** ⓴, on the coast of Puget Sound and northwest of Green Lake, winds and plunges down into a maze of wooded pathways, over the railroad tracks and onto an unfettered stretch of beach. The park was named for Morgan and Emily Carkeek, early Seattle contractors and philanthropists. Locals are laboring to re-establish the park's Piper's Creek as a salmon-spawning site.

Following the railroad tracks south leads towards the proud-hearted neighborhood of Ballard. The tracks run through **Golden Gardens Park** ㉑ (on Seaview Place NW), neatly dividing it into two distinct sections: a forested hill side and a golden beach stretching along **Shilshole Bay**, Seattle's coast of blue. Sunbathe, scuba dive, dig for clams, or watch the sailboats breezing out toward the Puget isles. Wind up Golden Gardens Drive and go south until a "scenic drive" sign at NW 77th denotes the aptly named **Sunset Hill**.

Ballard

Scandinavians were drawn here by the fishing, lumber and boat-building opportunities found in such a majestic and watery region, much like their homeland. When downtown Seattle was rebuilt after the great fire of 1889 and Washington

Map on page 124

Seattle is reputedly the best place in America to have a heart attack. More than 50 percent of the adult population has had some sort of CPR training.

BELOW: taking a break outside a Ballard club.

Map on page 124

Ray's Boathouse, tel: 206-789 3770, has a fantastic view of Puget Sound and serves simple dishes.

BELOW: the Hiram M. Chittenden Locks are also known as the Ballard Locks.

entered the Union as the 42nd state, Gilman Park, with nearly 2,000 residents, hurried to be the first to incorporate, naming their boomtown **Ballard** ㉒.

Early Ballard was a bastion of pioneer revelry, said to hold 27 saloons on a four-block strip. It has fewer today, but Ballard still sports its share of bars and plays a key role in Seattle's music scene. It's a fun neighborhood to be in, with independently owned stores and businesses, and individual-looking young people thronging the streets.

The "Dream of America," an exhibit at the **Nordic Heritage Museum** ㉓ (3014 NW 67th Street; tel: 206-789 5707; Tues–Sun 10am–4pm, Sun from noon; admission charge; www.nordicmuseum.org), tells a graphic story of the immigrants' travel to the new land. Five rooms describe the cultural legacy of Sweden, Norway, Iceland, Finland and Denmark.

Every year, about 100,000 commercial and pleasure vessels navigate through the 1917-era **Hiram M. Chittenden Locks** ㉔ – also known as the **Ballard Locks** – two masonry gates on the north bank of the canal and opposite Discovery Park, which raise and lower boats between the level of the saltwater of Puget Sound and the freshwater of Lake Washington.

Salmon ladder

About 500,000 sockeye, chinook and coho salmon use the same channel to get to their spawning grounds in Lake Washington and streams farther along in the Cascade Range to the east, climbing a 21-level fish ladder built to preserve the migrating runs. In summer, visitors can watch their passage upstream through six lit underwater viewing windows, a moving portrait of creatures driven by a mandate of nature and against all odds back to their birthplace.

Not far away are the terraced lawns and roses of the waterside **Carl S. English, Jr Ornamental Gardens** ㉕. Named after one of the region's top horticulturalists in the early 1900s, the gardens make an excellent picnic spot. ❑

RESTAURANTS

Asteroid
3601 Fremont Avenue N
Tel: 206-547 9000
www.asteroidcafe.com
Open: D Wed–Sun. **$$–$$$**
For years, this Italian restaurant was in a tiny Wallingford store front, but moved in 2006 to Fremont. The food is still the draw: spicy *puttanesca*, vegetarian ravioli *ai funghi*, and wine-by-the-glass specials.

Bizzarro Italian Café
1307 N 46th Street
Tel: 206-632 7277
Open: D daily. **$**
This funky Wallingford joint serves good Italian fare with décor to reflect the name: bizarre.

Brad's Swingside Café
4212 Fremont Avenue N
Tel: 206-633 4057
Open: D Tues–Sat. **$$**
Walk in the door of this funky Fremont bungalow and you might think you'd walked into a private party in someone's home. Start with antipasti, and move on to pastas and specials.

Brouwer's Café
400 N 35th Street
Tel: 206-267-BIER
www.brouwerscafe.com
Open: L and D daily. **$$**
Beer is big here: 50 on tap and 100 by the bottle. The traditional Belgian alehouse also serves Scotch (more than 30 kinds) and an à la carte pub-type menu.

Canlis
2576 Aurora Avenue N
Tel: 206-283 3313
www.canlis.com
Open: D Mon–Sat. **$$$$**
Canlis is where restaurant critics spend their own money on special dinners. A spectacular view over Lake Union, elegant, understated décor and service, and top-notch food, not to mention a legendary valet service.

Carmelita
7314 Greenwood Avenue N
Tel: 206-706 7703
www.carmelita.net
Open: D Tues–Sun. **$$**
This artful spot on Phinney Ridge seats 100 for vegetarian fine dining.

Essential Baking Co.
1604 N 34th Street
Tel: 206-545 0444
www.essentialbaking.com
Open: B, L daily. **$**
This Fremont bakery is crowded morning and noon, with folks stopping by for coffee and pastries, and at lunch for the wonderful sandwiches.

Eva Restaurant & Wine Bar
2227 N 56th Street
Tel: 206-633 3538
Open: D Tues–Sun. **$$**
This Green Lake spot serves Mediterranean-influenced cuisine with a lengthy wine list.

Le Gourmand
425 NW Market Street
Tel: 206-784 3463
Open: D Wed–Sat. **$$$**
Good French food has been served at this Ballard favorite since 1985.

Lockspot Café
3005 NW 54th Street
Tel: 206-789 4865
Open: B, L, D daily. **$**
Right by Ballard Locks is this dive, great for breakfasts and fish & chips.

Mona's Bistro & Lounge
6421 Latona Ave NE
Tel: 206-526 1188
Open: D daily. **$$$**
A sexy spot near Green Lake, perfect for a romantic evening.

Ponti Seafood Grill
3014 3rd Avenue N
Tel: 206-284 3000
www.pontigrill.com
Open: D daily. **$$$**
A local favorite for more than 15 years, Ponti serves Northwest seafood in a location overlooking the Lake Washington Ship Canal and the Fremont drawbridge.

Volterra
5411 Ballard Avenue NW
Tel: 206-789 5100
www.volterrarestaurant.com
Open: Br Sat–Sun, D daily. **$$$**
Said by some to serve the best Italian food in the city: try the creamy polenta with wild mushroom *ragu*, or the wild boar tenderloin with gorgonzola sauce.

PRICE CATEGORIES

Prices for a three-course dinner per person with half a bottle of wine:
$ = under $20
$$ = $20–45
$$$ = $45–60
$$$$ = more than $60

RIGHT: stop in at the Lockspot for fish & chips.

WEST AND SOUTH SEATTLE

The "birthplace of Seattle" has views, flowers and
sandy beaches, while South Seattle is the place
for new homeowners and urban pioneers

I t was on the windswept shores of
what is now Alki Beach that
Seattle's pioneers first built a
community. The area's original residents, led by Arthur Denny, came
from the state of Illinois, in the
American Midwest, seeking a better
life. After one blustery winter on
Alki (pronounced Al-khi, to rhyme
with "pie"), however, most of the
Denny party moved away from the
beach's winds to the shelter and
deeper anchorage of Elliott Bay.

That exodus seems surprising
given Alki's current popularity. In
summer, the sandy beach is a mass
of tanned bodies, and on sunny days
year-round, the footpath and its
adjacent bike-and-skating path are
crowded with promenading, strut-
ting, jogging people.

West Seattle

Geographically the southern part of
the city, known locally as West Seattle, is on a peninsula, separated from
downtown Seattle by the Duwamish
River. The West Seattle bridge connects the area to the rest of the city,
arcing over busy Harbor Island and
the Duwamish River which flows
into Elliott Bay, like the back of a
brontosaurus, its tail the Spokane
Street Viaduct, its neck the sweep of
the freeway, up a tree-covered hill
dotted with houses. Harbor Island,

at the river's mouth where it empties
into Elliott Bay, is an artificially
created industrial island, and operates as a storage depot for much of
the equipment that serves the busy
Port of Seattle.

The present high-level bridge is
still known by many longtime residents as the "new bridge," even
though it was completed in 1984. It
replaced one of two bascule bridges
which stopped traffic too often, opening to let sailboats and freighters
pass along the river.

**Map
on page
136**

LEFT: water, water
everywhere in
West Seattle.
BELOW: "Honey, I
shrunk the kid,"
Georgetown.

Jogging, promenading and strolling are popular pastimes near Alki Beach.

The Junction

Downtown West Seattle is better known as **The Junction ❶**. It is centered around California Avenue SW, and SW Alaska Street, but this central shopping area has had its ups and downs. Some businesses have made passing appearances while others have stood unchanged for several decades.

The Junction's murals are remarkable. More than half a dozen wall-sized paintings decorate the retail and commerciail buildings, most depicting the area as it was over a century ago. The best of these is on the wall at California and Edmunds, and looks as if one could walk right into a 19th-century street scene.

North of the junction on California is the rolling **Admiral District**, named for Admiral Way, which climbs the hill from the West Seattle Bridge on the east and slides down to Alki Beach on the west. The district is home to the last of West Seattle's movie theaters, the **Admiral Theatre**, which screens second-run films at discount prices. A lovely old brick public library is here with some restaurants, coffeehouses and West Seattle High School.

This part of Seattle is on two hills, Gatewood and Genesee, which give it plenty of view-enhanced property. Homes on the west sides of both hills overlook Puget Sound and the Olympic Mountains, while those on the east have views over Downtown and Harbor Island. At the top of Genesee Hill are scenic outlooks including **Hamilton Viewpoint**, at the north end of California Avenue, and **Belvedere Viewpoint**, which is on Admiral Way.

Alki Beach

The closest thing the city has to a Southern California outdoor scene is **Alki Beach ❷**, which for many years was a summer place where teenagers brought their cars. Anti-

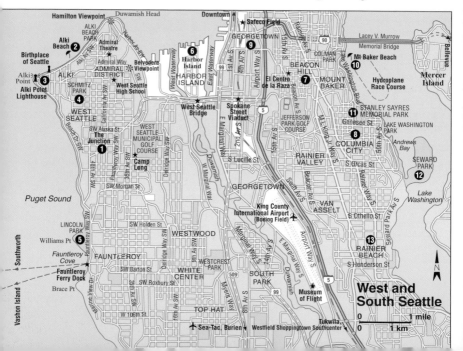

West and South Seattle

0 ___ 1 mile
0 ___ 1 km

cruising laws were enacted to restrict drivers to a single pass along the beach's Alki Avenue every four hours, cutting down considerably the noise and traffic nuisance that so irked local residents – many of them occupants of the shiny condo complexes across from the beach.

The beach park is technically closed between 11pm and 6am, mid-April through September. In summer, though, Alki attracts a good crowd of shiny cars, bronzed bodies in bikinis and teenagers out to see and be seen. Beach volleyball courts are usually bouncing with players and lined with spectators.

In the fall, winter and spring, Alki is still a wonderful place for a beach stroll under swirling clouds and squawking seagulls. If the wind and rain that drove the Denny party across the bay do get to be too much, the area also offers plenty of shelter and places to eat, ranging from bakeries and delis to a chain seafood restaurant with an excellent view of the downtown skyline.

The oldest landmark here is a concrete column marking the beach as the "Birthplace of Seattle." It was presented to the city in 1905 by Arthur Denny's daughter and stands now at 63rd Avenue SW and Alki Avenue. In 1926, when the column was moved from its original location on the other side of the street, a hunk of the Plymouth Rock, the Massachusetts boulder which the Pilgrims steered towards in 1620, was embedded in its base.

At the southern end of the beach – just before it becomes residential – is the **Alki Point Lighthouse ❸**, established in 1881. The present lighthouse, standing on a small reservation behind apartments and condominiums, dates from 1913. The lighthouse offers guided tours to summer visitors, although only by appointment (tel: 206-217 6203 or 206-217 6128).

Schmitz Park ❹, just east of Alki, is a 50-acre (20-hectare) nature preserve with narrow trails through thick woods, but no picnic areas or playgrounds. Just off 35th Avenue SW, the hill-side West Seattle Municipal Golf Course offers views of downtown Seattle, Elliott Bay

Map on page 136

Alki Point Lighthouse marks the southern entrance to Seattle's busy harbor.

BELOW: summer in the city, Alki Beach.

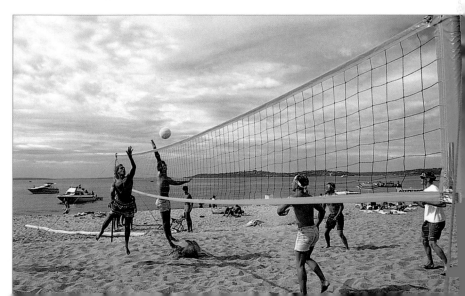

Alki's landmark includes a chunk of Plymouth Rock from Massachusetts.

BELOW: CEO John Buller of Tully's, the coffee company based in South Seattle.

and the Duwamish waterway. The 18-hole, par-72 golf course was laid out here in 1940.

City parks

Continue along the waterfront, which becomes **Beach Drive**, passing beach-side homes both extravagant and funky, as well as apartment buildings and open spaces such as Emma Schmitz Memorial Park. Beach Drive culminates in the lower part of Lincoln Park, at the foot of Gatewood Hill. Alki may be the most visible of this area's city parks, but it is certainly not the only one.

Most prominent is 130-acre (50-hectare) **Lincoln Park ❺**, designed by the Olmsted brothers, creators of New York's Central Park, and with miles of wooded and waterfront trails. Colman Pool is a heated 164-ft (50-meter) Olympic-size outdoor pool open only in summer. Filled partly with chlorinated freshwater and part saltwater, Colman Pool is accessible only on foot; the roads through the park are restricted to park vehicles. At the south end of Lincoln Park is the **Fauntleroy Ferry Dock**,

where boats depart for Vashon Island and Southworth. Either destination makes a pleasant day trip. Vashon *(see page 185)*, just 20 minutes from the dock, is a charming rural area far from the rush of city life. Many residents farm as a hobby and make the daily commute to Seattle or Tacoma via ferry; a few have found work on the island itself, in bucolic pursuits like orchid growing.

One of the city's few parks to offer overnight facilities, **Camp Long**, just off 35th Avenue SW at Dawson, is 68 acres (27 hectares) of wilderness. Open to organized groups for camping and wilderness-skills programs, Camp Long is a popular site for weddings and also features a decent rock wall for climbing instruction and practice. **Schurman Rock** is open Tues–Sat 10am–6pm.

Southeast of West Seattle is the area named **White Center**, for George W. H. White, a partner in the railway that served this part of the city. White Center was then a rugged logging district. Government housing projects went up after World

War II, and later, taverns were built just outside the city limits, earning White Center the nickname Rat City in the 1960s. Nowadays, White Center is one of the few places left with affordable real estate for first-time home buyers, partly because of the low-income housing nearby.

Harbor Island ❻, between Downtown and West Seattle, is home to the city's shipyards and loading facilities for freighters. It is a landfill of more than 25 million cubic yards (19 million cubic meters), all of it dredged up and reclaimed from the bottom of the Duwamish River.

When it was completed in 1912, Harbor Island was the largest man-made island in the world. Shortly after the island was created, the meandering Duwamish was straightened, allowing much greater space along its banks for industrial development. South from Elliott Bay, past busy Harbor Island and through Seattle's industrial corridor, the river passes salvage ships, commercial shipping lanes, Boeing Field and the town of Tukwila.

South Seattle

Overlooked for many years, South Seattle is now enjoying the thrill of being discovered by "urban pioneers." Three neighborhoods in particular – Beacon Hill, Columbia City and Georgetown – are areas to keep an eye on.

On the east side of Interstate 5 is **Beacon Hill ❼**, an affordable residential area with a diverse ethnic mix. The view from Beacon Hill itself is fantastic *(see photo on page 58)*, stretching out over Downtown all the way down to Seattle's waterfront. Highlights here include the city-owned Jefferson Park Golf Course, where pro Fred Couples perfected his swing; the Latino community center El Centro de la Raza; and an Asian grocery store with exotic Asian foods and tanks of live fish.

Beacon Hill is also home to success-story **Amazon.com**, who are headquartered in a tall, towering Art Deco building, part of a old hospital. Amazon.com can be recognized from far below, a towering landmark near the top of the hill. Their offices are not open to the public.

Map on page 136

TIP

Don't jaywalk in Seattle; police are vigilant at handing out tickets. As a result, pedestrians here wait for lights to change at crosswalks, even when there isn't a car anywhere in sight.

BELOW: gentrification in Georgetown.

Another neighborhood that has been gentrified in recent years is **Columbia City ❽**. The area now has a small cinema, a good bakery, a weekly farmers' market, several popular restaurants and watering holes – even a wine bar. Older houses are sporting fresh coats of paint and attention is being paid to detail, a sure sign that real-estate values are buoyant.

Farther south is **Georgetown ❾**, which has recently seen a surge in counter-cultural types. The Georgetown neighborhood website, maintained by the community council, labels it "Seattle's Feisty, Intensely Creative Neighborhood." With some of the city's more affordable real estate, the area has sprouted artists' studios, parks and museums, as well as the requisite coffeehouses and a microbrewery. It's not exactly trendy yet, but watch this space.

East of Beacon Hill is the comfortable neighborhood of **Mount Baker**, which has fine old homes, a few interesting shops, and a diverse population. Wind down the hill through Mount Baker and you're on the shores of Lake Washington. At **Mount Baker Beach ❿**, a large, blue boathouse holds rowing shells, which are taken out daily by rowers young and old.

Along the west side of the lake runs **Lake Washington Boulevard**, which begins at the University of Washington in North Seattle and continues all the way down to Seward Park. The road gives eastward views of the Cascade Range and meanders past the string of grassy Lake Washington beach-front parks. An adjacent cycle path follows the road for miles.

May through September the road closes to automobiles some weekends, usually the second Saturday and third Sunday of each month for Bicycle Saturdays and Sundays. A beautiful ride any time, the event makes it even more appealing.

The stretch of lake shoreline from just south of the bridge which carries Interstate 90 to Andrews Bay is hydro heaven during the Rainier Cup Hydroplane Race in August. The races, part of the annual Seafair celebration and first staged in 1950,

The headquarters of Amazon.com are in an Art Deco building on Beacon Hill.

BELOW: co-workers at Amazon.com.

have become a tradition, drawing thousands of spectators despite the noise of engines on 150-mph (240-kph) boats. Seafair's official viewing beach is **Stan Sayres Memorial Park ⓫**, where the hydro pits are, but many fans watch from homes along the lake, and hundreds pay a per-foot charge to moor their boats along the challenging course.

The Lake Washington parks culminate in **Seward Park ⓬**, 279 acres (113 hectares) of greenery, trails and waterfront. Bald eagles have bred here, and it has been home to a flock of now-wild parrots, domesticated birds that escaped. The park has an art studio, an outdoor amphitheater and a short lakeside trail for cyclists and runners.

Southcenter and shopping

In **Rainier Valley**, named for the views of Mount Rainier that it offers, the old Sicks Stadium once stood, home successively to baseball teams the Seattle Rainiers and the Seattle Pilots. Neighborhoods near the Duwamish River as it winds south from Elliott Bay include Holly Park, Highland Park, South Park, Beverly Park and, farther southwest, Burien. To the east on the edge of the lake is **Rainier Beach ⓭**.

Limited real estate in the city's International District lured Asian immigrants to search out new areas for development, including the area south of Safeco Field and which now has a substantial Asian population, mostly Vietnamese, and some good restaurants. Many more Asian restaurants line Pacific Highway South towards Sea-Tac International Airport. **Westfield Southcenter**, at the southern confluence of interstates 5 and 405, is one of Seattle's larger covered shopping malls. The complex has almost 200 shops, with department stores Nordstrom and Macy's, a good Made in Washington store, specialty retailers and a busy food court.

Nearby is Boeing country and the home of the aerospace firm's test field, at the south end of Lake Washington. The Museum of Flight *(see page 167)* is also here, while other Boeing plants are located in Renton, Auburn and Kent. ❏

Map on page 136

Time to eat fish & chips near the sand on Alki Beach.

RESTAURANTS

Columbia City Ale House
4914 Rainier Ave S. Tel: 206-723 5123. Open: L, D daily. **$**
www.seattlealehouses.com
Local and seasonal microbrews are on tap, as well as good pub fare.

Elliott Bay Brewery Pub
4720 California Ave SW. Tel: 206-932 8695. Open: L, D daily. **$**
www.elliottbaybrewing.com
West Seattle's brewpub serves good pub food as well as a selection of more than a dozen of their own beers.

Endolyne Joe's
9261 45th Avenue SW. Tel: 206-937-JOES. Open: B, L, D daily. **$–$$**
www.chowfoods.com
Quarterly, this West Seattle restaurant changes its regional cuisine; the French Quarter, tropical islands or Little Italy.

La Medusa
4857 Rainier Ave S Tel: 206-723 2192
www.lamedusarestaurant.com
Open: D Tues–Sat. **$$–$$$**
One of the best established restaurants in Columbia City, La Medusa serves sensual Sicilian fare – often using fresh produce from the local farmers' market.

La Rustica
4100 Beach Drive SW. Tel: 206-932 3020. Open: D Tues–Sun. **$$**
You have to hunt for La Rustica, but the rustic Italian specialties are worth the search.

Mission
2325 California Ave SW. Tel: 206-937 8220. Open: D daily. **$$**
Some come to this West Seattle restaurant for the modern Latin cuisine – others for the drinks and the scene, both of which are best enjoyed late at night.

Stellar Pizza
5513 Airport Way. Tel: 206-763 1660. Open: L Mon–Fri, D daily. **$**
www.stellarpizza.com
This family-owned pizza place in Georgetown serves huge, hand-tossed pizzas, *calzones*, sandwiches and pastas amid retro artifacts.

● ● ● ● ● ● ● ● ● ● ● ● ●
Prices for a three-course dinner per person with half a bottle of wine: $ under $20, $$ $20–$45, $$$ $45–$60, $$$$ over $60

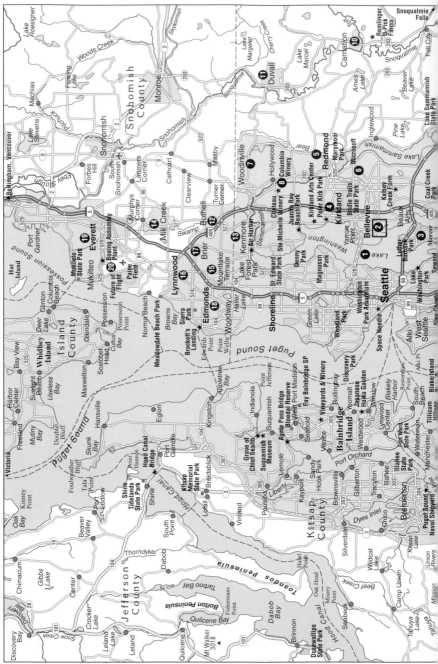

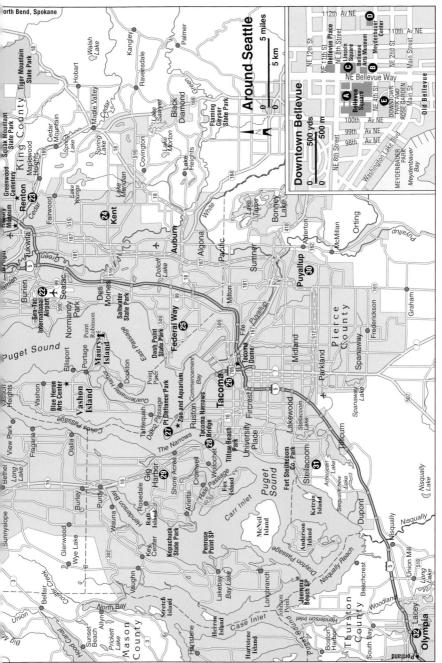

EASTSIDE

The Eastside – east of Lake Washington – is a
lush location of big homes, fine wineries
and high-tech, high-profile companies
like Microsoft. Bring a boat

T he Eastside is smooth and
sleek, well-heeled and well-
connected. Stroll along the
Kirkland waterfront, espresso in
hand. Stop for an outdoor lunch on
a sunlit deck overlooking Lake
Washington. Head to downtown
Bellevue for an afternoon at the arts
museum. Visit the velodrome in
Redmond's Marymoor Park and
cheer on champion cyclists. Drive
into Issaquah for an evening of theater, or head out to Woodinville for
an afternoon of wine tasting and
music at Chateau Ste Michelle.

Although these scenes are taken
for granted by Eastsiders, they are
often overlooked by visitors intent
on seeing just the sites of Seattle's
city center.

Go east, young man

It wasn't long ago that visiting the
Eastside from Seattle meant pack-
ing a picnic lunch and going for a
drive in the country. Today, all of
that has changed. Seattleites zip
back and forth across Lake Washington to the east side of the lake (20
minutes one-way, if the traffic gods
are with you, over an hour if they're
not) with regularity. In fact, increasing numbers that can afford it pack
up and move to the Eastside permanently, making the trip across the
lake twice a day as commuters.

Some don't even need to commute.
Formerly sleepy cities like Bellevue
and Redmond now have high-profile identities as financial or technology centers, or, like Kirkland and
Woodinville, as increasingly sophisticated recreation centers.

Several Seattle-based companies
have made a leap across the lake and
relocated permanently onto the
Eastside, while office space is still
available and affordable. Microsoft,
Nintendo and Google have led the
way, and many eagerly follow.

PRECEDING PAGES:
aerial view of homes
on Lake Washington.
LEFT: crossword puzzle
the Microsoft way.
BELOW: Chateau Ste
Michelle winery.

TIP

Public boat launches in both Bellevue and Kirkland make Lake Washington accessible to all kinds of floating craft, from sailboats and motorboats to cabin cruisers and canoes. If you're taking the organized lake cruise, ask the pilot to point out Bill Gates' multimillion dollar waterfront house in Medina.

BELOW:
Lake Washington in the sunshine.

Lake Washington

It's **Lake Washington ❶** that provides the frame of reference for the term "Eastside," a designation that applies to the cities, towns and rural areas that dot the hills and valleys to the east of the lake. Navigating the waterways and highways of the Eastside requires a few reference points, and the most useful are the bridges that run east and west across Lake Washington. The **Evergreen Point Floating Bridge** (SR 520) connects Seattle from just south of the University District in North Seattle to Kirkland and continues on to Redmond.

Both the **Lacey V. Murrow Memorial Bridge** and the **Homer M. Hadley Bridge** on Interstate 90 connect South Seattle with southern Bellevue via Mercer Island, a residential community about midway across Lake Washington.

The main north-south route on the east side of the lake is Interstate 405, which runs the length of the state and goes directly through Bellevue, Kirkland and north on to Bothell and Woodinville. Interstate

405 eventually leads farther north to the Canadian border and to Vancouver, British Columbia.

In many ways the Eastside owes its development to the bridges that connect it to Seattle in a truly love-hate relationship. As well as some of the most spectacular scenic views, these bridges can be the scenes of horrendous traffic congestion. It may be, in fact, that the scenery contributes to the traffic problems. Residents rarely seem blasé about Lake Washington, or the spectacular vistas of Mount Rainier, also visible from the bridges.

Bellevue

Given the beauty of Lake Washington and the finite aspect of its waterfront, it's no surprise that from **Bellevue ❷** north to Bothell (*see page 161*), waterfront property is prime real estate. Properties with private docks, private beaches and multi-level houses cascading down the hills can be seen from the highways; they look even more spectacular from a boat on the lake.

Bellevue's **Meydenbauer Bay** is an area of luxury homes and condominiums on the lake west of Bellevue's downtown area which was named for William Meydenbauer, a Seattle baker. North of Meydenbauer Bay, the exclusive communities of Medina, Yarrow Point and Clyde Hill are other prominent Bellevue-area waterfront places. Public-beach access to the lake around Bellevue is limited, but **Chism Beach** (1175 96th Avenue SE) offers swimming, trails and picnic facilities. Other reasonable beaches in Bellevue include Meydenbauer, Newcastle and Enatai.

Aside from Lake Washington, the strongest attraction in Bellevue for visitors is **Bellevue Square ♈** (on NE 8th Street and Bellevue Way; tel: 425-454 8096; Mon–Sat 9.30am–9.30pm, Sun 11am–7pm), known to

Maps on pages 144–45

locals as **Bel Square**. Opened in 1946 as one of the first suburban shopping centers in the country, the upscale mall now has some of the area's trendiest shops. The **Bellevue Arts Museum** Ⓑ (510 Bellevue Way, tel: 425-519 0770; Tues–Thur and Sat 10am–5.30pm, Fri 10am–9pm, Sun 11am–5.30pm; admission charge) is across from the mall. The museum specializes in the decorative arts.

Also in the area is the **Lincoln Square** Ⓒ complex (700 Bellevue Way NE), featuring a shopping center on the ground floor with a home-related focus. It also has fine restaurants as well as a smoking-not-permitted billiards club and a 16-screen cinema. But much of Lincoln Square's space is rented out as offices for companies including Microsoft and Eddie Bauer. The top 23 floors are occupied by 148 high-priced condos with premium views.

Roses and fairs

One of Bellevue's most popular annual events, the Bellevue Arts and Crafts Fair, began the year Bel Square opened. What is now one of the largest outdoor art shows in the western US started in 1946 with a few paintings on the sidewalk. Always slated for the last weekend in July (one of the weekends when rain is least likely to fall), the show attracts artists, collectors and the curious from all over North America.

Lovers of the performing arts are also very well catered for in the **Meydenbauer Center** Ⓓ (11100 NE 6th Street, tel: 425-637 1020). This convention facility features a 36,000-sq-ft (3,350-sq-meter) exhibition hall and a 410-seat performing-arts theater.

Across the street from the southern side of Bel Square is Bellevue's **Downtown Park and Rose Garden** Ⓔ (10201 NE 4th Street), a 20-acre (8-hectare) site in the heart of the shopping district. It includes a high, cascading waterfall, a canal enclosing a large meadow and a 28-ft (8-meter) wide promenade.

Just south of the park is **Old Bellevue**, the city's first shopping district before the arrival of Bel Square. The two-block precinct

Home decoration on the Eastside.

BELOW: retail therapy in Bel Square, Bellevue.

includes a cafeteria-style Mexican café and several art galleries. Keep in mind that in Bellevue "old" means dating to about 1940.

Bellevue's **Kelsey Creek Farm** (410 130th Avenue SE, tel: 425-452 7688; free) has pigs, horses, chickens and rabbits as well as walking trails, picnic tables and plenty of room to roam.

Mercer Island

Named for Aaron Mercer, one of the first local homesteaders, **Mercer Island ❸** sits directly west of Bellevue, about midway in Lake Washington between Bellevue and the southern part of Seattle. A thriving community of almost 22,000, it was incorporated in 1960. There are still people around who remember Mercer Island as a summertime vacation area, accessible only by ferry. Interstate 90 and the bridges that linked the island to Seattle and the Eastside changed all that.

Today, it's a residential community known for some incredible luxury homes, including the $30-million spread built by Microsoft

co-founder and Experience Music Project supremo Paul Allen, and an excellent theater. Worth a stop is **Luther Burbank Park** (2040 84th Avenue SE). Originally a private estate, the park has 77 gorgeous acres (31 hectares) of lake front, tennis courts, an outdoor amphitheater and a playground for kids. The sandy beach completes this great spot for summer.

Kirkland

Just north of Bellevue, with much of its shopping, restaurants and commercial areas hugging the shore of Lake Washington, is **Kirkland ❹**. This city of 47,000 has more public access to waterfront through parks, open space and walkways than any other city in the state of Washington. Public access to the waterfront has been a priority here since the city was first incorporated in 1905. A walk along **Lake Street** passes by a number of green, grassy parks which provide public access to the lake and to its waterfront restaurants. Clancy's Bistro (6023 Lake Washington Blvd NE, tel: 425-827

Mercer Island, where Microsoft co-founder Paul Allen lives, has about 476 acres (193 hectares) of parks and open space, and two off-leash areas for dogs. Around 275 pooper-scooper bags are used each day in the island's parks.

BELOW: dog-day afternoon in a well-groomed Kirkland park.

Map on pages 144–45

0654; Sun–Thur 5–9.30pm, Fri–Sat 5–10pm), for example, is one that provides its own dock for the use of restaurant patrons.

A central part of Kirkland's downtown is **Peter Kirk Park** (202 3rd Street), with tennis courts, a ball field, one of the few public outdoor swimming pools on the Eastside and a children's playground. On summer evenings, the floodlit baseball field is a big draw. **Kirkland Parkplace** (on 6th Street and Central Way) has movie theaters, gift shops, a book store, a gym and a great selection of places to eat.

In downtown Kirkland, many antiques dealers congregate to display their wares. Art walks are periodically scheduled when galleries stay open late, and the public are invited to meet the artists whose work is on view. The **Kirkland Arts Center** (620 Market Street, tel: 425-822 7161; Mon–Fri 11am–6pm, Sat 11am–5pm; free) offers classes and exhibits for children and adults. Kirkland also has numerous outdoor art works.

Carillon Point (on Lake Washington Boulevard at Lakeview Drive) is a waterfront complex which includes a luxury hotel, restaurants, waterfront walkways and docks as well as shops and restaurants, a mile or two south of Downtown. Two large office towers and a hill-side of condominiums initially drew complaints from nearby residents, but the views from the hotel, the restaurants and the docks *are* spectacular.

A few miles north of Downtown (from the northern end of Lake Street, turn left onto Central Way, right onto Market and then left onto Juanita Drive) is **Juanita Bay Beach Park** (2201 Market Street), a county-run beach that has summertime lifeguards, roped-off swimming areas and a snack bar. The park is open year-round. There are picnic areas, a children's playground and a number of piers jutting into the lake.

Other Kirkland beach parks include O.O. Denny, Waverly and Houghton. **Bridle Trails State Park** (NE 53rd Street and 116th Avenue NE), right in the middle of residential neighborhoods, is a heavily wooded haven for horseback riders and hikers who don't mind sharing the trails with horses. The park is located in south Kirkland near the Bellevue border and can be accessed off 132nd Avenue NE.

Redmond

In the past two decades **Redmond ❺** has tripled its population to nearly 49,000 residents (the number climbs to 100,000 during the workday) and shows no signs of slowing. Fortunately, there's still enough open space in the city for one of the signature activities, hot-air ballooning. Look out toward the northern part of the city along the Sammamish River on just about any summer or fall evening and chances are you'll see colorful hot-air balloons drifting

Seattle has more pleasure-boat owners per capita than any other city in the US.

BELOW: the living is easy in the Eastside.

peacefully in the sky. Balloon rides are available from several companies and in a variety of styles: some offer "red carpet" romantic rides complete with champagne and gourmet lunches or dinners; others offer family prices.

The **Sammamish River** (often called the Sammamish Slough) winds its way south from Bothell to Marymoor Park, passing through Redmond and Woodinville. An asphalt pathway alongside the slough makes a perfect path for cyclists, and on weekends the place gets a mix of visitors with a wide range of bicycling skills.

Toward the southern end of Redmond, the Sammamish River drifts past **Marymoor Park** (6046 West Lake Sammamish Parkway NE; 8am–dusk), a pretty 640-acre (259-hectare) county-operated park which includes a museum housed in an old mansion, bicycle and hiking trails, and the largest off-leash dog area in the state.

The park is also the home of the **Marymoor Velodrome**. One of only six of its kind in the United States, the banked racing course attracts professional cyclists from all around the world.

Microsoft

Since the 1980s, Redmond has probably become best-known as the headquarters of **Microsoft** ❻. The company employs more than 60,000 people in 80 countries, but it all began – and continues – here. Locally, Microsoft occupies office space in 99 buildings in Redmond, Bellevue, Seattle and Issaquah, most of them numbered accordingly, ie, Building 33, Building 34, etc.

Unfortunately for the curious, the ambitious or the simply digitally desperate, its campuses are closed to the public and guarded around the clock. There is, however, the **Microsoft Visitor Center** (4420 148th Avenue NE, tel: 425-703 6214; Mon–Fri 9am–7pm) in Redmond. Here, visitors can learn all about the company's history via a timeline, and play in the Video Games Room with tech toys like multiscreens, the Xbox 360, and screen interfaces controlled by hand movements.

Local economists estimate that there are about 10,000 millionaires in the Seattle area. According to a 2005 survey, it's also America's most literate city.

BELOW: the President of China was entertained in this part of the Microsoft campus during his 2006 American trip.

Map
on pages
144–45

Although the software giant dominates Redmond, video-game company **Nintendo** of America has its headquarters for the Western hemisphere right down the street. Nintendo has big plans to grow in Redmond, with its sights set on an additional 550,000 sq ft (51,000 sq meters) by 2010.

To complete the tech trio, search-engine giant **Google** moved into nearby Kirkland in 2004.

Woodinville

There are several attractions in **Woodinville** ❼, the best-known being **Chateau Ste Michelle** winery (14111 NE 145th Street, tel: 425-415 3300; daily 10am–5pm; free), just west of the Sammamish River and a frequent stop for bicyclists on the slough route.

The winery, the largest in the state of Washington, has 87 acres (35 hectares) of picnic grounds, a pond with ducks and swans, a tasting room and test vineyards. The attractive facilities are popular for weddings and receptions. Tours of the winery's operations (the main vineyards are actually in eastern Washington) are offered daily, along with wine tastings. Premium tastings can also be arranged for a fee.

Just a few hundred feet away, in a large, gingerbread-style building, is **Columbia Winery** ❽ (14030 NE 145th Street, tel: 425-488 2776; daily 10am–6pm; free), another excellent regional wine producer. Columbia also gives daily tours for a small fee, with wine tastings. Private tours with tastings of signature wines are another possibility. Although best known for white grapes, the wineries of western Washington are increasingly producing fine table wines, both red and white *(see page 154)*.

The **Redhook Ale Brewery** (14300 NE 145th Street, tel: 425-483 3232; call for hours) and the **Forecasters Public House** are next door to the ColumbiaWinery. More than a quarter of a century old and one of Seattle's original microbreweries, Redhook brews ESB, an India Pale Ale; Hefe-Weizen; and other beers in this Eastside facility. The Forcasters pub is open every day

Every summer, on the grounds of Chateau Ste Michelle, there's a series of concerts featuring big-draw performers.

LEFT:
Microserfs surfing.
BELOW:
Columbia Winery.

Washington Wines

The Pacific Northwest is known for its pioneering spirit, as is its wine industry. The Northwest's wineries have established themselves in world tasting circles in just a few decades, which is no small feat for an industry known for its picky noses. In 1980, Washington state had fewer than 20 wineries; today it is the nation's second-largest producer of wine (after California), with more than 460 wineries. It's said a new winery opens here every 15 days – which is good news for wine lovers, though this *can* make the choice of what to buy and where to visit a little overwhelming.

While often processed in the Seattle region (specifically Woodinville), Washington-grown grapes are mostly nurtured on the eastern side of the Cascades in an arid environment that has long, warm, sunny days and cool nights. The state has ideal geography and conditions for growing premium *vinifera* wine grapes. More than 30,000 acres (12,140 hectares) in the state are currently planted with wine grapes of more than 15 different varieties. Leading red varieties include merlot, cabernet sauvignon, syrah, cabernet franc and sangiovese; white varieties include chardonnay, riesling, sauvignon blanc, semillon and viognier.

Washington's potential for premium wine was discovered in 1966 when renowned wine critic Andre Tchelistcheff first sampled a home-made Washington gewurztraminer and called it the best produced in the United States. In 2001, *Wine Enthusiast Magazine* cited Washington as "Wine Region of the Year" for quickly emerging as a global wine industry recognized for quality.

In 2006, the state's Quilceda Creek Vintners (coincidentally owned by Tchelistcheff's nephew, Alex Golitzen) made history by earning its second consecutive 100-point wine rating from Robert Parker's *Wine Advocate* for its cabernet sauvignon.

Seattle-area wineries: Though most of the state's wineries are situated closer to where the grapes are grown, on the east side of the Cascade Mountains, a certain number are located in the Seattle area, primarily on the Eastside. Chateau Ste Michelle, the largest winery in the Pacific Northwest, has its headquarters in Woodinville. Across the street is Columbia Winery, another well-established producer. The majority of the state's wineries are smaller, family-owned operations, however, many of which have tasting rooms open to the public on weekends, if not more frequently.

Woodinville wineries worth a visit include Chatter Creek (www.chattercreek.com), Cuillin Hills (www.cuillinhills.com) and Di Stefano (www.destefanowinery.com). Also in the Seattle area: Market Cellar (www.marketcellar winery.com) at Pike Place Market; Hedges Family Estate (www.hedgescellars.com) in Issaquah; Wilridge (www.wilridgewinery.com) in Madrona; and E.B. Foote (www.ebfoote winery.com) in Burien.

Puget Sound wineries: A little bit farther from the city, about 50 wineries are within a couple of hours' drive. Two of the most accessible are Bainbridge Island Vineyards & Winery (www.bainbridgevineyards.com), on one of the main ferry routes to the Olympic Peninsula, and the Mount Baker Winery, just outside Bellingham. ❑

LEFT: of Washington state's wine-grape varieties, 47 percent are red and 53 percent are white.

(and night) and features live music on weekends. A tour of the brewery can be taken and the small fee includes tastings and a souvenir glass. Children are welcome.

From Woodinville, hikers can walk the **Tolt Pipeline Trail**, either westward to Bothell or eastward to the Snoqualmie Valley. Its wooded and open terrain makes this a very popular pastime.

Molbak's (13625 NE 175th Street, tel: 425-483 5000; Sun–Fri 10am–6pm, Sat 9am–6pm) greenhouse and nursery is probably the most popular downtown stop. Thousands of varieties of plants, a greenhouse, fountains and flowers are the attractions. At Christmas, when the greenhouses are filled with seemingly endless rows of blooming poinsettias, it's a local holiday tradition to head for Molbak's to pose for family photographs against this festive background.

Issaquah

Southeast of Bellevue and nestled in a valley between Squak, Tiger and Cougar mountains is the little town of **Issaquah ❾**. The developers chose a country theme for the shopping center. They scoured the vicinity for old clapboard-style homes, then moved and arranged them into a village setting at the edge of Downtown. Then they built wooden boardwalks, planted flowers and set to work attracting a particular kind of retailer. **Gilman Village** is the result, a "destination shopping center" of specialty shops and restaurants which draws people from many miles around.

Also in Issaquah, the **Village Theater** (303 Front Street N, tel: 425-392 2202) puts on regular dramatic performances, popular with locals. A few blocks east of Gilman Village is Boehm's Candies (255 NE Gilman Blvd, tel: 425-392 6652), a family-owned confectionery that has been in Issaquah since 1956. Swiss-style chocolate candies are still hand-dipped here the old-fashioned way.

Next to Boehm's is a winery, **Hedges Family Estate** (195 NE Gilman Blvd, tel: 425-391 6056), which offers individual and group

The Eastside takes on a rural aspect east of Issaquah.

BELOW: the Columbia Winery's tasting bar is the largest in the state.

Map on pages 144–45

Farms and country life make up most of the Far Eastside, with the possibility of even seeing a bear.

tastings as well as tours of the winery itself. Wildlife enthusiasts love **Cougar Mountain Zoological Park** (19525 SE 54th Street, tel: 425-391 5508; Wed–Sun 9am–5pm; admission charge), and every fall salmon head up Issaquah Creek via a fish ladder at the **Issaquah State Salmon Hatchery** (125 W Sunset Way, tel: 425-391 9094). The early-October Issaquah Salmon Days Festival celebrates their return.

Lake Sammamish State Park, just north of downtown Issaquah, provides access to the trails, baseball fields, picnic tables and barbecue spots of the lake's south shore. Lake Sammamish is popular for boating in summer, despite the noise of waterskiers' speedboats.

Into the countryside

Past Issaquah, the scene around Interstate 90 becomes more rural the farther east one travels. Bears have been seen in the region, and Carnation and Fall City have enough attractions to fill a whole weekend's visit, Snoqualmie Falls especially *(see pages 63 and 204)*.

In the heart of the Snoqualmie Valley in **Carnation** ❿ is the popular 450-acre (180-hectare) **Tolt MacDonald Park** and Campground (31020 NE 40th Street), spanning both sides of the Snoqualmie River. The park has 40 camp sites, play fields, picnic shelters and meandering bicycle and hiking trails. The 40-minute tour can be topped off with a picnic in the park.

South of Carnation is **Remlinger U-Pick Farms** (tel: 425-333 4135; open May–Oct), a great place to prove to the kids that there is a connection between the land and the food they eat. Remlinger has fruits and vegetables aplenty, a restaurant, a petting farm, and seasonal events and entertainment.

Duvall ⓫ is the outer limits of the Eastside; its one-street Downtown has several antiques stores. The town celebrates its rural atmosphere with Duvall Days every spring around Mothers' Day. A street fair, a parade and a pancake breakfast are the highlights of the event. ❑

● *For sites and attractions farther east, see page 204.*

RESTAURANTS, BARS & CAFES

Restaurants

Barking Frog
14582 NE 145th Street,
Woodinville
Tel: 425-424 2999
www.willowslodge.com/
culinary-barkingfrog.php
Open: B and D daily, L
Mon–Fri, Br Sat–Sun. **$$$$**
The elegant restaurant in
the Willows Lodge fea-
tures fresh Northwest
cuisine. Dine in the
courtyard, or cozy up by
the fireplace.

Café Juanita
9702 NE 120th Place,
Kirkland
Tel: 425-823 1505
www.cafejuanita.com
Open: D Tues–Sun. **$$$**
The oft-changing menu at
this Kirkland hot spot fea-
tures the best foods of
the season cooked in the
tradition of northern Italy.

Daniel's Broiler
10500 NE 8th Street,
21st floor, Bellevue
Tel: 425-462 4662
www.schwartzbros.com
Open: L Mon–Fri, D daily.
$$$$
This Bellevue steak-
house serves prime
steaks and seafood spe-
cialties. The restaurant
also has a piano bar.

The Herbfarm
14590 NE 145th Street,
Woodinville
Tel: 425-485 5300
www.theherbfarm.com
Open: D Thur–Sun. **$$$$**

Dinner doesn't get more
sumptuous than Wood-
inville's five-hour, nine-
course, fixed-price
extravaganza. The menu
changes seasonally to
feature fresh foods, some
grown on the premises.

Maggiano's Little Italy
10455 NE 8th Street,
Bellevue
Tel: 425-519 6476
www.maggianos.com
Open: L Mon–Sat, D daily. **$$**
Italian food, always
made from scratch and
served family style.

**Seastar Restaurant
and Raw Bar**
205 108th Avenue NE,
Bellevue
Tel: 425-456 0010
www.seastarrestaurant.com
Open: L Mon–Fri, D daily.
$$$$
A seafood restaurant with
plenty to please vegetar-
ian diners. Don't miss the
local oysters or the crab
cakes, halibut and soups.

Szechuan Chef
15015 Main Street, Suite 107
Tel: 425-746 9008
Open: L and D daily. **$$**
Fantastic Chinese food
and good service. Spicy
rice-cake noodles or pea
vines are divine.

Typhoon!
8936 161st Avenue NE,
Redmond
Tel: 425-558 7666
www.typhoonrestaurants.com
Open: L Mon–Sat, D daily. **$$**
Authentic Thai food with

sweat-inducing spice lev-
els, all utterly delicious.

What the Pho!
10680 NE 8th Street, Bellevue
Tel: 425-462 5600
Open: L and D daily. **$**
Stylish Bellevue restaur-
ant offering tasty bowls
of *pho* and other Viet-
namese specialties.

**Yarrow Bay Grill and
Beach Café**
1270 Carillon Point, Kirkland
Tel: 425-889 9052
www.ybgrill.com
Open: D daily. **$$$$**
A romantic waterfront setting for seafood served
with flair. The Beach
Café downstairs offers
less pricey lunches.

Bars and Cafés

Cypress Lounge, 600
Bellevue Way NE, is a

contemporary lounge
inside the Westin Hotel.

**The Parlor Billiards &
Spirits**, 700 Bellevue
Way NE, Suite 30, is an
elegant, upscale billiards
club, which also offers
full-service meals.

Purple Café & Wine Bar,
323 Park Place (Kirk-
land). The specialty here
is a selection of hun-
dreds of bottles of wine
served in a sophisti-
cated but comfily casual
café atmosphere.

PRICE CATEGORIES

Prices for a three-course
dinner per person with
half a bottle of wine:
$ = under $20
$$ = $20–45
$$$ = $45–60
$$$$ = more than $60

RIGHT: chef Jerry Traunfeld of The Herbfarm gathering
nasturtium blossoms to use in salads.

NORTHWESTERN WILDLIFE

Pacific wildlife ranges from black bears to moles and from bald eagles to songbirds

Despite Seattle's urban – and suburban – growth, wildlife is still at home in this corner of the Northwest. Though expanding residential areas have shrunk the number and extent of natural wild habitats, many species have adapted and made their homes in Seattle's parks and fertile green spaces.

Inside the city limits, the most common creatures are eastern gray squirrels, opossums, raccoons and a range of birds including robins, seagulls, pigeons and crows. Beaver and otter sightings are also not uncommon, and harbor seals are the highlight of most cruises around the port. A little farther away – in the suburbs – chances increase of spotting cougar, deer or coyotes (they occasionally make a meal of someone's cat or small dog). Black bears are seen at Tiger Mountain, near Issaquah.

Even closer to home, in May 2006, a black bear cub was spotted on Seattle's University of Washington campus; he is thought to have been roaming the city at night for some time. Two nesting pairs of bald eagles are known to reside in the Seattle area, and are occasionally spotted near Green Lake and Seward Park. Popular places for birds in the city include Lake Union, as well as Discovery Park and the Washington Park Arboretum, home to shorebirds and freshwater ducks.

LEFT: The northern elephant seal or "sea elephant" *(Mirounga angustirostris)* is an occasional visitor to Puget Sound, and usually travels solo.

ABOVE: in the fall, sockeye salmon *(Oncorhynchus nerka)* spawn in streams such as Issaquah Creek and the Sammamish Slough.

BELOW: a mother and baby sea otter *(Enhydra lutris)* rest on a kelp bed. Though wild in the area, the best places in the city to find these playful animals are Woodland Park Zoo or the Seattle Aquarium.

SWIMMING FOR HOME

Five species of salmon migrate through Puget Sound. King, sockeye, coho, chum and pink salmon all return from the saltwater to spawn in rivers and streams from early June through November.

Their most spectacular appearance in Seattle is in early July, when thousands of sockeye salmon fight their way from Puget Sound up the fish ladder at Ballard's Hiram M. Chittenden Locks, heading for the Cedar River and other streams. The fish ladder bypasses the locks, and viewing windows are provided for the public, along with an explanation of the salmon's life-cycle.

Issaquah's annual Salmon Days Festival is held in the first week of October. In Seattle, the Salmon Homecoming event is celebrated around the second week of September, with Northwest tribal gatherings, pow wows, sacred sites exhibits, cedar-canoe events and an environmental fair. There is a huge salmon bake every day from mid-morning till evening.

ABOVE: watch for the black dorsal fins of killer whales *(Orcinus orca)* in Puget Sound. The Sound was designated a critical habitat for orcas in 2006; they are most commonly sighted in the San Juan Islands.

RIGHT: bears are frequently spotted on Tiger Mountain, east of Issaquah on Interstate 90, in the Seattle suburbs. Black bear cubs are agile climbers, and, unlike most young mammals, will follow their mother sometimes for as long as two years. Bear cubs tend to be alert, with a developed sense of smell and exceptional hearing, though they have only moderate eyesight.

BELOW: the bald eagle *(Haliaeetus leucocephalus)* is the only eagle unique to North America, and can sometimes be seen in Seattle's Green Lake area, Discovery Park and Seward Park. Curbs on pesticides mean that the eagles, endangered only 30 years ago, are now a fairly common sight.

2

HEADING NORTH

Growing in populararity with locals spreading their roots, the lure of towns like Bothell, Edmonds and Everett are subtle and understated

S hortly after Seattle was named America's "most livable city" by *Money* magazine for the first time, scores of young, affluent people settled the suburbs just outside the city, searching for that prize of prosperity known as "quality of life." From the northern frontier of Seattle at 145th Street to the city of Everett, 25 miles (40 km) north on Gardner Bay, a stretch of satellite communities with award-winning parks and progressive public schools seem to offer the modern suburban idyll.

With a population of more than 600,000 people and rising, the commuter communities on these great expanses of verdant rolling hills, lakes and sparkling streams on the northern tip of King County and the southern stretch of Snohomish County are among the nation's fastest-growing regions.

Technology Corridor

The very earliest European settlers – mill owners, homesteaders and land developers – relied on the Mosquito Fleet steamship line for transportation up and down Puget Sound, but railroads and electric trolleys soon followed to speed the flow of goods and passengers. Today's commuters head to jobs in downtown Seattle or, more likely, to one of the business

parks in the Technology Corridor, a path of commercial communities stretching along Interstate 405 between Bothell and Everett. Hundreds of businesses in electronics, software, telecommunications and computing cluster in campus-like neighborhoods where high-tech execs cycle along groomed cycle paths at lunch or work out in the company gym after hours.

Bothell ⓬ is the gateway to the corridor, a town of 32,000 people northeast of Lake Washington and

Map on pages 144–45

LEFT: Kenmore Air Harbor. **BELOW:** publications for consumption.

Between Everett and Mount Vernon is the Pilchuck Glass School in Stanwood, regarded by many as the best in the world.

BELOW: auction in aid of the Pilchuck Glass School, founded by Dale Chihuly.

nestled in the winding Sammamish River Valley, only 30 minutes' drive from Seattle or the Boeing plant in Everett. The Sammamish River biking and hiking trail joins the Burke-Gilman Trail *(see page 123)* in Bothell and curves along 33 acres (13 hectares) of a natural wildlife habitat south of the river, and continues uninterrupted to Marymoor Park on the east side of Lake Washington. The trail connects by a pedestrian bridge to the north side of the river, where **Bothell Landing**, with its historic buildings, serves as a focal point for the community.

Seaplanes

Also in the vicinity is **Kenmore ⓭**, known for water sports, a spectacular view of Lake Washington and the **Kenmore Air Harbor** (6321 NE 175th Street, tel: 425-486 1257), the country's largest seaplane base, with scenic flights over Seattle and scheduled flights to Victoria and Vancouver in British Columbia.

Mill Creek ⓮ began as a designed community in 1976, with almost 3,000 homes developed around a country club, a private 18-hole golf course, tennis courts, swimming pools and a nature preserve. It was incorporated as a city in 1983, and remains very popular.

Mountlake Terrace

The National Park Service awarded a commendation for the parks of **Mountlake Terrace ⓯** – a lavish sprinkling of little neighborhood parks and a 9-hole golf course (23000 Lakeview Drive, tel: 425-697 GOLF) on Lake Ballinger. The largest and one of the fastest-growing commercial and manufacturing centers in the north is **Lynnwood ⓰**, with a large middle-class population, a good percentage of whom are commuters to Seattle.

The only truly rural community is **Brier ⓱**, a small town of approximately 6,500 people. A strict no-growth policy keeps stores and traffic to a minimum.

Edmonds

Flower boxes and hanging planters dot the main street of **Edmonds ⓲**, the self-proclaimed "Gem of Puget

Sound," a modern community of around 40,000 on the shore 15 miles (24 km) north of Seattle.

Property values here are such that few people under 40 can afford the taxes, much less the mortgage payments. Few big business interests bother with this growth-resistant town either, but artsy-craftsy Edmonds doesn't mind. Residents know that their prestigious Amtrak station, ferry terminal, waterfront shops, restaurants and stylish parks draw plenty of weekend visitors.

One of three waterfront parks in Edmonds' **Brackett's Landing** (just north of the Edmond/Kingston Pier) includes the oldest and most popular **underwater park** in Washington, dedicated as a marine preserve in 1971. Divers can explore the 300-ft (90-meter) long DeLion dry dock, which dropped to the sandy bottom in 1935, and a number of other sunken structures. The dock is a maze-like haven for schools of fish and aquatic plant life.

Visitors are encouraged to feel the texture of leaves, needles and tree bark at **Sierra Park** (190th and 81st avenues W). The park was innovatively designed around the aroma and fragrance of plants, and created with the blind in mind. The park provides paths and braille signs for sight-impaired visitors.

Views from Marina Beach include the Unocal oil refinery loading dock at Edwards Point just off the beach to the south and the port of Edmonds to the north. At Olympic Beach, be sure to see the sea-lion sculpture and watch the activities at the **Edmonds Fishing Pier**, open year-round for fishing.

Other parks along this stretch of waterfront include the woodsy **Meadowdale Beach Park** (6026 156th SW) and the high, sandy cliffs of Norma Beach Boathouse. At the center of Edmonds is **Old Mill Town**, a living museum with historic mementos, shops, and the Edmonds Antiques Mall (10117 Edmonds Way; tel: 425-670 0770), in the old shingle mill, a wood building with plank floors and soaring timbers. Among Edmonds' cultural attractions is a community theater and a symphony.

Map on pages 144–45

TIP

See Seattle from the air on one of the Kenmore Air Harbor's tours. Highlights include the Space Needle, Green Lake and the campus of the University of Washington. Tel: 425-486 1257; www.kenmoreair.com

BELOW:
Everett by night.

Map on pages 144–45

Tours of Everett's Boeing facility are conducted every day.

Everett

Tacoma lumberman Henry Hewitt hoped the Great Northern Railroad would site its western terminus where **Everett ⑲** sits today. He persuaded investors to develop an industrial timber site on Port Gardner Bay, and although the town boomed in 1891, it went bust almost immediately. This cycle continued to haunt the town through the next century. More recently, Everett's emphasis on lumber shifted to an economy based on technology.

In 1966, Boeing constructed the **Boeing Assembly Plant** in Everett, the largest building in the world, bigger by volume than NASA's Vertical Assembly Building in Florida. Boeing was the world's largest maker of commercial aircraft in the second half of the 20th century, and the area's prime employer. For some time, Seattle's economy was intimately linked to Boeing's.

Boeing tour

The **Future of Flight ⑳** (8415 Paine Field Boulevard; tel: 425-438 8100; daily 8.30am–5.30pm, tours 9am–3pm; admission charge includes both; www.futureofflight.org) is an aviation center which provides visitors with displays and and experiences of flight-related exhibits. Upon entering the main lobby of the center, the first sight is of an aircraft flying directly above, while further along the runway, a 727 is poised nose-up for takeoff. Interactive programs explain the finer points of the design and technology.

Visitors are given the opportunity to digitally design and test an airplane of their own. Other interactive exhibits include flight simulators, a virtual tour of the 787 flight deck, plane components to touch and examine, a multimedia presentation of the 787, and more.

This is also the place to join the **Boeing Tour**, which gives a first-hand view of the company's planes – including the 787 Dreamliner – in construction. Visitors walk through the largest building by volume in the world and see airplanes at various stages, including manufacture and flight testing. Please note that Boeing does not allow photography. ❑

Boeing

Although Boeing's headquarters are no longer in Seattle, the company still exerts a huge influence on the city and the region.

Seattle has been the home of Boeing since the company began in the early 20th century, so its announcement in 2001 that it was moving its headquarters to Chicago was a shock. Major production facilities are still located in the region, though, and the company continues to play a significant role in the area's economy.

Boeing's planes, and the parts that they are comprised of, are made in large, helter-skelter complexes reflecting the hopscotch way the company grew from the red barn on the shores of Lake Union in 1916. Only in one place would you know at a glance this was one of the world's biggest industrial enterprises. That's in Everett. The original hangar, built in 1968 for the 747, enclosed 200 million cubic ft (5.7 million cubic meters), the world's largest building at the time; it then doubled in size. Tours are offered daily between 8:30am and 5:30pm *(see opposite)*.

Bill Boeing, the company's founder, was a prosperous Seattle lumberman who developed a fascination with planes. In 1916, he asked George Westervelt, a Navy engineer, to design one – a pontooned biplane made of spruce and linen, which he called the B&W for the two men's initials. Only two B&Ws were built, but they impressed the government and earned the fledgling Boeing Company new contracts to build military trainers in World War I.

During World War II, Boeing supplied huge numbers of the successful B-17 and B-29 bombers. Over the next decades, the company moved from strength to strength, but by the 1970s, a downturn in Boeing's success had a profound impact on the area's economy. Thousands of families packed up and left.

A billboard on the outskirts of Seattle exhorted "Will the last person leaving Seattle please turn off the lights?" Boeing won back commercial dominance in the 1980s but lost its lead to the European consortium Airbus by the end of the 1990s. For three decades, Boeing and Airbus have battled for supremacy in the global market. Downturns have been the result of a number of influences, significantly including the 1990s meltdown of the Asian economies and the impact of the 9/11 terrorist attacks of 2001.

With soaring oil prices as well as increasing pressure from governments and environmental groups over carbon dioxide (CO_2) emissions, the battleground is increasingly shifting towards fuel efficiency.

Boeing's strategy is to build aircraft like the 787 Dreamliner from composite materials with reduced weight and therefore less fuel use and CO_2 emissions. Airbus, meanwhile, is responsible for the A380, whose sheer size, seating 550 passengers, or 800 fitted in an economy configuration, reduces the amount of fuel used per passenger mile, and it's adding the A350, a mid-sized, long-haul jet, as a direct rival to the 787.

In 2006, Airbus revised its production schedule, delaying delivery of the A380, a move expected to cost the company about $2.5 billion in earnings from 2007 to 2010. This, coupled with recent successes of Boeing's, have propelled the Seattle-born company back into the air race. ❏

RIGHT: props of Boeing's success.

HEADING SOUTH

South of Seattle are superlative mountain views, glassworks as great as any in the world, a museum of the story of flight and one of the prettiest state capitals in the US

Southern of Seattle is a region of rapid growth and enduring natural beauty. Plus first-rate attractions. No trip to the Seattle area would be complete without a visit to the **Museum of Flight** ㉑ (9404 E Marginal Way S; tel: 206-764 5720; daily 10am–5pm; admission charge; www.museumofflight. org), at Boeing Field, just south of the city. The museum is a stalwart local favorite, predating the Future of Flight Aviation Center *(see page 164)* by several years.

Flight patterns

The impressive collection of aircraft and aviation ephemera represents the entire aero industry, not only Boeing's contribution. It occupies the original 1909 Boeing building, known as the **Red Barn**, which was part of a shipyard along the Duwamish River, and the adjacent Great Gallery, added in the 1980s. Inside the Red Barn are restored early planes, as well as historical photographs and drawings. The main-hall gallery has high ceilings and an assortment of flying craft, ranging from hang-gliders to fighter jets, including an F-104 Starfighter and a Russian MiG 21.

Interesting exhibits include an airplane car that looks like (and in fact is) a shiny, red sports car with wings; a flight simulator (actually, a simulation of a simulator); and, just outside the gallery, the country's first presidential jet, a Boeing 707. From the museum is a clear view of Boeing's airfield.

Most visitors arrive in the Seattle area by air, touching down in one of Washington's newer cities – aptly, if unpoetically, named **SeaTac**, after the **Sea-Tac International Airport** ㉒. The cumbersome name is a combination of the names of the two cities the airport serves, Seattle and Tacoma.

Map on pages 144–45

LEFT: close up of the Venetian Wall, Chihuly Bridge of Glass.
BELOW: exhibits in the Museum of Flight.

BELOW: glass-blowing is demonstrated at the Museum of Glass.

Renton

Renton ㉓, a city of 50,000 at the southern end of Lake Washington, is home to the Boeing facilities where the 737 and 757 jets were produced, as well as its own municipal airport. Renton's attractive outdoor offerings include **Liberty Park** beside the Cedar River – the site of the annual Renton River Days – and **Gene Coulon Memorial Beach Park**, on the lake.

The **Renton History Museum** (235 Mill Ave. S; tel: 425-255 2330; Tues–Sat 10am–4pm; admission charge; www.rentonhistory.org), not far from Liberty Park, recounts the city's beginnings as a coal-mining community, Black River Bridge. On view are a number of old photographs and some mining equipment, as well as maps showing the mining shafts that criss-cross underneath the expensive contemporary homes that now perch on Renton Hill.

The valley around **Kent ㉔**, south of Renton, formerly produced much of the Puget Sound area's agriculture; now it sprouts manufacturing plants and warehouses. Farther south are the waterfront communities of **Normandy Park** and **Des Moines**, named by a founder from Des Moines, Iowa, who persuaded friends in the Midwest to finance his venture in 1887.

Federal Way ㉕, south of Seattle along Interstate 5 and named for the federally funded Highway 99, is home to **Dash Point State Park** and the **Wild Waves Water Park and Enchanted Village**, popular summer attractions for children. Also in Federal Way are the **Rhododendron Species Botanical Gardens** (on Weyerhaeuser Way S; tel: 253-661 9377; Mar–May Fri–Wed 10am–4pm, June–Feb Sat–Wed 11am–4pm; admission charge; www.rhodygarden.org), at Weyerhaeuser corporate headquarters.

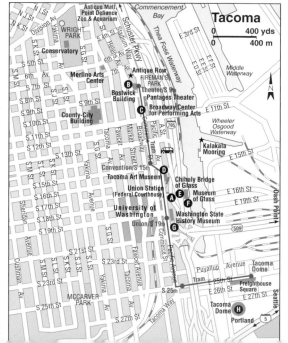

One of the world's largest collections of rhododendrons, the 22-acre (9-hectare) gardens feature 450 varieties of Washington's state flower – from the 100-ft (30-meter) high trees of the lower Himalaya to the ground-hugging species of Tibet and China. Adjacent to the gardens is the **Pacific Rim Bonsai Collection** (Mar–Sept Fri–Wed 10am–4pm, Oct–Feb Sat–Wed 11am–4pm; free; tel: 253-924 3153), with fine examples of bonsai plants from Asia and North America.

Tacoma

Just south of Federal Way and an hour's drive south of Seattle, **Tacoma** 26 is the state's third-largest city, with almost 200,000 people. Approaching the city with the bay in front and Mount Rainier behind, it's easy to understand why the city founders had such high hopes for Tacoma. It is one of the few cities with a setting that rivals – surpasses, locals would argue – Seattle in beauty. In the quality and variety of its architecture, Tacoma also stands out; just about every major architectural style of the past

100 years is represented in the city and its neighborhoods.

Originally called Commencement City – after Commencement Bay, in turn so-called because it was the origin of an 1841 surveying expedition – Tacoma was named after the Nisqually and Puyallup tribal name for Mount Rainier, 40 miles (65 km) to the southeast. It began as a 19th-century timber boomtown that in its 1890s heyday rivaled Seattle in importance, but the city went bust in the nationwide slump of 1893 and has been trying to catch up ever since.

In the heady, early days, Tacoma dubbed itself the City of Destiny, but for much of the 20th century, Tacoma's nickname seemed amusingly at odds with reality. Its smelly air (known as "Tacoma Aroma" and derived from pulp-mill emissions), crime rate, and defunct Downtown made it the butt of Seattle jokes.

Quietly and without too much fuss, Tacoma has been transforming itself from a blue-collar mill town with LA-style gangs to an economically diverse and environmentally

The Italian-style clock tower of Tacoma City Hall.

BELOW:
downtown Tacoma.

The Crystal Towers on the Chihuly Bridge of Glass glow at night.

BELOW: cycling to work is popular both in Seattle and Tacoma.

aware city with a vibrant cultural life. The economic center of a larger metropolitan area of some 750,000 people, Tacoma serves as a major port facility in the Pacific Northwest and as a gateway to two of the Northwest's most popular attractions: the Olympic Peninsula *(see page 187)* and Mount Rainier National Park *(see page 203)*.

An effort to revive the downtown area is bringing commerce and culture back to the city center. Yet despite the changes, Tacoma maintains its unpretentious and slightly eccentric ways. You can still get served a mean burger and shake at Frisko Freeze (1201 Division Ave; tel: 253-272 6843) and listen to rock 'n' roll at the teapot-shaped Bob's Java Jive (2102 S Tacoma Way; tel: 253-475 9843).

An energetic preservation movement is writing new leases of life for Tacoma's old buildings. The movement began with the transformation of the long-vacant Beaux Arts **Union Station** **A** into an elegant venue for the Federal courthouse. Across the street, once-empty warehouses serve as the locale for a University of Washington campus.

On Broadway, at the entry to so-called **Antique Row**, the triangular-shaped **Bostwick Building** **B**, built in 1889 as a hotel, has turned its downstairs into a coffeehouse and jazz club. Antiques stores and specialty shops occupy the rest of the block. A brass plaque on the Bostwick makes a claim to fame: that here in 1893, Civil War veteran Russell O'Brien started the tradition of standing for the national anthem.

Art and glass

A lively arts scene has also contributed to the revival of Downtown. The excellent **Broadway Center for the Performing Arts** **C** (tel: 253-591 5894 for tickets) puts on dance, music and stage productions at the restored **Rialto Theater** and Pantages, and at the postmodernist **Theatre On the Square**. A 1,100-seat vaudeville palace dating back to 1916, the **Pantages Theater** was designed by B. Marcus Priteca, a European-trained architect known for his neoclassical style and the designer of more than 150 theaters throughout North America.

The **Tacoma Art Museum** **D** (1701 Pacific Ave; tel: 253-272 4258; daily except Mon, 10am–5pm, Sun from noon, every third Thur until 8pm; admission charge; www.tacomaartmuseum.org) was designed by architect Antoine Predock. It features major traveling exhibitions, TAM's permanent collection, interactive activities, and a café. The museum is building a top collection of works by Northwest artists, and on permanent display is a collection of early glass works by world-renowned and Tacoma-born glass artist Dale Chihuly.

Dale Chihuly has done much to raise the profile of the city. The dazzling **Chihuly Bridge of Glass** **E** *(see photo on page 46)* over the

Thea Foss Waterway that connects the Museum of Glass with Union Station and the Art and State History museums is the most famous contribution. The sculptures nearest Union Station make up the Seaform Pavilion; the middle section has the glittering Crystal Towers; while the walkway nearest to the Museum of Glass is the Venetian Wall, featuring 109 Chihuly sculptures in miniature.

"Hot glass. Cool art" is the catchphrase of the **Museum of Glass ⒡** (1801 Dock Street; tel: 253-284 4750; Mon–Sat 10am–5pm, Sun noon–5pm, every third Thur until 8pm in summer, closed Mon–Tues in other seasons; admission charge; www.museumofglass.org). This is one of the few museums in the country to concentrate on contemporary glass art, and glass-blowing techniques are demonstrated to would-be Chihulys.

The **Washington State History Museum ⒢** (1911 Pacific Ave; tel: 888-238 4373 or 253-272 3500; open Tues–Sun 10am–5pm, Sun from noon, Thur until 8pm; admission charge; www.wshs.org), housed in a handsome brick building next to Union Station, has a substantial collection of pioneer and Native American exhibits.

Tacoma attractions

Popular culture and sports have a venue at the **Tacoma Dome ⒣**. Built in 1983, the 152-ft (46-meter) tall dome, one of the world's largest wooden-domed structures, is well-known for its acoustics. A popular venue for rock acts, the arena seats up to 27,000 people and has hosted events ranging from the Billy Graham Crusade to truck-and-tractor pulls to the Dixie Chicks.

Freighthouse Square has the distinction of being a mom-and-pop shopping mall. More precisely, this mom-and-son enterprise is an early-1900s freighthouse for the Milwaukee/St Paul Railroad converted into a marketplace. The three block-long building, managed by the owner with assistance from his mother, Freighthouse Square is made up of small specialty stores, New Age health services, and an international food court with everything from

Maps:
Area 145
City 168

TIP

Walking tours of sites created by or which inspired glass artist Dale Chihuly are organized by the Tacoma Art Museum. It is also available by cellphone. Go to: www tacomaartmuseum.org

BELOW: Tacoma Dome and Mount Rainier.

The yellow "smiley face" is said to have originated in Seattle. The smiley "berry face" – with legs – originated in Tacoma.

Korean barbecue to Greek salads. The oldest residential neighborhood, **North End**, is evidence of Tacoma's glory days when the new city on the hill held promise of becoming the West Coast's center of industry and finance. Stroll along broad, tree-lined **Yakima Avenue** past colonnaded mansions built by Tacoma's 19th-century industrial barons. The neighborhood's best building (at 111 North E Street) is a French chateau lookalike, complete with towers and turrets.

The building was commissioned by the Northern Pacific Railroad in 1891 as a hotel for its passengers after Tacoma became the terminus for the railroad. But before it was finished, the railroad went bankrupt and the hotel became (and still is) **Stadium High School**. Scenes were filmed at Stadium for the movie *Ten Things I Hate About You*, a 1990s teen take on *The Taming of the Shrew*.

Below the North End, along the south shore of Commencement Bay, **Ruston Way** has trails, parks and piers as well as enough waterfront restaurants to earn it the nickname

Restaurant Row. Follow Ruston Way inland a few miles, and plan to spend some time on one of Tacoma's most engaging landmarks. At 700-acres (280-hectares) one of the largest urban parks in the United States, **Point Defiance Park** ㉗ is on a finger of land jutting out into Puget Sound. It has formal gardens, a swimming beach, a replica of a 19th-century trading post, a children's storybook park, a zoo and aquarium and a logging camp, complete with a 1929 steam train chugging around the camp.

The **Point Defiance Zoo and Aquarium** (daily 9:30am–6pm in summer, seasonal hours at other times of the year; admission charge; tel: 253-404 3678; www.pdza.org), founded in 1888, is both animal- and people-friendly; it isn't unusual to encounter a llama, a pig or even an elephant with its keeper on an afternoon walk. With a Pacific Rim focus, the zoo is known for its humane and innovative approach.

Galloping Gertie

On the west side of Tacoma, the **Tacoma Narrows Bridge** ㉘ is the world's fifth-largest suspension bridge. The first bridge, opened in 1940 across the Tacoma Narrows, was called "Galloping Gertie" for the undulating winds that whip through the narrows. Gertie galloped too much, though, and just a few months after opening, collapsed. Pieces of the old bridge shelter marine life, and entice scuba divers into the waters. Just over the Narrows Bridge is **Gig Harbor** ㉙, a pleasant harbor town with old-fashioned shops, restaurants and bed-and-breakfast inns.

Puyallup

Although much of the surrounding farmland has been lined with strip malls, **Puyallup** ㉚ is still primarily a farming community. This is one of

those Washington place names where the pronunciation separates locals from outsiders: it's pronounced *pyew-allup*. The Native American tribe of the same name has casino interests in the area.

In the 1880s, this fertile valley was a huge producer of hops, used for brewing beer. Most were exported to Europe. Hop yards were later converted to berry and rhubarb farms. Today, the area produces daffodils, tulips and Christmas trees. A revival of the downtown area has brought back some of the small-town ambiance, lost when a mall was built on the outskirts of town.

Contributing to the effort is the Arts Downtown program, a changing exhibit of outdoor art by local and outside artists. Shown in parks, shops, and on public buildings, pieces range from a sculpture of a pet pig made from scrap metal, to a Russian-born artist's elegant bronze tribute to a mother's love.

The town is restoring the **Ezra Meeker mansion** (312 Spring St, tel: 253-848 1770), a 17-room, Italianate house built in 1890 by Puyallup's first mayor. Three rooms are currently open to the public. In 1906, 54 years after crossing the Oregon Trail in a covered wagon, Meeker, aged 76, made the trip in reverse, clearing the overgrown trail. Some of his stone markers still remain. He continued his journey by foot and covered wagon to Washington, DC.

Steilacoom

A 20-minute drive southeast of Tacoma, **Steilacoom** ㉛ (pronounced *stilacum*) is Washington's oldest incorporated town. It is hard to believe that this small waterfront village once was a busy frontier port and seat of government. It was one of the first places in the area to develop a sense of its own historic importance: years ago, its preservation-minded citizens registered the downtown area as a national historic site, ensuring that Steilacoom was protected from development.

The town's old drugstore, **Bair Drug & Hardware**, was built in 1895. The traditional combination pharmacy, hardware store, post office and gathering place has been

Map on pages 144–45

A glass slipper fit for a 21st-century Cinderella.

BELOW: the Puyallup Fair is a 17-day event held every September.

Olympia's liberal arts college means the town's residents include more than just politicians.

turned into a museum and café (1617 Lafayette St; tel: 253-588 9668; opens daily at 8am, hours vary by season; www.thebairrestaurant.com). The museum shows patent medicines and other original items, and the café serves ice-cream sodas from a 1906 marble-topped soda fountain.

The **Steilacoom Historical Museum** (1801 Rainier Ave; tel: 253-584 4133; Apr–Oct Fri–Sun 1–4pm; www.steilacoomhistorical.org; donations) documents early town life with realistic displays of a living room, kitchen and parlor in a late 1890s-era home.

At the other end of the block, the **Steilacoom Tribal Museum and Cultural Center** (1515 Lafayette St; tel: 253-584 6308; Tues–Sun 10am–4pm; admission charge) is one of the few tribal-run museums in the state of Washington, and tells the story of Native American life and Pacific Northwest and local history from the tribal point of view.

Olympia

Thirty miles (50 km) south of Tacoma at the southernmost point of Puget Sound, the Washington state capital of **Olympia** ③ brings to mind a comment made about another capital, Washington, DC – it's a city for people who don't like cities. The city's low-rise architecture and leisurely pace gives the place a friendly, small-town feel, while Evergreen State College, a progressive liberal arts college established in 1972, provides enough of a countercultural edge to keep the city interesting.

After Washington became a territory in 1853, Olympia was named its capital. City fathers spent the next 40 years fighting off claims to the title by Vancouver, Tacoma and Seattle, among others.

It wasn't until 1890 that Olympia was officially named Washington's state capital, and it took another 60 or so years for it to wrestle several

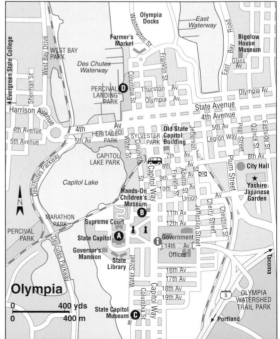

Olympia

state government offices away from Seattle. It is easy to forget that Olympia is Washington's state capital until the beautifully landscaped grounds and stately buildings of the **State Capitol Ⓐ** compound loom on a hill, overlooking the water with the snowcapped Cascades in the distance. Olympia has one of the loveliest and most impressive capitol sites in the country. Dominating the 55-acre (22-hectare) campus is the Washington State **Legislative Building**.

Constructed in 1927, the handsome Romanesque structure, with its 287-ft (87-meter) dome, brings to mind the capitol building in Washington, DC. The chandelier hanging in the rotunda was designed by Louis Tiffany, an American artist and designer who established a firm in New York specializing in glass work and whose father founded the venerable Tiffany and Co.

Embedded in the floor underneath it, the state seal bears an image of George Washington worn smooth by the feet of visitors. During a visit to the capitol in the late 1940s, President Harry S Truman objected to the image being defaced in this way, and the state seal has been cordoned off ever since.

Other buildings in the State Capitol compound include the handsome **Governor's Mansion**, the **State Library**, which houses a collection of artworks by Northwest artists, and the **State Greenhouse**, which provides all the flowers and plants for the capitol complex. War memorials and sculptural works also grace the lovely grounds.

Guided hour-long tours (tel: 360-902 8889; www.ga.wa.gov/visitor) of the Legislative Building are provided on a daily basis. More detailed information, including special appointments for group tours is available from the **Visitor Center** (tel: 360-586 3460).

Kids in the capital

If politics is a little dry for young visitors, try taking them to the **Hands On Children's Museum Ⓑ** (106 11th Ave. SW; tel: 360-956 0818; daily 10am–5pm, every first Fri until 9pm, Sun from noon; admission charge; www.hocm.org), which offers enough activities to keep kids busy for a whole afternoon.

In a residential neighborhood of lovely old homes, the **Washington State Capitol Museum Ⓒ** (211 21st Ave SW; tel: 360-753 2580; Tues–Sat 10am–4pm, Sat from noon; admission charge; www.wshs.org/wscm/) is housed in a 1920s Renaissance Revival-style mansion. Among the museum's exhibits is a collection of rare baskets made by weavers of the Nisqually, Puyallup and Skokomish tribes.

Tourists and locals mingle at the shops, restaurants and cafés at cute **Percival Landing Park Ⓓ**, a waterfront park and boardwalk. Next to the landing is Washington state's largest **farmers' market**, a good place to buy local produce, crafts and foods.   ❏

Maps:
Area 145
City 174

TIP

Even if you don't live locally, you can be a part of Olympia's thriving arts scene. The cute website www.buyolympia.com not only has unusual mail-order gifts, but also lists events.

BELOW: Olympia is the state capital of Washington.

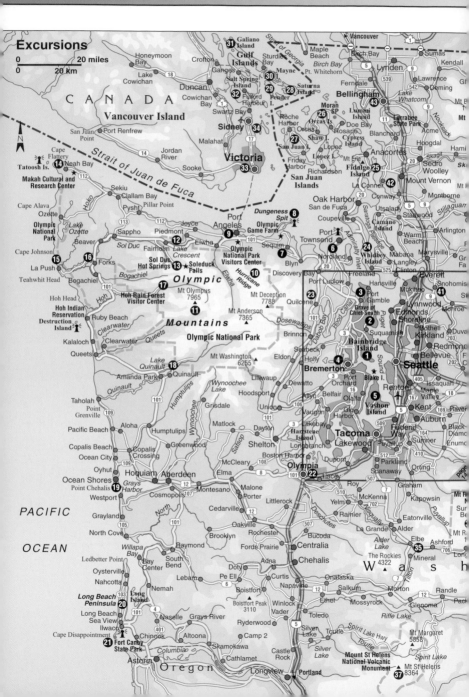

Excursions

0   20 miles
0   20 km

EXCURSIONS

One of the main reasons people live in Seattle is, ironically, the ease with which they can go somewhere else

Escaping the urban bustle can be as easy as a 35-minute ferry trip to Bainbridge Island, or as bracing as several days' trek across the majestic Cascade Mountains. The jewels of Puget Sound are the San Juan Islands, the archipelago that gets more sunshine than the surrounding area, so in winter the weather is pleasant; in summer it's even better.

Jagged mountain peaks, temperate rainforests, Victorian towns and remote, sandy islands: all are just a few hours from downtown Seattle. The middle of the Olympic Peninsula is Mount Olympus, towering 7,965 ft (2,428 meters) over the surrounding mountains. The crown is 922,000-acre (375,000-hectare) Olympic National Park, with glacial rivers roaring down folds and crevices to empty into the Pacific Ocean, the Strait of Juan de Fuca, and Puget Sound itself.

The park encompasses one of the last wilderness forests on the US mainland. Rain and fog, coupled with a mild coastal climate, are essential for the temperate rainforest to thrive. Sitka spruce are dominant, and soaring trees draped in moss, shot through by hazy sunlight, make a lasting impression. One of the first expeditions across the mountains on foot took nearly six months, but now you can do it in four or five days.

Puget Sound is known for its wildlife, including orcas, bald eagles and bears. Also in the area is the Olympic short-tailed weasel, found nowhere else in the world.

The ski slopes and hiking trails of the Cascades, the glacial Mount Rainier, Mount St Helens and Mount Baker, plus more than 370 islands, with beaches, fishing and water sports, all mean there's plenty to enjoy outside Seattle for either a day out, or a trip lasting several weeks. ❑

PRECEDING PAGES: a ferry glides by the Victorian town of Port Townsend on the Olympic Peninsula.

ACROSS PUGET SOUND

Just a short ferry ride from downtown
Seattle are rural lanes, upscale
amenities and small towns

A good ferry system, a few art-
fully placed bridges, and excellent roadways link Seattle to
the nearby islands, peninsulas and
waterways that surround the city.
Day trips can easily extend into
longer excursions, with the assurance
that all roads – and ferries – lead via a
highly scenic route back to Seattle.

Some of the islands are developed
and have good tourist amenities.
Others give a glimpse of the wild
without an expedition into the out-
back. The small, uninhabited **Blake
Island** for example, accessible only
by boat, has a park with 16 miles (26
km) of trails and driftwood-strewn
beaches. Deer and bald eagles are
among the plentiful wildlife.

Blake Island is the location of
Tillicum Village. Designed as a
tourist attraction in the early 1960s,
boats still leave from downtown
Seattle on organized excursions. Visitors can see a Northwest American
Indian longhouse, lunch on salmon,
traditionally baked over alder fires,
and watch a dance interpretation of
local tribal myths and legends. The
show is a little stagey, but the setting
is beautiful, especially at sunset.

Bainbridge Island

Nearby **Bainbridge Island** ❶
belongs jurisdictionally to rural Kitsap County (to which it is connected

by Route 305), but culturally the
increasingly upscale island, with its
pricey homes and proliferating
BMWs, is closer to Seattle, a pleasant 35-minute ferry ride away. The
farmers, fishermen and wealthy
"summer people" from the city who
once populated the island are being
replaced by Seattle-commuting pro-
fessionals or wealthy retirees.

At the end of the 19th century, little Bainbridge was home to the
world's largest sawmill, at Port
Blakely. Later, the economy turned

Map
on pages
178–9

LEFT: reflections on
Bainbridge Island.
BELOW: sailing to the
islands from Seattle.

For 26 years, the Bainbridge Island Winery was located in this pretty blue barn. Now the vintners have moved up the road to be nearer to their vineyards.

BELOW: Bainbridge Island is only 35 minutes from Seattle.

to berry farming. Many of the farmers were Japanese immigrants – arriving in the 1880s as laborers for the sawmills and later becoming farmers – whose internment in government camps (some in California but most in Idaho) during World War II was vividly described in the 1995 best-selling novel, *Snow Falling on Cedars*, written by Bainbridge resident David Guterson.

The big berry farms that once anchored the island's economy are gone, though there are still enough small farms left to justify a strawberry festival put on by the local Filipino-American community. Most of the pretty summer homes have been turned into year-round residences or bed-and-breakfast inns.

Winslow

Winslow is a tidy cluster of gift shops, cafés and restaurants. At the Bainbridge Island Library, the **Japanese Haiku Garden**, part of the library's attractive grounds, commemorates the island's *issei* (first generation) Japanese-Americans. *Haiku*-inscribed plaques are scattered throughout the stone-and-bonsai garden: "Ice and water/their differences resolved/are friends again," reads one poem, hinting at the World War II internment.

At the **Bainbridge Island Historical Society**'s small museum (May–Sept Tues, Thur, Sat and Sun 1–4pm; donations; tel: 206-842 2773), two photographs vividly underscore the impact of the internment on island life.

The photographs show Bainbridge High School's 1942 and 1943 graduating classes. In the first picture, about one third of the faces are Japanese; the second shows a smaller, all-white class.

Most descendants of the *issei* have moved away for opportunities on the mainland. One who has remained is nursery-owner Junkoh Harui. He restored the nursery, **Bainbridge Gardens** (tel: 206-842 5888), which his father started in the early 1900s from Japanese seeds, and then lost during the internment. The nursery sells an excellent selection of trees, shrubs, perennials and bonsai, as well as garden statuary.

It's a pleasant place to stroll around.

Four miles (6½ miles) from the ferry dock is **Bainbridge Island Vineyards & Winery** (8989 Day Road East; tel: 206-842 9463; Fri–Sun, 11am–5pm; free), a family-run business making wines solely from its own grapes (which you can see growing in the valley) or fruit wines from the island's berries.

Take Route 305 north towards the Agate Pass bridge to the Kitsap Peninsula. Before crossing the bridge you can visit the **Bloedel Reserve** (Wed–Sun 10am–4pm; admission charge; tel: 206-842 7631). The former summer retreat of a Seattle mayor's widow is a 150-acre (60-hectare) preserve of woodland and meadows which make a perfect wildlife habitat.

Kitsap Peninsula

The Agate Pass Bridge onto the Kitsap Peninsula leads to **Suquamish**, where a right turn on Suquamish Way leads to the **grave of Chief Sealth ②**, the tribal chief for whom Seattle is named. The tribal cemetery is peaceful and small, but as befits his importance, the leader is commemorated with a tall, white marker. Just up the highway, the **Suquamish Museum** (May–Sept daily 10am–5pm, Oct–Apr Fri–Sun 11am–4pm; admission charge) has historical photos and tribal artifacts.

Along Route 305 is **Poulsbo**, a Scandinavian fishing village turned tourist town. It was nicknamed "Little Norway" for its setting on Liberty Bay, which is reminiscent of the Scandinavian fjords. This may have been the attraction for the Nordic families who emigrated here a century ago. Poulsbo is noted throughout the state for Poulsbo bread, baked fresh daily at Sluys Poulsbo Bakery.

Heading northward towards the Olympic Peninsula is a worthwhile diversion. This takes you to **Port Gamble ③** which, until a few years ago, was one of the last lumber towns to have a fully operational mill.

Built by the Pope and Talbot timber families, who arrived by clipper ship from Maine in the 1850s, the town's original trading center has been converted into a combination gift store, café and museum. The tiny

In June 2005, the Suquamish tribe received the deeds to small Old Man House Park. Chief Seattle had lived on the land, and its return by the Washington State Parks department helped to heal wounds. Old Man House Park is still managed by the department, but under tribal control.

BELOW:
aerial view of
Bainbridge harbor.

town, with refurbished Victorian clapboard houses, is a picture of a prim-and-pretty New England village – but one that is set against a dramatic Northwestern backdrop.

Bremerton

South from Poulsbo is the seaport town of **Bremerton ④**. Founded in 1891 by William Bremer, a German immigrant, Bremerton is one of those towns in the West that for years was controlled by one family. Plotted by Bremer on land he had purchased, the town – today's downtown area – stayed in the hands of the Bremer family until the second of the two sons died in 1986. Neither son married – according to local lore, in accordance with their mother's wishes – and after the second son died, local Olympic College inherited most of Downtown.

To the outside world, Bremerton is known for the **Puget Sound Naval Shipyard**. The shipyard is still a large force in the local economy and culture, but gentrification has brought about a transformation in the town. The result is art galleries, specialty

Sunset picnic on Puget Sound.

BELOW: island inlet.

shops and espresso cafés, mixed in with a few reminders of older days, like tattoo parlors and gritty bars.

The former Woolworth department store has been converted into an indoor **antique market**, with more than 40 vendors proffering a lively assortment of junk and treasure.

The **Harborside District** is a big, glossy development designed to lure corporations to the town, and with a conference center to attract the business trade. There's a marina, a boardwalk, fountains and restaurants.

For years Bremerton's biggest tourist attraction was the battleship USS *Missouri*, but Bremerton lost the most highly decorated ship of World War II to Honolulu in 1999. In its place now is an interesting footnote to the Vietnam War: the destroyer **USS *Turner Joy*** (Fri–Sun 10am–4pm; admission charge), which was one of the ships in the Tonkin Gulf incident that escalated the Vietnam War. Nearby is **Bremerton Naval Museum** (Mon–Sat 10am–4pm, Sun from 1pm; donations; tel: 360-377 4186) which focuses on World War II, and on the shipyard's contribution.

Mysterious Myths

Myths are plentiful across the waters of Puget Sound and on the slopes of the Cascade mountains. Sea serpents up to 100 ft (30 meters) long with heads like horses and snouts like camels were reported in the Pacific Northwest waters long before the white man arrived. Centuries old petroglyphs of these creatures adorn rock surfaces, while paintings and wood carvings depict them too. The creatures were named "Cadborosaurus" by a 1930s newspaperman after sightings in Cadboro Bay, Victoria. Mountain tales of the elusive Bigfoot or Sasquatch are among the most popular and persistent in North American folk memory. A giant, hairy hominid who roams the forests has been recounted in stories and depicted on totem poles from northern California to British Columbia. Both native and white witnesses describe the creature as 6–11 ft (1.8–3.4 meters) tall and weighing between 700 and 2,500 pounds (320–1,100 kg), walking erect or slightly stooped with long arms that swing back and forth. Its hair is black or brown. There is no solid evidence, however, to convince researchers of Bigfoot's existence.

Vashon Island

Southwest of Bremerton is a ferry link to **Vashon Island ❺**, which is also accessible by ferry from Tacoma and from the Kitsap Peninsula. Without a bridge connecting it to the mainland, Vashon remains the most rural and least developed of Puget Sound's nearby islands, and that's the way the residents like it.

The island's sense of rural priority is nicely symbolized by a famous landmark: the bike in the tree. It seems that, years ago, someone planted a bike in the fork of a tree and left it to rust. Today, the bike is completely engulfed by the tree, with only the handlebars sticking out the front of the trunk and part of the rear wheel sticking out the back. It's thriving in the woods, on Vashon Highway a few miles south of Downtown, but you may have to ask for directions locally.

Unfortunately, there isn't enough industry to support the island's 10,000 residents, so most commute to Seattle or Tacoma. But there are a few who manage to live on the island and work here, too, usually by running one of the small specialty shops (including four booksellers) that sell knick-knacks like candles and gifts.

Vashon is perfect for visitors who like their pleasures low-key. During the summer months, they can pick their own strawberries, rent a kayak, or go swimming. At other times of the year, the main leisure activities include hiking to Point Robinson Lighthouse or taking one of the horse-drawn hayrides.

In the 1960s and 1970s, Vashon was a counterculture retreat. "There was only one cop on the island, so you could get away with a lot," one alumnus of the era reminisces. Today, intermingling with the locals is a lively community of artists, some of whose work is displayed in New York, San Francisco and elsewhere, not to mention the galleries scattered across the island.

Vashon Allied Arts, which is headquartered in the **Blue Heron Arts Center** (Vashon Highway SW; tel: 206-463 5131), presents a well-attended monthly show featuring local and regional artists. ❑

Map on pages 178–9

Street scene in Winslow.

BELOW: Puget Sound Naval Shipyard in Bremerton.

THE OLYMPIC PENINSULA

A rainforest, a Victorian town, a tribal reservation
and magnificent Mount Olympus urge travelers
to "go west" to this lovely peninsula

All over Puget Sound, the peaks of the **Olympic Mountains** dominate the western skyline. Few regions can offer visitors such rugged coasts, prairies and forests with views, above the timber line, of snowy, glacier-capped peaks.

To reach the peninsula from Seattle, take a ferry to Bremerton *(see page 184)* and head north 19 miles (30 km) on State Route 3. Pass through Poulsbo *(see page 183)*, Washington's Little Norway, and about 7 miles (11 km) farther on State Route 3 is the **Hood Canal Bridge**. This floating bridge is a major gateway to the Olympic Peninsula, the only one over tidal waters and at 1½ miles (2.5 km) long, one of the world's longest.

A section swings aside for ships to pass, and Trident submarines from the base at Bangor may hold up traffic. Before crossing the bridge, you might want to take a short trip to historic Port Gamble just east of the bridge *(see page 183)*.

Port Townsend

Port Townsend ❻ is about 30 miles (50 km) north of the bridge. The harbor here was discovered by Captain George Vancouver in 1792 while surveying the coast for the British Admiralty. In 1851 the city was created, planned to be the main West Coast port. By the end of the century, the city was booming, but the dreams relied on a railroad connection to Tacoma, which never came.

Urban renewal and development passed it by, so Port Townsend has many lovely Victorian buildings, some of them now hotels or inns. **Water Street** has art galleries, antique and clothing stores, and restaurants in the old commercial center. Some of these back up onto the water, as they were built in the late 19th century to transport goods

Map on pages 178–9

LEFT: Hoh Rainforest.
BELOW: bald eagle.

Stop for chocolate or coffee on Water Street, Port Townsend.

BELOW LEFT: Point Wilson Lighthouse.
BELOW RIGHT: St Paul's Church.

from sailing vessels. Many people use Port Townsend as a base to explore the surrounding area, returning each night to accommodation in an historic building and to dine in one of the town's excellent restaurants. The **Visitor Center** (daily; tel: 360-385 2722; www.enjoypt.com) has maps and information.

Fort Warden

North of the city are the 434 acres (175 hectares) of historic Fort Worden, keystone of an 1880s network of forts, which guarded the entrance to Puget Sound until the end of World War II. The fort is now a state park, and the parade ground was featured in the movie *An Officer and a Gentleman*. The Coast Artillery Museum (daily 10am–4pm in summer, weekends at other times; donation; tel: 360-385 0373) illustrates the history of the fort.

Fine accommodation is available in restored officers' homes (tel: 365-344 4400), less luxurious lodging is in the barracks and the hostel. Campgrounds are also available.

Sharing the flat point with gun emplacements is the **Point Wilson Lighthouse**, built in 1922. The **Marine Science Center** (Wed–Mon 11am–5pm in summer, Fri–Mon noon–4pm at other times; admission charge; tel: 360-385 5582) on the waterfront has exhibits and touch tanks of local marine life. The Marine Science Center also sponsors marine-science activities and summer camps for kids.

Heading west

From Port Townsend, 13 miles (21 km) south on State Route 20 and then north and west another 13 miles on US 101, is the sunny town of **Sequim ⑦** (pronounced *skwim*), in the Dungeness Valley.

The arid area was first homesteaded in 1854 and irrigated four decades later as Sequim became a farming community. The **Museum and Arts Center** (Tues–Sat 8am–4pm; donation; tel: 360-683 8110) has exhibits of farming, Salish and pioneer life, and displays by local artists. Sequim's mild climate, in the rain shadow of the Olympic Mountains, attracts many retirees.

Map on pages 178–9

Head north 5 miles (8 km) on Ward Road to the **Olympic Game Farm** (open daily 9am, with variable closing times; admission charge; tel: 360-683 4295 or 1-800 778 4295), where animals like bears, bison, elk, zebras and lions live. Over the years it has supplied animal "actors" for movies and television. There's a selection of walking and driving tours.

Dungeness Spit ❽ is farther north. At 6 miles (8 km) and growing, the spit is the longest sand hook (a sand spit growing out from the shore then parallelling it) in the United States. The Dungeness Recreation Area includes a 6-mile (8-km) hike along the spit, and around the shore of the salt water lagoon. The lagoon is a national wildlife refuge for migrating water fowl. At the end of the spit is the **New Dungeness Lighthouse**, built in 1857.

Follow US 101 west 17 miles (27 km) to **Port Angeles ❾**, the largest port city on the northern Olympic Peninsula. Port Angeles' huge harbor for Asian and Pacific ocean-going ships is formed by Ediz Hook, another long sand spit with a Coast Guard air station at its end. The car ferry *Coho* (tel: 360-457 4491) operates year-round to Victoria *(see page 198)* on Vancouver Island, in Canada's province of British Columbia. A passenger-only ferry – *Victoria Express* – also sails to Victoria from here, and to Friday Harbor on San Juan Island.

Within an historic Georgian-style courthouse, the **Clallam County Historical Museum** (Mon–Fri 10am–4pm; donation; tel: 360-417 2364) has displays on local history, fishing, genealogy and Native American artifacts. There are spectacular views of both the Strait of Juan de Fuca and Vancouver Island to the north, and of the Olympic Mountains to the south.

Olympic National Park

The **Olympic National Park Visitor Center** (daily 8.30am–6pm in summer, 9am–4pm the rest of the year; tel: 360-565 3130) in Port Angeles has maps and park information, and displays on the wildlife, plants, geology and the tribal culture of the Northwest coast.

The Strait of Juan de Fuca, the narrow passage between the Olympic Peninsula and Canada's Vancouver Island, was named for a Greek captain sailing under the Spanish flag who may have sailed the strait in 1592.

BELOW LEFT: Water Street, Port Townsend.
BELOW RIGHT: the Ann Starrett mansion is now a hotel.

To enter the park, follow Race Street in Port Angeles to the well-marked Hurricane Ridge Road, and then make the steep 17-mile (27-km) ascent through dense forest to reach **Hurricane Ridge ⑩**, 5,200 ft (1,600 meters) above sea level. From here are views of mountains, meadows with wildflowers, and forests.

To the southwest is glacier-capped **Mount Olympus ⑪**, at 7,965 ft (2,428 meters) the highest peak in the Olympics. No roads lead to Mount Olympus, only hiking trails. In winter months, Hurricane Ridge is the only place in the Olympics for cross-country and downhill skiing.

Return to US 101 and head west for 5 miles (8 km) beyond Port Angeles; the road curves south around **Lake Crescent ⑫**, an immense cobalt-blue glacier lake surrounded by tall-timbered forest. Gorgeous **Lake Crescent Lodge** (tel: 360-928 3211), on the southern shore, is where President Franklin D. Roosevelt stayed in 1937 before he signed the act creating the 922,000-acre (373,000-hectare) Olympic National Park. Continue west along US 101 and turn south onto Sole-duck River Road to reach **Sol Duc Hot Springs ⑬**, where you can take a dip in the Olympic-sized pool or hot mineral pools, which are a pleasant 102–109°F (39–43°C). A short rainforest hike leads to Soleduck Falls and a less fancy geothermal spring, Olympic Hot Springs.

In 1999, the Makah exerted their whaling rights and harpooned a gray whale from the vantage point of a dugout canoe. The action drew protests from animal rights groups, even though the whale was not on any endangered species list.

BELOW: Olympic National Park has lush glades and gorges.

Neah Bay

Continue west on US 101 to **Sappho** and then north on State Route 113. At the intersection with SR 112, turn and head west 27 miles (43 km) through Clallam Bay and Sekiu to **Neah Bay ⑭**, at the northwesterly tip of the peninsula. Alternatively, follow SR 112 from Port Angeles along the picturesque shore of the Strait of Juan de Fuca, bypassing Lake Crescent.

The remote village of Neah Bay is on the **Makah Indian Reservation**. The Makah, who call themselves Kwih-dich-chuh-ahtx – "people who live by the rocks and seagulls" – have been here for hundreds of years. Majestic red cedars provided housing, tools, and sea-going canoes, in which they hunted migrating gray whales and seals.

The Makah still have the right by treaty to hunt whales, but commercial fishing is a mainstay. Sports fishing for salmon and halibut is an important industry for the Makah and a big attraction for thousands of anglers who visit annually; Neah Bay is home port more for than 200 commercial and sports-fishing boats. The Makah welcome visitors to visit a hatchery, where salmon migrate up the fish ladders.

For information on this and more, contact the **Makah Cultural and Research Center** (daily in summer 10am–5pm, Wed–Sun 10am–5pm the rest of the year; admission charge; tel: 360-645 2711). This is a useful source of information as well as a museum, with Northwest Indian

artifacts and a replica longhouse, the hub of Makah village life. Edward S. Curtis' photomurals are from more than 40,000 images of a 34-year photo-essay he began on the North American Indians in 1896.

Most of the 55,000-plus artifacts are from the archeological dig on the Ozette Indian Reservation on the coast, south of Neah Bay and the Makah lands. The village, buried by a mudslide more than 500 years ago, was sealed in clay soil, the contents of the houses closed off for posterity. The Ozette dig remains one of the most important archeological finds in North America.

Many beaches in the area are closed to non-Native Americans. At the Cultural and Research Center, maps of the reservation show open areas, and the car route and walking trail to **Cape Flattery**, on the northwestern tip of the Peninsula. The boardwalk trail threads through a forest to observation decks on the 60-ft (18-meter) cliffs of the cape. Vistas are spectacular, with waves crashing on rocky shores and pristine beaches. In spring and late fall, migrating gray whales can sometimes be seen, as well as seals and birds.

A few hundred yards offshore is **Tatoosh Island**, home to seals, sea lions and the **Cape Flattery Light**, begun in 1857. The light overlooks the funnel-like entrance to the Strait of Juan de Fuca, a graveyard for the many ships wrecked on the Washington coast or Vancouver Island by storms, ocean currents and fog.

South along the coast

South from the Makah Reservation is a national wildlife refuge: 57 miles (98 km) of spectacular cliffs, sea stacks and beaches. Just north of Forks is a turnoff – SR 110 – to the coast, leading to Rialto Beach and the Quileute village of La Push. **Rialto Beach** is a favorite spot for fashion photographers. **La Push ⓯** has a jagged rock-lined beach, offshore sea stacks, and a justly famous 16-mile (26-km) beach walk.

Century-old **Forks ⓰**, with a population of around 3,000, is on a broad prairie on the northwest of the peninsula and is the only sizable town. The **Forks Timber Museum**

Map on pages 178–9

Life is lived at a different pace on the Olympic Peninsula.

BELOW: Olympic National Park's glacier-capped mountains are perfect for hikers.

On Dabob Bay is the town of Quilcene, which has a huge oyster factory.

BELOW: Great Blue Heron sits on kelp near Neah Bay.

(daily 10am–4pm; donation; tel: 360-374 9663), displays a pioneer kitchen, farm and logging equipment, vintage newspapers and photos. The town is a good base for hiking the rainforests and rugged coast.

The **Hoh Rainforest Visitor Center** ⑰ (daily; tel: 360-374 6925) is south of Forks off US 101 and about 20 miles (30 km) into the national park. There is a wealth of information here on the wildlife, flora and the history of the temperate rainforest. Moisture-laden air from the Pacific drenches the area with more than 150 inches (380 cm) of rain annually – this is the wettest place in the 48 states. Three loop trails (and a wheelchair-accessible mini-trail) lead into the rainforest of moss-draped trees, ferns and a clear, glacial-fed river. Elk, deer and other animals are often seen.

Farther south of the turnoff, US 101 swings west to the coast and follows cliffs overlooking beautiful beaches, from **Ruby Beach** and the **Hoh Indian Reservation** in the north to **Kalaloch** (pronounced *clay-lock*) **Beach** in the south. Part of Olympic National Park's coastal strip, the coast has a rugged and picturesque beauty. Waves crash against rocks and offshore islands, casting tree trunks up on the shore like toothpicks. A few miles offshore is reef-girdled **Destruction Island** and its lighthouse, built in 1890. On a foggy day, the mournful foghorn disturbs thousands of auklets – small sea birds – on the island.

The forest surrounding **Lake Quinault** ⑱ – at the southwest corner of Olympic National Park – is often called "the other rainforest." It's possible to drive a 25-mile (40-km) loop around the glacial lake. **Lake Quinault Lodge** (tel: 360-288 2900), a huge, old-fashioned cedar hotel built in 1926 on the lake's southern shore, is a landmark. Winding trails lead from the lodge into the rainforest, including to **Big Acre**, a grove of huge, centuries-old trees.

Ocean Shores

Head south to **Ocean Shores** ⑲, on a 6-mile (10-km) long peninsula, and enter through an imposing gateway. Originally homesteaded in the

1860s, Ocean Shores was only incorporated as a city in 1970, when investors, including singer Pat Boone, got the town under way. Ocean Shores is now a town of motels and vacation homes. **Grays Harbor** was discovered in 1792 by an American trader, Captain Robert Gray, who also discovered the Columbia River. The harbor is the only deep-water port on the outer Washington coast, and is a major terminal for Asia-bound lumber.

The tall ship *Lady Washington* (tel: 360-532 8611), a replica of Gray's ship, embarks on cruises from the Grays Harbor Historical Seaport, a working tall-ship dockyard.

Southward and eastward

South on US 101 and along the east shore of **Willapa Bay** is one of the nicest stretches of beach in Washington. This is the lovely **Long Beach Peninsula ⑳**, fronted by a 28-mile (45-km) shore. The lively town of **Long Beach** is a miniature Coney Island – the main street filled with huge chainsaw art sculptures (a near-naked mermaid, the Louis and Clark

duo, and more). The historic town of **Oysterville** had its heyday in California's 1850s Gold Rush, shipping oysters to San Francisco at the equivalent of $19 each in today's money.

At the base of the Olympic Peninsula is one of the most spectacular spots on the Washington coast: **Cape Disappointment ㉑**, overlooking the treacherous mouth of the Columbia River, a graveyard for ships and sailors. This graveyard is **Fort Canby State Park**, home to two lighthouses. **Cape Disappointment Light**, one of the first on the West Coast, has warned sailors for over 150 years. **North Head Light** was built later to guide ships coming from the north.

To complete the trip around the Olympic Peninsula, head east from Grays Harbor to the state capital at **Olympia ㉒** *(see page 174)*. A highway runs north along **Hood Canal**, known for oysters, through **Shelton** (Christmas trees and oysters) and Hoodsport. **Quilcene ㉓**, on Dabob Bay, has one of the world's largest oyster factories. Stop by for tangy oysters or clams to take home. ❑

Map on pages 178–9

Eight kinds of plants and five species of animal in Olympic National Park are found nowhere else in the world.

BELOW: Cape Disappointment Light.

ISLANDS AND MOUNTAINS

Watch orcas by the islands of the San Juan archipelago, visit a Victorian town in Canada, discover the magnificent Cascade Mountains, and end up only a couple of hours away from Seattle

L ike points on a compass, breathtaking trips into the Northwest radiate from Seattle in all directions. To the north are the coastal islands of the US and Canada, perfect for sunsets and picnics. The Cascade Mountains, with the volcanic showstoppers Mount Rainier, Mount St Helens and Mount Baker, are geographically to the east, but their snowcapped glacial peaks can be seen from everywhere. Short trips from Seattle include a spectacular waterfall; a miniature railroad and downhill and cross-country skiing.

ISLANDS OF THE NORTH

Whidbey Island ㉔ is the longest contiguous island in the US. The Keystone ferry travels from Port Townsend on the Olympic Peninsula to the rolling hills and rocky beaches of Whidbey, a hideaway place for hikers and walkers. A ferry at Mukilteo, 45 minutes north of Seattle, also goes to the island. The town of **Langley** perches on a cliff over Saratoga Passage, with water and mountain views a backdrop to the century-old shops, restaurants, art galleries and inns. **Coupeville** has Victorian homes and shops. **Oak Harbor** is the largest town, with Whidbey Naval Air Station nearby.

At the northern tip of the island, narrow **Deception Pass** is spanned

by a 976-ft-long (297-meter), 180-ft-high (55-meter) steel bridge to **Fidalgo Island** ㉕. Attractive, 19th-century **Anacortes** is the ferry terminal for the San Juan Islands and Vancouver Island. Views from nearby Mount Erie are well worth the drive to this lovely spot.

San Juan Islands

Of the 172 San Juans, only four – the islands of Shaw, Lopez, Orcas and San Juan – have regular ferry service; the others can be reached by float-

Map on pages 178–9

LEFT: Mount Rainier.
BELOW: a good oyster catch on the San Juan Islands.

plane or chartered sailboat, via narrow channels and open water, passing on the way sandy beaches, shallow bays, sand spits, grassy estuaries and forested slopes. Orcas (killer whales), seabirds, harbor seals, otters and bald eagles can be spotted on this leisurely route. The flat rural terrain of Lopez, Shaw and San Juan are great for bicycling.

Orcas Island ㉖ was named not for killer whales but for the Spanish patron of an explorer of the region in 1792. Bed-and-breakfast inns are all over the island, but the only traditional resort is **Rosario** (tel: 866-801 ROCK), the handsome 1904 estate of ship-builder and former Seattle mayor Robert Moran, for whom **Moran State Park** is named. A paved road and hiking trail winds up the mountain to a 50-ft (15-meter) high stone lookout tower. At the top is a 360° view of the islands and, on a clear day, Mount Baker 50 miles (80 km) east in the Cascade Range.

On **San Juan Island ㉗**, the ferry docks at **Friday Harbor**, a highly attractive village of restaurants, hotels and shops. The **Whale Museum**

(62 1st Street N; tel: 360-378 4710; July–Aug daily 9am–6pm, hours vary in off-season; admission charge) explains whale behavior and sounds, and has skeletons of an adult orca and a baby gray whale. Also on display are photos of the region's resident orcas, whose distinctive markings enable researchers to follow individuals in each "pod;" in 2006, Puget Sound was designated a critical habitat for orcas. The museum organizes whale-watching tours in season.

Relics of a dispute between Great Britain and the US between 1859–72 are in the **San Juan Island National Historical Park**. Charming **Roche Harbor**, once the richest deposit of limestone west of the Mississippi, is at the island's north end. At the harbor's edge is the delightful 1880s **Hotel de Haro** (tel: 800-451 8910).

Canada's Gulf Islands

The southern part of the Gulf Islands – Salt Spring, Galiano, Mayne, the Penders and Saturna – are near Victoria and mainland British Columbia. Activities range from shopping and dining to bicycling, hiking, golf and

tennis, kayaking, fishing and scuba diving. All, of course, offer shores to relax on, with gorgeous sunsets.

Saturna Island ㉘, the most southerly, is large in area but tiny in population – about 350. The ferry from Swartz Bay on Vancouver Island docks at Lyall Harbour. The island is a rural hideaway with wildlife, quiet roads, scenic walks and accessible beaches. Rent a boat for fishing or a kayak to tour the shoreline. **Winter Cove Marine Park** has an excellent harbor, a boat launch, picnic areas, walking trails, and a tidal marsh with wildlife. A stiff hike leads to Mount Warburton Pike for a panoramic view of the Gulf and San Juan Islands.

The **Pender Islands** ㉙, with a population of around 2,000, are two islands connected by a wooden bridge. The ferry from Vancouver Island docks at Otter Bay on North Pender. Explore the islands by car, bicycle, scooter or on foot to discover hidden coves and beaches. Bedwell Harbour on South Pender has a large resort with a full range of facilities, including a marina. It is a port of

entry for boats to Canada from the San Juan Islands.

Mayne Island ㉚, with fewer than 1,000 people, was the center of commercial and social life in the Gulf Islands during the Fraser River/Cariboo Gold Rush in the 1850s. Would-be miners rested at **Miners Bay** before rowing across the Strait of Georgia. Miners Bay now has shops, eateries and a museum in the old jail. The island has lovely hiking trails to peaks, and beaches with sandstone caves.

Skinny **Galiano Island** ㉛ lies just east of the larger Salt Spring Island. It is reached from the west through Active Pass, an S-shaped passage with Mayne Island on the south. Currents are strong, with eddies when the tides are flowing. Sea birds, eagles, herons and – sometimes – orcas can be seen, though these mighty predators are threatened by shrinking salmon stocks. Ferries between Vancouver Island and mainland British Columbia use Active Pass.

Wildflowers and migrating birds draw naturalists in the spring. Hike through meadows and forests of

Map on pages 178–9

Deer Harbor road-signs, Orcas Island.

BELOW: Friday Harbor on San Juan Island.

TIP

The Gulf Islands and Victoria fall under Canadian territory, so US and other foreign visitors need to take a passport. Passengers on cruise ships may be exempt from this ruling, but be sure to check in advance.

Douglas fir to high views, or along the shoreline. Kayakers and other boaters enjoy the protected west coast, while the waters of Active Pass and Porlier Pass at the north end attract scuba divers and fishermen.

Salt Spring Island ㉜ has 14 salt springs, ranging in size from a few feet to 100 ft (30 meters) in diameter. It is the largest of the Gulf Islands, with a population of around 10,000, mostly in the flatter northern part of the island. **Ganges** is the only town. Salt Spring is home to many artists, and there is a summer-long arts-and-crafts fair. Cyclists enjoy flat roads, and hikers find trails on the level, up mountain slopes or along beaches. Freshwater lakes are lovely for swimming and fishing.

The south is punctuated by two mountain ranges separated by a valley. The ferry from Swartz Bay docks at Fulford Harbour at the south end of the valley, but ferries from mainland British Columbia and the other Gulf Islands dock at Long Harbour, on the east coast. Yet another ferry connects Vesuvius Bay, in the northwest, to Crofton, north of Victoria.

BELOW: BC Government Parliament Buildings, Victoria.

Vancouver Island

On the south tip of **Vancouver Island** is **Victoria** ㉝, the capital of British Columbia. Victoria is known as the City of Flowers – flowers in gardens, window boxes, road dividers, and, in summer, hanging from the blue lamp-posts Downtown. The world-famous Butchart Gardens north of Victoria are the floral masterpiece *(see pages 201 and 202)*. It rains just enough to keep plants and lawns green, and a warm offshore current moderates the temperatures. Visitors are drawn to this classy little town from around the world. The Hudson's Bay Company built a trading fort on the site of modern-day Victoria in 1843, and the city retains a pleasing English ambience with tea rooms, double-decker buses, horse-drawn carriages, and, of course, flowers.

Victoria's center of activity is the **Inner Harbour,** where float planes, pleasure and fishing boats and tiny harbor ferries scurry like water bugs among larger ferries. The harbor is dominated by two buildings. The first is the **BC Government Parliament Buildings** (tours every half hour during summer months; tel: 1-250-387 3046). It was designed in 1898 by 25-year-old English architect Francis Rattenbury, who made a fortune in British Columbia's Gold Rush. An imposing mix of European styles, Parliament is especially impressive at night when illuminated by thousands of light bulbs. Curiously, Rattenbury neglected to include any washrooms in the main building.

Building began on the **Empress Hotel** (tel: 250-384 8111), the harbor's other structure, in 1904 on what had been muddy James Bay. The Empress sits on 2,855 pilings of Douglas fir, 50 ft (15 meters) through the mud of the bay. Ever since this French château-style hotel opened in 1908, it has played host to royalty, ghosts (allegedly), intrigue and movie stars. Few people come to Victoria

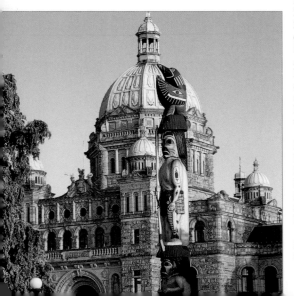

without partaking of traditional afternoon tea at the Empress Hotel, where appropriate dress is appreciated. In fine weather, artists and street musicians attract crowds to the **Lower Causeway** in front of the hotel.

Victoria's history

A good way to learn about the province is to visit the **Royal British Columbia Museum** (daily 9am–5pm; admission charge; tel: 250-356 7226 or 888-447 7977), which has exhibits that document the culture of the original native inhabitants, early life in Victoria, and an IMAX theater. The Native American exhibit centers on a replica of a Northwest longhouse, with canoes and tribal clothes. Adjacent to the museum is **Thunderbird Park**, where Native American carvers produce totem poles and gifts for sale. Replicas and real totems are scattered around the green lawns, and in front of a couple of historic buildings.

Head north on Victoria's main boulevard, **Government Street**, with its many stores, most in 19th-century buildings, and be pulled into

shops selling chocolate, Scottish woollens or Irish linens. A wonderful bookstore occupies an old bank building. A few steps farther, aromas of fine cigars and pipe tobaccos waft from a 100-year-old tobacconist's store. At the corner of Fort Street is the four-story **Eaton Centre**, a huge indoor mall looking out of place in a 19th-century environment. Turn right on Fort Street for the section known as Antique Row.

Opposite the north end of Eaton Centre, a pedestrian walkway leads west to **Bastion Square**, the former site of Fort Victoria (no longer in evidence). If time allows, explore the **Maritime Museum of British Columbia** (daily 9.30am–4.30pm; admission charge; tel: 250-385 4222) in the old Law Courts building where Matthew Begbie, the "hanging judge," worked. Begbie was the first judge in British Columbia, and rode on horseback to mining camps to dispense justice from a tent.

Heading up Government Street leads to Wharf and Store streets and the waterfront. This is **Old Town**, where fine 19th-century buildings

Map on pages 178–9

Shop for Native American crafts in Victoria.

BELOW: Victoria's Empress Hotel was built in 1908.

Totem Poles

Northwest Indians are carvers by tradition, and the totem pole is one of the more notable of their crafts. The extent of totem pole carving ranged from the Puget Sound area north to Alaska. The natives of British Columbia and Alaska, however, were the first to carve them. The history of these works is surprisingly brief, for it wasn't until the mid-1700s, when European explorers first encountered these remote people, that the unique sculptures began to appear. Although the local tribes were already expert carvers of canoes, tools, longhouses and furniture, they lacked the iron tools necessary to fell a massive tree in one piece and carve its length.

With the iron axes for which they traded, the coastal tribes could now take advantage of the trees that grew so tall and straight in their wet climate. Initially, the poles were made to stand against the front of a home, with figures facing out and a door cut through the base, so all would enter the house through the pole. In these cases, the totem pole functioned as a family crest, recounting genealogies, stories or legends that in some way identified the owner.

Poles served the function of recording the lore of the clan, much like a book. The top figure on the pole identified the owner's clan, and the succeeding characters (read from top to bottom) tell their stories. There is a story behind almost every image on a pole. If a legendary animal – Raven, the trickster, for example – had the power to transform into, say, a person, then the carver would depict Raven with both wings and limbs or with a human face and a raven's beak.

Towards the end of the 1800s, the poles stood free on the beach or in the village outside the carvers' homes. Some villages were virtual forests of hundreds of poles. The family that carved the pole held a *potlatch* (ceremony) with feasting, games and gift-giving. These gatherings were costly and required a great deal of preparation and participation. The custom frustrated white men trying to "civilize" the tribes, especially local missionaries, who solved the problem by chopping down the poles. Employers, too, complained that their Native American workers were unreliable when a pole was being carved or a potlatch planned. Eventually, both the Canadian and United States' governments banned potlatches, and pole carving nearly died out. (The ban was finally lifted in the 1950s.)

The Tlingit, on the southeastern coast of Alaska, are especially noted for their poles. On a tour in 1899, a group of Seattle businessmen visited the Tlingit village of Tongass and took one of the poles. They erected it in Seattle, where, at 60 ft (18 meters), it became one of the city's most distinctive monuments. In 1938, Tlingit carvers copied the pole after the original was destroyed by an arsonist; the copy is today in Seattle's Pioneer Square.

Learning to read – and appreciate – totem poles is like learning to read a language. The poles speak of history, mythology, social structure and spirituality. They serve many purposes, for both individual and community, and continue to be carved by descendants of the original carvers. ❏

LEFT: coastal tribes are adept at totems; learn more about them in Victoria's Thunderbird Park.

survived the "urban renewal" after World War II. **Market Square**, once a produce market, has been rejuvenated with shops and restaurants.

Farther along Government is Fisgard Street and the "Gate of Harmonious Interest," a red-tiled arch emblazoned with Chinese art, supported by two red columns. Stone lions guard each side. This is the entrance to Victoria's **Chinatown**, once the largest on the North American West Coast but now only a fragment of the original. Look out for **Fan Tan Alley**. Only 5 ft (1.5 meters) wide in places, it is one of the narrowest roads in Canada.

The Johnson Street Bridge (Blue Bridge) leads to the town of **Esquimalt**, home of Canada's Pacific Fleet. Britain used the deep-water anchorage as early as 1837, and it's been in use ever since.

Beyond Esquimalt is the community of **Colwood** and Royal Roads University, a former military college. **Fort Rodd Hill National Historic Park** (daily Mar–Oct 10am–5.30pm, Nov–Feb 9am–4.30pm; admission charge; tel: 250-478 5849) was a

coastal defense complex, used between 1895 and 1956. Visitors can explore underground magazines and barracks. **Fisgard Lighthouse**, on the shoreline of the fort, was built in 1860, the first in British Columbia.

Coastal views

For spectacular coastal views, drive west past the motels and hotels on Belleville Street, follow the waterfront past the Canadian Coast Guard base and the docks for cruise ships at Ogden Point. This is Dallas Road, the beginning of **Marine Drive**, a marked scenic route. Between Dallas and the shore are walks along the cliffs and beaches on the Strait of Juan de Fuca.

On the left is **Beacon Hill Park** with flowers and a lookout with a view of the Strait and the Olympic Mountains. Beyond, the road becomes **Beach Drive**, lined by the fairways and greens of the ocean-front Victoria Golf Club. This is **Oak Bay**, said to be "behind the tweed curtain" because of its many British residents. About 20 miles (30 km) north of Victoria is **Sidney ㉞**, site

Map on pages 178–9

Visit Victoria's Butterfly Gardens and Butchart Gardens in the same day.

BELOW: Butchart Gardens is a popular excursion from both Victoria and Seattle.

of Victoria's international airport and a ferry connection to the San Juans. The **British Columbia Aviation Museum** (daily 10am–4pm in summer, 11am–3pm the rest of the year; admission charge; tel: 250-655 3300), is by the airport, and it has several historic aircraft.

Butchart Gardens (open daily 9am but closing times vary; admission charge; tel: 250-652 4422) is world famous, and it showcases 55 acres (22 hectares) of flowers in the Rose Garden, Japanese Garden and the Show Greenhouse. Conceived by Jennie Butchart, the wife of a cement tycoon, in order to fill the gap created by her husband's exhausted limestone quarry, the gardens blossomed, literally, into the Sunken Gardens, which achieved considerable fame for its exotic plantings. By the 1920s more than 50,000 people came each year to see her creation.

When is the best time to visit? There's something all year round. In April, the results of the fall planting of more than 250,000 bulbs reach their peak; in wintertime when the trees are bare, you can go ice-skating.

Naturalists are drawn to the Pacific Northwest for its marvelous marine life.

BELOW:
bird over water.
RIGHT: ferry tales
on the violin.

Not far from Butchart are the pretty **Butterfly Gardens** (daily Mar–Oct, closed in winter; admission charge; tel: 250-652 3822), an indoor tropical garden with numerous species of free-flying butterflies and birds. In cold weather, the butterflies seldom fly, and are easily admired.

THE CASCADE MOUNTAINS

For more on the Cascade Mountains, see pages 206–7.

All over Puget Sound, views are dominated by the majestic Cascade Mountains, and their lure is constant. From the Tacoma area south of Seattle, follow the Nisqually River south to the tiny town of **Elbe** ㉟, the only train town this side of Strasberg, Pennsylvania. Dine or even stay the night in a railroad caboose at the **Hobo Inn** (tel: 360-569 2500), or hop aboard the steam-powered **Mount Rainier Scenic Railroad** (tel: 360-569 2588) as it chugs into the mountain forests on short excursions (mainly during the summer months). Behind the depot is the "tiniest church in the world," according to *Ripley's Believe It or Not*.

Mount Rainier

First named Tahoma – "The Mountain That Was God" – by Native Americans, **Mount Rainier** was renamed in 1792 by English explorer Captain George Vancouver. Visible for more than 100 miles (160 km) in all directions, thousands of feet above the other peaks of the Cascades, Rainier is the fifth-highest summit in the contiguous United States.

A single road loops the mountain, through much of the 378-sq-mile (980-sq-km) **Mount Rainier National Park**. The park is open all year, but in winter months passes at Cayuse and Chinook are closed.

Mount Rainier's history dates back more than 75,000 years when volcanism drove the peak to its 16,000-ft (5,000-meter) height. Erosion by glaciers stripped 2,000 feet (600 meters) off its top. Rainier has the largest glacier system – 26 glaciers – in the lower 48 states. The dormant peak erupted 500–600 years ago, with a lava flow just 150 years ago.

There are four entrances to the park. At **Longmire**, just inside the southwestern border near the Nisqually entrance, the modestly priced **National Park Inn** (tel: 360-569 2275) is the only lodge open all year; the rustic inn has a wildlife museum and stuffed animals on display. Longmire is also the only place in the park to buy gas. Follow the road to where a short hike leads into the **Grove of the Patriarchs**, the tallest trees in the park.

Paradise is the most popular destination and has paved parking, the **Henry M. Jackson Memorial Visitors' Center**, a gift shop and a cafeteria. There are spectacular views of **Narada Falls** and **Nisqually Glacier**, as well as of Mount Rainier. The fabulous **Paradise Inn** (tel: 360-569 2275), built in 1917, is closed for renovation until 2008.

Head east, then north at the Stevens Canyon entrance in the park's southeast corner, to the 4,675-ft (1,425-meter) **Cayuse Pass**. Just beyond the pass is the White River entrance. Turn left to stop by the **Sunrise Visitors' Center** (at 6,400 ft/1,950 meters), a breathtaking entry to lush wildflower meadows. The Emmons Glacier, largest in the lower 48 states, is visible from a trail by the visitors' center.

North of the White River entrance is **Crystal Mountain**, with some of the best winter skiing in the state of Washington. In summer, riders in chair lifts get to catch glimpses of Mount Rainier, while tennis, horseback riding and easy park access all entice tourists during the months when skiing is not possible.

Mount St Helens

Only two hours south of Elbe is **Mount St Helens** , the active volcano that erupted in May of 1980 (*see page 207*). The area is designated as the **Mount St Helens National Volcanic Monument** (tel: 360-449 7800). Five visitors' centers dot the Spirit Lake highway, all supplying information on the eruption.

Map on pages 178–9

TIP

The town of Ashford is the best place to stay outside of Mount Rainier Park itself. Accommodations range from log cabins to inns to B&Bs. Go to: www.mountrainier. worldweb.com/ Ashford/WheretoStay for info.

BELOW: orcas with baby.

TIP

One of the most spectacular train journeys in America is the trip north from Seattle to Vancouver. The track hugs the coast and glides through the beautiful Skagit Valley. It takes under four hours, and you can have breakfast or dinner on board, admiring the views.

BELOW: go paddling in the summer and skiing in the winter at Skykomish.

EAST OF SEATTLE

There are many wonderful excursions into the countryside from Seattle, some just a couple of hours' drive away. For instance, east of Issaquah on the Eastside of Seattle *(see page 155)* is **Snoqualmie Falls ㊳**, a sensational 268-ft (82-meter) avalanche of water, far higher than Niagara Falls *(see photo on page 63)*.

Perched above the falls is **Salish Lodge & Spa** (tel: 800-272 5474), made famous by the *Twin Peaks* TV series and known locally for huge Paul Bunyan-size country brunches. Much of the TV series was shot in the small town of **North Bend**, on Interstate 90, and Twedes Cafe still serves cherry pies. Long a stopping point for Snoqualmie Pass skiers, the city also draws shoppers to its outlet mall, the **Factory Stores of North Bend**.

Another 25 miles (40 km) farther is 3,022-ft (921-meter) **Snoqualmie Pass**, with trailheads into the mountains and three easily accessible winter ski areas near the summit.

Continuing east on US 2 is a route along the Skykomish River through the **Mount Baker-Snoqualmie National Forest**, towards the jagged peaks of the Cascade Range. The road is breathtaking in the fall, when the leaves of the vine maple trees turn scarlet. At **Wallace Falls State Park**, a 7-mile (11-km) round-trip trail leads to the 365-ft (111-meter) cascade and a view of **Mount Index**, nearly 6,000 ft (1,800 meters) high.

Kayaking, fishing and river-rafting are popular along the Skykomish, and trailheads lead off the route. Stop at the US Forest Service Ranger Station in **Skykomish ㊴** itself for maps and information. In winter, the downhill and cross-country ski slopes are at 4,061-ft (1,237-meter) **Stevens Pass ㊵**, 25 miles (40 km) past Skykomish. There are also slopes at Mission Ridge, southwest of Wenatchee, on the east of the Cascades.

NORTH OF SEATTLE

From Everett, north of Seattle *(see page 164)*, head east to arrive at one of Washington's oldest communities. **Snohomish ㊶** was founded in 1859. The town is an antique center of the Northwest, and its downtown historic district is a pleasant place to stroll

around. Six miles (10 km) east is Highway 203, which joins up with **Snoqualmie** *(see page 204)*. Climb aboard the **Snoqualmie Valley Railroad** for a scenic tour after visiting the **Northwest Railway Museum** (tel: 425-888 3030).

Back on Interstate 5, head north to Mount Vernon, and then west for the busy tourist town of **La Conner ㊷**. In the 1970s, local entrepreneurs filled their tiny shops with art galleries, antique stores and restaurants. The best-known town in the **Skagit Valley**, La Conner's claim to fame is tulips *(see photo on page 61)*. Visitors in busloads come each April to attend the Skagit Valley Tulip Festival.

Chuckanut Drive, a historic part of the old Pacific Highway, goes through the valley and along the coast. It's one of the state's most scenic drives, an alternative to the interstate. The train from Seattle to Vancouver does the same.

The roadway curves north about 25 miles (40 km) and follows the water up to **Bellingham ㊸**, where a good number of top-notch restaurants serve regional oysters and seafood.

North Cascades Park

From La Conner, SR 20 shoots east into the Cascade Range, which divides the eastern and western parts of the state of Washington. The mountains are 700 miles (1,100 km) in length, and extend from northern California, where they join the Sierra Nevada Range, to the Fraser River just south of Vancouver, in British Columbia.

The entire mountain range is a jigsaw puzzle of different national parks, national forests and wilderness areas. Five hundred miles (800 km) of scenic highway loop through **North Cascades National Park ㊹**, traversing snow-covered mountains, rushing rivers and pretty towns.

Prominent on the skyline directly west is **Mount Baker ㊺**, at 10,778 ft (3,285 meters) one of several volcanic mountains *(see pages 206–7)*.

On the southern end is **Glacier Peak Wilderness**, the heart of the North Cascades named after 10,541-ft (3,213-meter) **Glacier Peak ㊻**. Its glaciers end in ice-blue lakes, and meadows blanket small corners between broken rock spires. ❏

Map on pages 178–79

Twedes Cafe, North Bend, of Twin Peaks *fame, still serves cherry pies.*

BELOW: Rainy Pass, North Cascades.

MOUNTAINS OF GREAT BEAUTY AND DANGER

The city of Seattle sits within the "Ring of Fire," an area of volcanoes that have the potential to erupt at any time

Local tribal mythology tells the story of a pair of warriors, Wyeast and Pahto, who fought each other for the love of a beautiful maiden.

Their monumental battle involved earthquakes and firing volleys of rock and fire across the Columbia River. To settle the dispute, the gods transformed the warriors into mountains along the Cascade Chain: Wyeast became Mount Hood and Pahto became Mount Rainier.

Seattle sits on the Pacific Rim, where 850 active volcanoes in mountain ranges on all sides of the Pacific Ocean form a "Ring of Fire." This includes the Cascade Range, a 700-mile (1,130-km) chain of mountains that runs north-south through the state of Washington. The most recent major volcanic eruption in the Cascades occurred in May 1980, when Mount St Helens gave a powerful demonstration of the natural forces that created much of the Northwest landscape. The eruption of ash and molten lava transfigured the hillsides and sent a gray cloud across the state. Repercussions were said to have been felt as far away as Europe.

Almost 60 people died, as well as 7,000 big game animals (deer, elk, and bear). Many small animals survived, however, because they were below ground level or the water surface.

ABOVE: Mount St Helens began erupting on March 16th 1980, and continued until the magnitude 5.1 eruption at 8:32am on May 18th. It was the most destructive ever recorded in the United States.

ABOVE: 11,235-ft (3,424-meter) Mount Hood is in northern Oregon state. Here it is reflected in the water of Trillium Lake.

LEFT: the 700-mile (1,130-km) Cascade mountain range stretches from southern British Columbia to northern California. It includes Mount Baker, north of Seattle; Mount Hood, near Portland; and Mount Rainier – all of which have the potential for volcanic activity.

MOUNT ST HELENS ERUPTION

On May 18, 1980, skies darkened as far away as Seattle as Mount St Helens, in southwestern Washington state, literally blew its top. The explosion took a cubic mile off the summit, reducing the mountain's elevation from 9,677 ft (2,950 meters) to 8,364 ft (2,550 meters).

The volcano had shown signs of activity well before the blast, and although the region had been evacuated, the death toll reached 57, as lava and mud slides flattened 230 sq miles (595 sq km) of forest. There was extensive damage to wildlife, and the ash-covered slopes and fallen trees serve as modern reminders of the day. The mountain continued to shudder with minor eruptions into the 21st century.

RIGHT: vegetation has slowly recovered since the eruption of Mount St Helens in 1980.

BELOW: when Seattle residents have a clear view of Mount Rainier (seen here from the south), they say, "the Mountain is out."

ABOVE: Mount Rainier National Park is popular with sightseers and hikers, as well as climbers of varying experience.

BELOW: the lava dome on the volcano of Mount St Helens is still growing, almost 30 years after its last major eruption.

TRANSPORTATION

GETTING THERE AND GETTING AROUND

GETTING THERE

By Air

Seattle-Tacoma International Airport, known as **Sea-Tac**, is located 13 miles (20 km) south of Seattle.

For information on the airport, its services, parking or security, call the Sea-Tac International information line, tel: 206-431 4444, 206-433 5388, or 1-800-544 1965.

Access to Sea-Tac is via Interstate-5 (take exit 154 from south I-5 or exit 152 from north I-5), or via Highway 99/509 and 518. Stop-and-go traffic on I-5 is not uncommon, especially during rush hours, so the alternative route on the highway is often much quicker.

At the Airport

Many services are available at Sea-Tac to ease the transition from air to ground; some are especially helpful to foreigners, as this can be a confusing airport, especially if arriving jetlagged after a long flight.

In 2004, the Port of Seattle (which operates the airport) completed a $586 million expansion project of the airport's south terminal. Along with a large public space with an expansive view of Mount Rainier, the sleek, modern 880,000-sq-ft (81,755-sq-meter) project added shops and other conveniences for travelers.

Aside from restaurants, restrooms, gift shops, and resort-wear clothing stores, three Travelex **currency exchange booths** are scattered throughout the airport. Two are in the main terminal; the third booth is located in the south satellite (open 6am–2:30pm). Tel: 206-433 5388 for more information.

At **Laptop Lane**, located in the north terminal, fax (outgoing only) and copy machines are available, as are desks, a small conference room (on a first-come, first-served basis), and telephones for the hearing impaired.

A **children's area** with an

INTERNATIONAL AIRLINES

Major airlines flying into and out of Seattle include:
Air Canada/Air BC
Tel: 1-888-247 2262
Alaska Airlines
Tel: 1-800-252 7522
American Airlines
Tel: 1-800-433 7300
British Airways
Tel: 1-800-247 9297
Continental Airlines
Tel: 1-800-231 0856
Delta
Tel: 1-800-221 1212

Hawaiian Airlines
Tel: 1-800-367 5320
Horizon Air
Tel: 1-800-547 9308
Japan Airlines
Tel: 1-800-525 3663
Korean Air
Tel: 1-800-438 5000
Lufthansa
Tel: 1-800-645 3880
Northwest Airlines/KLM
Tel: 1-800-225 2525
Qantas
Tel: 1-800-227 4500

Scandinavian Airlines
Tel: 1-800-221 2350
Southwest Airlines
Tel: 1-800-435 9792
United Airlines
Tel: 1-800-241 6522
US Air
Tel: 1-800-428 4322
US Airways
Tel: 1-800-235 9292

Check the *Yellow Pages* under "Airline Companies" or tel: 206-555 1212 for further information.

CITY	FROM SEATTLE	DRIVING TIME
Spokane, WA	280 miles (450 km)	5 hours approx.
San Francisco, CA	850 miles (1,370 km)	15 hours approx.
Portland, OR	175 miles (280 km)	3 hours approx.
Vancouver, BC	140 miles (225 km)	3 hours approx.

This is a list of estimated times and distances to several cities within a day or two, driving a car under safe road conditions.

enclosed carpeted play area, a crib and a nursing room with pleasing rocking chairs, will provide relief for stressed parents *and* kid-sized travelers.

A **meditation room**/chapel is available on the mezzanine level that has a Sunday only interdenominational service. For the chaplain, tel: 206-433 5505.

In the inspection booths at Customs and Immigration, and at the **Airport Information Booth**, right outside the exit from the B gates (pre-security, south of the Central Security Checkpoint), are Language Phone Lines that connect travelers and inspectors to interpreters for more than 150 different languages.

The **Seattle Convention and Visitors Bureau** operates a tourist information booth near the baggage claim area. Tel: 206-461 5888.

The **Lost and Found** is located on the mezzanine level in the main terminal. It is open Monday–Friday 7am–5pm, tel: 206-433 5312.

Last but not least, **Ken's Baggage**, on the baggage level, under the escalators between carousels 12 and 13, will take care of odds and ends for travelers, such as coats and boot storage, dry cleaning services, UPS and Federal Express package services, as well as notary public, ticket- and key-holding services and much more. Hours: 5:30am–12:30am, seven days. Tel: 206-433 5333.

By Bus

Transcontinental bus lines providing services throughout Seattle and the United States include the following:

Greyhound
811 Stewart Street
(corner of 8th Avenue and Stewart Street)
Tel: 1-800-231 2222
www.greyhound.com
The ubiquitous Greyhound bus service offers the most comprehensive service of scheduled routes from Seattle and across the North American continent.

Green Tortoise
Tel: 415-956 7500
1-800-867 8647
www.greentortoise.com
This famous bus service is an alternative (in both senses of the word) form of bus travel connecting Seattle to San Francisco and Portland. Here, easy chairs replace bus seats, music plays in the background, and stops are scheduled for soaking in hot springs and having a campfire cookout.

Quick Shuttle
Tel: 1-800-665 2122
www.quickcoach.com
This company operates 4–6 daily express runs between Vancouver BC, and downtown Seattle and the airport.

By Rail

Amtrak is the USA's national rail network. It can be found in Seattle at 3rd Avenue and S. Jackson Street, tel: 1-800-USA-RAIL; www.amtrak.com.

The train is a convenient way of getting to the other "Pacific Rim" cities of Portland, San Francisco, and Vancouver in Canada's British Columbia. The distances are not far, and the train times flexible and frequent.

Amtrak connects Seattle with the east coast via the "Empire Builder" from Chicago. It connects with the south via the "Coast Starlight" from Los Angeles. The "Coast Starlight" is the most popular route with beautiful coastal scenery and stops in Tacoma, Olympia, Vancouver, Washington, and Portland, Oregon, along the way. Amtrak's "Mount Baker" run also connects Vancouver, over the Canadian border, and Seattle. In the summer months early reservations for this popular trip are essential.

BELOW: ferries are essential to Seattle's transportation system.

By Road

Major land routes into Seattle are the Interstate 5, known as "I-5" which stretches from the Canadian to the Mexican borders; and Interstate 90, or "I-90," which leaves downtown Seattle and travels eastward toward the cities of Chicago and Boston.

Federal and state highways are generally well maintained and policed, with refreshment areas and service stations located at regular intervals. There are no highway fees payable in or around Seattle, but there is a toll to cross the new Tacoma Narrows Bridge (scheduled to open in 2007).

Leave a lot of time for getting into the city, however. Traffic in Seattle itself and its outlying areas has increased dramatically in the last few years. So although you may make good time getting to the city limits, it doesn't mean you're there yet *(see page 211 for more information on driving in the city).*

GETTING AROUND

Maps

The Seattle Convention and Visitors' Bureau in the Washington State Convention Center, One Convention Place, 701 Pike St, Suite 800, Galleria Level, tel: 206-461 5840 *(see page 238 for further details)* offers free maps to tourists. If these maps are insufficient for a particular destination, the American Automobile Association, better known as the "Triple A", can offer advice on planning trips, the best routes to take and detailed maps, for a fee.
AAA, 330 6th Avenue N. Tel: 206-448 5353; www.aaa.com

The *Thomas Guides* contain detailed street maps in a book format. They are available in most bookstores. Don't forget to buy the *Insight Fleximap to Seattle* too. There's also a *Fleximap* to Vancouver, BC.

ABOVE: the Monorail passes through the Experience Music Project.

From the Airport

Shuttle buses and taxis can be found outside the terminal on the baggage claim level. The exact location of shuttle buses varies depending on destination and carrier. Check with the information booth at the north end of the main terminal on the baggage level. Taxis can be picked up at the north end of the terminal, too.

STITA (Seattle-Tacoma International Taxi Association), tel: 206-246 9999, provides services to and from the airport. The trip from the airport to downtown (or vice versa) costs about $30.

Bus or van companies that link the airport with metropolitan Seattle or Bellevue include:
The Grayline Airport Express, tel: 206-624 5077. Operates buses every 20–30 minutes between the airport and major downtown hotels.

Greyhound, tel: 206-628 5526 or 1-800-231 2222. Has several runs to and from the airport and to its downtown station at 8th Avenue and Stewart Street.

Shuttle Express, tel: 206-622 1424. Provides door-to-door van service to and from the airport 24 hours daily throughout the metropolitan Seattle area.

Metro Transit, tel: 206-553 3000. Buses link the airport with various points throughout the city and provide the least expensive

method of transportation. The 194 bus is the most direct, bringing passengers Downtown to bus tunnel stops in about 30 minutes. The 174 bus makes local stops on its way downtown. Both buses run on the half hour, seven days a week.

Quick Shuttle, tel: 604-684 2151 or 1-800-665 2122. Operates fast bus connections between the airport, downtown Seattle (Best Western Executive Inn, 200 Taylor Avenue N.) and Vancouver (Holiday Inn, 1110 House Street) four times daily. Trips between the two cities take four hours.

Washington Limousine Service, tel: 206-523 8000, a well-established and reliable service, is available by reservation only.

Local Transportation

Buses and Streetcars

Metro Transit buses have both peak and non-peak hour fares. Monthly passes are available. Metro also provides a **"Park Free and Ride Free"** in the Downtown core bordered by I-5 to the east, the waterfront to the west, Jackson Street to the south and Battery Street to the north. Buses operate 8am to midnight daily.
Metro Transit, tel: 206-553 3000 or 206-684 1739 for TTY/TDD users; www.metrotransit.org
Metro also operates a **water-**

TRANSPORTATION

front streetcar, a 1927 vintage trolley which runs 1½ miles (3 km) along the waterfront every 20–30 minutes from Myrtle Edwards Park to the Pioneer Square station. The ticket requires exact change.

You can also purchase a **Metro Visitors' Pass** at various Metro customer assistance offices which allows one day's unlimited travel on buses, streetcars, and the Monorail. Tel: 206-624-PASS.

Monorail

The **Monorail**, which was built for the 1962 World Fair, runs every 15 minutes between Seattle Center and Fourth and Pine streets to Westlake Center. The ride is just under 1 mile (2 km) and takes only 90 seconds. It's clean and spacious with large windows.

Taxis

There are **taxi stands** at major hotels, bus depots, train stations, and the airport. Taxi fares are regulated. There is an initial hire charge, with each additional mile (½ km) then costing a flat rate.
Taxi Companies:
Farwest Cab Tel: 206-622 1717
Orange Cab Tel: 206-522 8800
Yellow Cab Tel: 206-622 6500

Driving

Car Rental Tips

A wide selection of rental cars is available. Rental offices are located at the airport and Down-

CAR RENTAL COMPANIES

Alamo Tel: 206-433 0182
Avis Tel: 206-433 5231
airport: 1-800-831 2847
Budget Tel: 1-800-527 0700
Dollar Rent-A-Car Tel: 206-682 1316 or 1-800-800 4000
Enterprise Tel: 206-246 1953
airport: 1-800-736 8222
Hertz Tel: 206-433 5275
airport: 1-800-654 3131
National Tel: 206-433 5501
airport: 1-800-227 7368

town. Generally, a major credit card is required to rent a car and the driver must be 25 years old and possess a valid driver's license. Local rental companies sometimes offer less expensive rates. Be sure to check insurance provisions before signing any paperwork.

Road Tips

Driving around Seattle can be tricky. There are many one-way streets and steep hills, but also beautiful views in the downtown area, which is generally considered to lie between Denny Way and Yesler. Avenues run north–south, while streets run east–west. Streets and avenues can be designated with numbers or names. When trying to locate an address, be sure to note whether the address includes directionals (north, south, east or west). For example, E. Madison Street or Queen Anne Avenue N. will indicate the east or north part of town.

Avoid driving during the rush hours of 7–9am and 4–6pm. Although extra express lanes operate on parts of I-5 and I-90 to help alleviate the backup, it is a time-consuming and sometimes frustrating experience.

A right turn is permitted, after stopping, at a red light unless street signs indicate otherwise.

Parking laws in Seattle require that when facing downhill, the front wheels are turned into the curb and when facing uphill, front wheels are turned outward. Doing so will decrease the likelihood of the car rolling downhill. Also be sure to set the emergency brake.

Street signs, usually on corners, will indicate what type of parking is permitted for that side of the street. However, red-painted curbs mean no parking is allowed and yellow curbs indicate a loading area for trucks or buses only.

There are plenty of traffic police around (except when you need them) who earn their living by passing out fines and having

cars towed away. Picking up a towed car is not only inconvenient, but costly ($65–100 depending on where the car was parked).

Pedestrians always have the right of way. Although legal, except on freeways, picking up hitchhikers or hitchhiking is potentially dangerous.

By Ferry

On the Water

The **Washington State Ferry** system, the largest in the country, covers the Puget Sound area, linking Seattle (at Pier 52) with the Olympic Peninsula via Bremerton and Bainbridge Island. State ferries also depart from West Seattle to Vashon Island and Southworth and from Edmonds, 7 miles (11 km) north of Seattle, to Kingston on the Kitsap Peninsula. It also goes from Anacortes, 90 miles (145 km) northwest of Seattle, through the San Juan Islands to Victoria, on Canada's Vancouver Island. For information: tel: 206-464 6400 or 1-800-843 3779. Passengers to Canada should carry a passport.

Clipper Navigation operates a passenger-only ferry, the *Victoria Clipper*, year-round between Seattle and Victoria, BC. During summer catch the *Victoria Clipper* daily at 7:30am, 8:30am and 3:15pm from Pier 69 on the Seattle waterfront. The ride is 2¾ hours with food and shopping available on board. Reservations required. Tel: 206-448 5000.

The **Black Ball Ferry**, the *M.V Coho*, departs from Port Angeles on the Olympic Peninsula to Victoria, BC, four times a day in summer and twice daily the rest of the year. Ferries carry cars. Tel: 206-283 4400.

Victoria–San Juan Cruises, Bellingham Cruise Terminal, Bellingham. Tel: 1-800-443 4552. Passenger ferries to San Juan Island and Victoria, May to October; also day cruises.

A CCOMMODATIONS

SOME THINGS TO CONSIDER BEFORE YOU BOOK A ROOM

Choosing a Hotel

There are few really inexpensive hotels in downtown Seattle, but there are many along Pacific South Highway to Sea-Tac International Airport, most about halfway between the airport and Seattle around 141st Street.

Hotels in this guide are listed by city region and are among the best in their categories, for either facilities or value for money.

Bed & Breakfast Inns

Bed and breakfast inns tend to be reasonably priced and low-key, with a more intimate atmosphere than a hotel. Some rooms have a private bath; some a

B & B AGENCIES

Several bed and breakfast agencies assist in selecting accommodation:
Pacific Bed & Breakfast Registry
2040 Westlake Avenue N, #301
Seattle WA 98109
Tel: 206-439 7677, 1-800-684 2932
www.seattlebedandbreakfast.com
Seattle Bed & Breakfast Inn Association
Tel: 206-547 1020 or
1-800-348 5630

shared bath. Here is a small sampling of older, mostly Victorian places in the Seattle area.
Bacon Mansion
959 Broadway E., WA 98102
Tel: 206-329 1864 or
1-800-240 1864
www.baconmansion.com
This Tudor-style mansion has seven rooms, five with private baths. There is also a carriage house on the grounds, which is perfect for a family or a group touring together. **$–$$**
Bed & Breakfast on Broadway
722 Broadway Avenue E., WA 98102
Tel: 206-329 8933
www.bbonbroadway.com
Two spacious rooms with private baths, televisions and queen-sized beds, one block from neighborhood shops and restaurants. **$$**
Bed and Breakfast on Capitol Hill
739 Broadway Avenue E., WA 98102
Tel: 206-325 0320
www.bbcapitolhill.com
A home built in 1903 with three guest rooms (one with private bath). **$–$$**
Gaslight Inn and Howell Street Suites
1727 15th Avenue, WA 98122
Tel: 206-325 3654
www.gaslight-inn.com
This early 20th-century mansion has 10 guest rooms, each decorated in a different style. Outside

is a large heated pool. The proprietors are friendly and aim to please. No kids, pets or smoking. **$–$$**
Hill House B&B
1113 E. John Street, WA 98102
Tel: 206-323 4455
www.seattlehillhouse.com
Built in 1903, this restored Victorian house has five elegantly decorated rooms, three with private baths. Breakfast, cooked by the innkeeper, can be a gourmet experience. **$–$$**
Mildred's Bed & Breakfast
1202 15th Avenue E., WA 98112
Tel: 206-325 6072 or
1-800-327 9692
www.mildredsbnb.com
Four rooms have private baths, some with skylights or views of nearby Volunteer Park. **$–$$**
Salisbury House
750 16th Avenue E., WA 98112
Tel: 206-328 8682
www.salisburyhouse.com
Located in an historic Capitol Hill neighborhood near Volunteer Park, the house offers an inviting wraparound porch. The interior is just as special as its elegant surroundings. **$$**
Shafer-Baillie Mansion
907 14th Avenue E., WA 98112
Tel: 206-322 4654 or
1-800-985 4654
Spacious grounds, gourmet breakfasts, antique furnishings. **$$**

NEAR SEA-TAC AIRPORT

Ben Carol Motel
14110 International Boulevard
WA 98168
Tel: 206-244 6464
This motel is around half the price of even modest downtown equivalents. Near a comfortable, family-type restaurant and close to an enormous 24-hour supermarket. Pool. **$**

Best Western Airport Execute
20717 International Boulevard
Tukwila WA 98198
Tel: 206-878 3300
Amenities include a heated indoor pool, sauna, Jacuzzi, exercise room, airport transportation, restaurant, lounge, morning newspaper and laundry service. **$$**

Comfort Inn
19333 International Boulevard

SeaTac WA 98188
Tel: 206-878 1100
Cable television, exercise room, airport transportation, laundry service, breakfast. **$**

Doubletree Hotel Seattle Airport
18740 International Boulevard
Seattle WA 98188
Tel: 206-246 8600 or 1-800-222 8733
www.doubletree.hilton.com
With three restaurants, two lounges, and other amenities such as heated pool, video room, room service and airport shuttle. The hotel's fresh chocolate chip cookies are brought to your room as a welcome gift. **$$**

Hilton Seattle Airport & Conference Center
17620 International Boulevard

WA 98188
Tel: 206-244 4800 or 1-800-hiltons
www.hilton.com
Hotel geared to the needs of business travelers. Some rooms have work desks, voice mail and conference call facilities. **$$$**

Radisson Gateway
18118 International Boulevard
WA 98188
Tel: 206-244 6666
www.radisson.com
Comfortable rooms, some with internet access. **$$**

Red Lion Hotel Seattle Airport
18220 International Boulevard
WA 98188
Tel: 206-246 5535 or 1-800-733 5466
www.redlion.rdln.com
Bright, spacious rooms.

Jacuzzi, sauna, fitness center and restaurant. **$$**

Seattle Marriott
3201 S. 176th Street
SeaTac WA 98188
Tel: 206-241 2000 or 1-800-228 9290
www.marriott.com
Heated indoor pool, sauna, hot tub, exercise room, airport transportation, cable television, restaurant and lounge, facilities for handicapped. **$$**

DOWNTOWN SEATTLE

Ace Hotel
2423 1st Avenue
Seattle WA 98121
Tel: 206-448 4721
www.theacehotel.com
A minimalist and futuristic downtown hotel in an historic building. 34 rooms with hardwood floors, and a sink and vanity in each. Rooms

PRICE CATEGORIES
The following price categories indicate the price for a double room in high season:
$$$ More than $200
$$ $100–200
$ Under $100

are available with shared bathrooms or private. Beds are appointed with wool French army blankets. **$–$$**

The Alexis
1007 1st Avenue
Seattle WA 98104
Tel: 206-624 4844
www.alexishotel.com
Located in an early 20th-century building near the waterfront, this is an elegant hotel of 109 rooms (15 with whirlpools) that prides itself on attention to detail and personalized service. Rooms facing the courtyard are the

best; those facing 1st Avenue tend to be noisy. Amenities include: fireplaces, complimentary sherry, continental breakfast and morning newspaper, shoe shines and a reduced-price, guest membership at the nearby upscale Seattle Club. **$$$**

Crowne Plaza Seattle
1113 6th Avenue
Seattle WA 98101
Tel: 206-464 1980 or 1-800-521 2762
www.ichotelsgroup.com
Amenities include a health club with whirlpool, sauna, weight room on the fifth floor; a

gift shop and a restaurant. 415 rooms. **$$$**

Days Inn Town Center
2205 7th Avenue, WA 98121
Tel: 206-448 3434
www.daysinntownscenter.com
Clean, affordable rooms near Seattle Center with a 24-hour front desk. A Downtown

bargain. **$**

The Edgewater
2411 Alaskan Way, Pier 67
Seattle WA 98121
Tel: 206-728 7000 or
1-800-624 0670
www.edgewaterhotel.com
Built at the time of the
World Fair in 1962 and
completely remodeled in
1989, this is Seattle's
only Downtown water-
front hotel. It stands
right on Pier 67. Current
amenities include an
atrium lobby, stone fire-
places, and mountain
lodge décor. Compli-
mentary downtown
shuttle, banquet and
meeting facilities.
Restaurant features
Northwest cuisine.
Rates vary depending
on water- or city-view
rooms. **$$–$$$**

Eighth Avenue Inn
2213 8th Avenue at
Blanchard Seattle WA 98121
Tel: 206-624 6300
www.eighthavenueinn.com
This 72-room hotel
offers reasonably priced

accommodations down-
town. Free local calls;
free parking; pets OK. **$**

Executive Hotel Pacific
400 Spring Street
Tel: 1-800-426 1165
www.pacificplazahotel.com
Boutique-sized hotel
next door to downtown
public library was built
in 1928 and renovated
in 2004. Pet friendly. **$$**

**The Fairmont Olympic
Hotel, Seattle**
411 University Street
Seattle WA 98101
Tel: 206-621 1700/1-800-223
8772 (US) or 1-800-821 8106
(Washington State)
www.fairmont.com
A grand hotel in the
Italian Renaissance
style, built in 1924 and
renovated in 1982. It
features 450 spacious
guest rooms furnished
with period reproduc-
tions. Enjoy high tea in
the atrium-style Garden
Court and shopping off
the lobby. The hotel
receives the AAA five-
diamond award for ser-

vice. Amenities include
a health club, indoor
pool, saunas, Jacuzzis,
two restaurants, 24-
hour room service,
complimentary news-
paper and shoeshine,
bar, bath robes, and
supplies for parents
with small children. Fee
for valet parking and
massage. **$$$**

Hilton Seattle
1301 6th Avenue
Seattle WA 98101
Tel: 206-624 0500/1-800-445
8667 or 1-800-HILTONS
www.Hilton.com
Amenities include: bay
windows in each room;
Top of the Hilton
Lounge (a disco), 24-
hour room service,
valet/laundry service,
concierge, restaurant
and gift shop. **$$**

Hotel 1000
1000 1st Avenue
Seattle WA 98104
Tel: 206-957 1000 or
1-877-315 1088
www.hotel1000seattle.com
One of the city's newer
hotels, this smart and
stylish place offers LCD
HDTV's and high-speed
wireless in every room.
Other amenities include
a restaurant (BOKA), golf
club (simulating play on
some of the world's
best courses) and the
Spaahh. 120 guest
rooms and suites. **$$$**

Hotel Andra (formerly
Claremont Hotel)
2000 4th Avenue
Seattle WA 98121
Tel: 206-448 8600 or
1-877-448 8600
www.hotelandra.com
The original 1926 brick
building was renovated
in 2004 to create the
Andra with 119 rooms
and suites. The design
is Northwest/Scandina-
vian and amenities
include wireless inter-

net, in-room safes,
evening turndown ser-
vice and a Tom Douglas
restaurant, Lola, on the
main floor. **$$–$$$**

Hotel Max
620 Stewart Street
Seattle WA 98101
Tel: 206-728 6299 or
1-866-833 6299
www.hotelmaxseattle.com
This stylish hotel spe-
cializes in original art
throughout. The door to
each bedroom is
obscured by a black and
white photograph, so
strolling down a corridor
feels like being in a
gallery. (The smoking
floor has photos of rock
musicians, and is defi-
nitely the rowdiest.) The
Max attracts a hip
crowd, but the easy
welcome and low-key
service means that
everyone feels at home.
Comfy beds to die for, a
(free) 24-hour business
center, millions of
movies on the plasma
in-room screens – if you
stay here you might
never see the rest of
Seattle. **$$$**

Hotel Monaco
1101 4th Avenue
Seattle WA 98101
Tel: 206-621 1770 or
1-800-945 2240
www.monaco-seattle.com
With 189 rooms, this
recent addition to
Seattle prides itself on
service and function.
The hotel restaurant is
the Southern-inspired
Sazerac. **$$$**

Hotel Vintage Park
1100 5th Avenue
Seattle WA 98101
Tel: 206-624 8000 or
1-800-624 4433
www.hotelvintagepark.com
Care in attending to
guests is one feature of
this highly organized
hotel. The rooms are

BELOW: Hotel Max has original artwork throughout.

decorated in vintage style but with amenities such as fax machines, fast internet connections and phones in the bathrooms. Personal touches include irons and ironing boards, robes, hair dryers and speedy room service. **$$$**

Inn at Harbor Steps
1221 1st Avenue
Seattle WA 98101
Tel: 206-748 0973 or
1-888-728 8910
www.innatharborsteps.com

Part of a hotel chain based in California called "Four Sisters," this place is geared toward country-inn experiences. The inn has only 20 rooms, but each has a fireplace, a wet bar, and a sitting area. Amenities include a sauna, Jacuzzi and indoor pool along with complimentary *hors d'œuvres* and wine before dinner. **$$$**

Inn At The Market
86 Pine Street
Seattle WA 98101
Tel: 206-443 3600
www.innatthemarket.com

Located in the Pike Place Market, many of the 70 rooms have splendid views of Elliott Bay. The inn surrounds a landscaped courtyard that has shops, a spa and a good restaurant, Campagne, serving French country cuisine. A fifth-floor deck offers one of the best views in town. Amenities: complimentary downtown shuttle to shops; newspaper and coffee; room service from Campagne. **$$$**

Mayflower Park Hotel
405 Olive Way
Seattle WA 98101
Tel: 1-800-426 5100 or

206-623 8700
www.mayflowerpark.com

European-style moderately sized hotel of 187 rooms. Adjacent to Westlake Center. Amenities include cable television, the Mediterranean-style restaurant Andaluca, lounge, and laundry service. **$$$**

Moore Hotel
1926 2nd Avenue
Seattle WA 98101
Tel: 206-448 4851 or
1-800-421 5508
www.moorehotel.com

Non-smoking 140-room hotel connected to the historic Moore Theatre in Belltown. **$**

Pacific Guest Suites
2793 152nd Avenue NE
Redmond WA 98052
Tel: 1-800-962 6620 or
206-454 7888

One-, two- or three-bedroom condominium suites located in Seattle, Redmond or Bellevue. Three-night minimum stay. Rooms have full kitchens, washer, dryer, fireplace, cable television, concierge and housekeeping. **$$$**

Renaissance Seattle Hotel
515 Madison Street
Seattle WA 98104
Tel: 206-583 0300 or
1-800-546 9184
www.marriot.com

Top two floors are the executive level rooms, with concierge service, complimentary breakfast and appetizers. Amenities include: outstanding views, fitness center with heated indoor pool, complimentary morning coffee and newspaper delivered to your room, 24- hour room service, laundry, and hair salon, two restaurants. **$$$**

Residence Inn by Marriott

800 Fairview Avenue N.
Seattle WA 98109
Tel: 206-624 6000
www.marriott.com

The inn has 234 suites, each equipped with a full kitchen including microwave oven, coffeemaker, refrigerator, range-top stove and dishwasher (but the inn takes care of the dishes). Seventy per cent of the rooms overlook Lake Union. Amenities: continental breakfast in the atrium (complete with waterfall), fitness center with indoor pool, sauna, Jacuzzi, exercise room; free parking. **$$$**

Roosevelt Hotel
1531 7th Avenue
Seattle WA 98101
Tel: 206-621 1200
www.roosevelthotel.com

A moderately priced hotel for Downtown, it was built in Art Deco style in 1930. Rooms are not large, but the hotel is convenient to shopping and downtown sightseeing. **$$$**

Sheraton Seattle Hotel
1400 6th Avenue
Seattle WA 98101
Tel: 1-800-325 3535 or
206-621 9000
www.sheraton.com

The top floor (35th) has

a fitness center equipped with Jacuzzi, sauna, pool, bicycles and aerobics area and lounge with panoramic view of the city. There's also a good restaurant and a café. **$$$**

Sorrento Hotel
900 Madison Street
Seattle WA 98104
Tel: 206-622 6400 or
1-800-426 1265
www.hotelsorrento.com

This 1909 hotel was remodeled in 1981 after a castle in Sorrento, Italy, and rooms were refurbished with an Italian flavor. Then, in 2001, it was renovated again. The 76 guest rooms on seven floors are sophisticated and stylish, yet due to its moderate size, the hotel prides itself on attentive service. The Hunt Club restaurant continues the European theme. During summer months guests can

ABOVE: expect sleek service at the best hotels.

PRICE CATEGORIES

The following price categories indicate the price for a double room in high season:
$$$ More than $200
$$ $100–200
$ Under $100

enjoy dining outdoors in the hotel's courtyard. Afternoon tea with sandwiches and pastries is served daily in the fireside room accompanied by a pianist or guitarist. Other amenities: free limousine Downtown, mobile phones, newspapers, shoe shines and valet parking. In-house florist, robes, valet and *shiatzu* massage. **$$$**

Westin Hotel
1900 5th Avenue
Seattle WA 98101
Tel: 206-728 1000 or
1-800-228 3000
www.westin.com
This is the Westin chain's flagship hotel, adjacent to the Westlake Shopping Center. Amenities include two restaurants: Nikko, serving sushi and Japanese fare, and Roy's, for seafood presented with flair and Asian sauces, which first started in Hawaii. The rooms are coveted and spacious with views of Puget Sound or the city. There is a heated indoor pool, Jacuzzis, saunas and fitness center. An Airport Express stops here. **$$$**

W Seattle
1112 4th Avenue
Seattle WA 98101
Tel: 206-264 6000
www.starwoodhotels.com
Voted one of the 100 sexiest hotels in the world, the W Seattle has a cool, contemporary,

ABOVE: the Fairmont Olympic.

minimalist style throughout its 417 guestrooms and 9 suites. The Earth & Ocean restaurant has been voted one of the top ten places to eat, while the W Bar is a great place for flirting and cocktails. There's a business center, a "sweatness" center and an in-room spa service. Even pets are privileged and pampered. **$$$**

NORTH SEATTLE

Chambered Nautilus Bed and Breakfast Inn
5005 22nd Avenue NE.
Seattle WA 98105
Tel: 206-522 2536
www.chamberednautilus.com
This early 20th-century Georgian colonial-style hotel near the University of Washington has six rooms furnished with antiques and private baths. Four of the rooms open onto porches that have views of the Cascade Mountains. Amenities are lavish, including flowers, robes, bottled water, writing desks,

and reading material taken from the 2,000-plus books from the library. **$$**

College Inn
4000 University Way NE
Seattle WA 98105
Tel: 206-633 4441
www.collegeinnseattle.com
This historic building complex, just across from the University of Washington, contains 27 rooms with shared baths above the popular College Inn Pub and Café Allegro. **$**

Hotel Nexus
Seattle at Northgate
2140 N. Northgate Way
Seattle WA 98133
Tel: 206-365 0700
www.hotelnexus.com
Located 7 miles (11 km) north of Seattle, adjacent to Northgate Mall. Amenities include: heated pool, restaurant, laundry, room service, disabled facilities. **$$**

Silver Cloud Inn – University
5036 25th Avenue NE
Seattle WA 98105
Tel: 206-526 5200 or
1-800-205 6940
www.scinns.com
One block from the University of Washington campus, near the U Village shopping center, the Silver Cloud has 180 non-smoking rooms, an indoor pool, complimentary continental breakfast and free parking. **$$**

University Inn
4140 Roosevelt Way NE.
Seattle WA 98105
Tel: 206-632 5055 or
1-800-733 3855
www.universityinnseattle.com
This remodeled hotel is a well-run addition to the university district. Amenities include voice mail, off-street parking, free morning paper, data modem hook-up,

and even small safes in guest rooms. Right next to the hotel, the Portage Bay Café has a terrific breakfast menu worth getting up for. **$$**

Watertown
4242 Roosevelt Way NE
Seattle WA 98105
Tel: 206-826 4242 or
1- 866-944 4242
www.watertownseattle.com
Convenient to the University of Washington, this sister property to the University Inn has 100 non-smoking rooms. Evening wine tasting, Mon–Fri; free loaner bikes. **$$**

TRANSPORTATION

EASTSIDE

Bellevue

Bellevue Club Hotel
11200 SE. 6th Street
Bellevue WA 98004
Tel: 425-454 4424 or
1-800-579 1110
www.bellvueclubhotel.com
As part of the athletic
club, the hotel offers 67
rooms each with enor-
mous bathrooms with
spa-tubs and shower
stalls. Amenities offered
through the athletic club
include: five indoor
tennis courts, Olympic-
size swimming pool,
squash and racquetball
courts, and exercise
rooms. **$$$**

Bellevue Residence Inn
14455 NE. 29th Place
Bellevue WA 98007
Tel: 425-882 1222
www.marriott.com
Offers one- and two-bed-
room suites in a village-
type setting amid
landscaped grounds.
Suites are equipped
with kitchens, fireplaces
and balconies or
decks (depending on
level). Other amenities:
heated pool, Jacuzzis,
laundry, airport trans-
portation. **$$$**

Hilton Bellevue
300 112th SE.
Bellevue WA 98004
Tel: 425-455 1300 or
1-800-955 1300
www.hilton.com
This hotel has 353
deluxe oversized rooms,
some with balconies.
Heated pool, sauna and
Jacuzzi, health club
privileges, restaurant
and lounge. **$$$**

Hyatt Regency Bellevue
900 Bellevue Way NE.
Bellevue WA 98004
Tel: 425-462 1234
www.hyatt.com
This luxury hotel in the
Bellevue Place shopping
center has 382 rooms
and is the tallest hotel
in Bellevue, with 24
floors. The top two
floors offer the Regency
Club rooms featuring
concierge service,
continental breakfast
and appetizers in the
evening. Amenities
include Eques, a fine
dining restaurant. **$$$**

Red Lion Bellevue Inn
11211 Main Street
Bellevue WA 98004
Tel: 425-455 5240
http://redlion.rdln.com
Amenities include:
landscaped courtyard,
heated pool, health club
privileges, airport transportation, restaurant,
suites with fireplace. **$$**

Sheraton Bellevue Seattle East Hotel
100 112th Avenue NE.
Bellevue WA 98004
Tel: 425-455 3330
www.starwoodhotels.com
Built in 1980 in the
heart of downtown
Bellevue. Amenities
include: heated indoor
pool, saunas, Jacuzzi,
airport transportation,
cable TV. There are
three restaurants and a
lounge with entertain-
ment. At weekends all
standard rooms are
inexpensive. **$$$**

Issaquah

Holiday Inn
1801 12th Avenue
Issaquah WA 98027
Tel: 425-392 6421
www.ichotelsgroup.com
Opposite Lake Sam-
mamish State Park on
the south end of the
lake. Amenities: sea-
sonal pool, sauna,
Jacuzzi, restaurant and
laundry facilities. **$$**

Kirkland

Woodmark Hotel
1200 Carillon Point
Kirkland WA 98033
Tel: 425-822 3700
www.thewoodmark.com
Features 100 rooms,
some with views of Lake
Washington, in a ritzy
31-acre (12.5-hectare)
shopping/office com-
plex. Carillon Point also
features a marina and
the popular Ristorante
Stresa, Yarrow Bay
Restaurant and Beach
Café, plus the Library
Bar for afternoon tea
served on bone china,
surrounded by books.
Amenities include: mini-
bars, DVDs with free
movies, bath robes,
complimentary break-
fast with newspaper,
and the Waters Lake-
side Bistro. **$$$**

Redmond

Redmond Inn
17601 Redmond Way
Redmond WA 98052
Tel: 425-883 4900 or
1-800-634 8080
www.redmondinn.com
Amenities: cable TV,
pool, Jacuzzi, restau-
rant, airport trans-
portation, laundry. **$$**

Willows Lodge
14580 NE. 145th Street
Woodinville WA 98072
Tel: 425-424 3900 or
1-877-424 3930
www.willowslodge.com
A Northwest-style
lodge in Washington's
wine country, bordering
the Sammamish
River and adjacent
to the RedHook
Brewery, Chateau
Ste. Michelle and
Columbia wineries.
86 spacious rooms
and suites. **$$$**

YOUTH HOSTELS

Most hostels offer clean,
no-frills, low-budget
accommodation.

Green Tortoise Hostel
105 Pike Street
Seattle WA 98101
Tel: 206-340-1222
www.greentortoise.net
Hostel at Pike Place
Market offers dorm-
style accommodations
at reasonable prices.
Continental breakfast
included daily; dinner
three times a week.

Hostelling International Seattle
84 Union Street
Seattle WA 98101
Tel: 206-682 0462 or
1-888-622 5443
www.hiseattle.org
A 125-bed hostel with
lounge, library and self-
service kitchen, laundry
available. Free member-
ship for non-profit
groups. Discounts with
membership.

YMCA Accommodations
909 4th Avenue
Seattle WA 98104
Tel: 206-382 5000
www.seattleymca.org
A 178-room hostel.
Use of YMCA facilities
including lounge, hot
tub, indoor pool,
sauna, fitness center
and laundry service.
Weekly rates are
available.

ACCOMMODATIONS

ACTIVITIES

A – Z

THE ARTS, NIGHTLIFE, EVENTS, SHOPPING, SPORTS AND TOURS

THE ARTS

Art Galleries

On the first Thursday of every month, Pioneer Square art galleries host "First Thursday." Visitors may gallery hop, view new works, sip wine and nibble cheese from about 6–8:30pm. Maps are available at most of the Pioneer Square galleries. Many galleries are closed Mondays.

The local news weeklies *(Seattle Weekly* and *The Stranger)* offer information on gallery shows, as do the daily newspapers. Other good sources include the online *Art Guide Northwest* (www.artguidenw.com) and *Art Access* (www.artaccess.com).

Arthead Art Gallery
5411 Meridian Avenue N.
Tel: 206-633 5544
Features regional artists of sculpture, photography and painting.

Bluebottle Art Gallery and Store
415 E. Pine Street
Tel: 206-325 1592
www.bluebottleart.com
This gallery on Capitol Hill displays and sells arts and crafts from up-and-coming artisans.

Carolyn Staley Fine Prints
2001 Western Avenue, Ste 320
Tel: 206-621 1888
www.carolynstaleyprints.com

Japanese woodblock prints and better quality old prints.

Center On Contemporary Art (COCA)
410 Dexter Avenue N.
Tel: 206-728 1980
www.cocaseattle.org
Innovative and avant-garde works on display. Stages large exhibits off-site, performance art on-site.

Davidson Galleries
313 Occidental Avenue S.
Tel: 206-624 1324
www.davidsongalleries.com
Features antique and contemporary prints from around the world.

Foster/White Gallery
220 3rd Ave S., Ste 100
Tel: 206-622 2833
www.fosterwhite.com
Exhibits ceramics, sculpture, and paintings by established Northwest artists and work in glass by artists of the Pilchuck School.

Francine Seders Gallery
6701 Greenwood Avenue N.
Tel: 206-782 0355
www.sedersgallery.com
Seders represents a large group of minority artists including works of Jacob Lawrence, Robert Jones and Gwen Knight.

G. Gibson Gallery
300 S. Washington Street
Tel: 206-587 4033
www.ggibsongallery.com
Contemporary photography by both well known artists and young Northwesterners.

Greg Kucera Gallery
212 3rd Avenue S.
Tel: 206-624 0770
www.gregkucera.com
Carries established Northwest artists with national recognition and hosts an exhibit once a year on a controversial topic.

Sacred Circle Art Gallery of American Indian Art
Daybreak Star Cultural Arts Center
Discovery Park
Tel: 206-285 4425
www.unitedindians.com/sacredcircle.html
An exquisite collection of works by highly respected Native American artists from Canada and the US.

MUSEUM OF GLASS

Museum of Glass: International Center for Contemporary Art
1801 Dock Street
Tacoma
Tel: 253-284 4750 or 1-866-4MUSEUM
www.museumofglass.org
Opened in July 2002, the museum's 13,000 sq. ft (1,200 sq. meters) of gallery space is devoted to international artists; there's also a glass studio, theater, gift shop and café, all of it connected to downtown Tacoma by the Chihuly Bridge of Glass.

Woodside/Braseth Gallery
2101 9th Avenue
Tel: 206-622 7243
www.woodsidebrasethgallery.com
Paintings by Northwest artists.

William Traver Gallery
110 Union Street, Ste 200
Tel: 206-587 6501
www.travergallery.com
Works by Pilchuck Glass artists.
Second floor displays paintings,
photographs and sculpture by
regional artists.

Eastside Galleries

Art Collective Issaquah Up Front Artist Co-op
48 Front Street N
Issaquah, WA 98027
Tel: 425-996 8553
www.artcollectiveissaquah.org
Exhibits local art and offers
workshops.

Creations Gallery
10837 NE 2nd Place
Bellevue, WA 98004
Tel: 425-454 8535
Showcases an eclectic collection
of paintings and prints, including
hand-signed limited edition
lithographs and paintings by
local artists.

East Shore Gallery
12700 SE 32nd Street
Bellevue, WA 98005
Tel: 425-747 3780
www.eastshoreunitarian.com
Gallery in East Shore Unitarian
Church represents the burgeoning
local arts scene with watercolors,
jewelry, pottery and more.

Elements Gallery
10500 NE. 8th Street, Bellevue
Tel: 425-454 8242
Glassworks, jewelry, textiles and
sculpture.

Howard/Mandville Gallery
120 Park Lane, Suite D. Kirkland
Tel: 425-889 8212
www.howardmandville.com
Northwest and international
artists.

Lakeshore Gallery
107 Park Lane
Kirkland, WA
Tel: 425-827 0606
Original fine art, limited edition
prints and handcrafted glass,
ceramics and jewelry.

BUYING TICKETS

You can purchase theater tickets
at half price on the day of the
show, but you run the risk of a
sell-out and must take whatever
seats you can get (if you're lucky
they may be first row at half-
price.) This also applies to dance
performances and music concerts. All are cash and walkup
only. Ticket venues include:
Ticket/Ticket: sells last-minute
tickets at four locations and
charges a surcharge per seat.
www.ticketwindowonline.com
Ticket venues include:
Pacific Place, Seattle
6th and Pine, inside Pacific
Place, 4th Level. Tues–Sun
noon–6pm.
Broadway Market, Seattle
401 Broadway East, 2nd Level.

Ming's Asian Gallery
10217 Main Street
Bellevue, WA 98004
Tel: 425-462 4008
www.mingsgallery.com
Asian art and imports, including
rugs, silk wall hangings, vases,
bamboo furniture and fine
wooden and lacquer cabinets.

Patricia Rovzar Gallery
118 Central Way
Kirkland, WA
Tel: 425-889 4627
www.rovzargallery.com
Shows representational art in
all mediums.

Rosalie Whyel Doll Museum of Doll Art
1116 108th Avenue NE.
Bellevue
Tel: 425-455 1116
www.dollart.com
More a museum than a gallery,
and highly popular with collectors
and laypeople. It houses more
than 3,000 dolls on display and
for sale. Admission fee.

Music & Dance

Pacific Northwest Ballet
301 Mercer Street
Tel: 206-441 2424
www.pnb.org

Tues–Sat, noon–7pm, Sun
noon–6pm. Validated parking,
with any purchase, in the Broadway Market Parking Garage.
Pike Place Market, Seattle
1st Ave and Pike Street, in Pike
Place Market Information Booth.
Tues–Sun noon–6pm. One hour
free parking at the Public Market Parking Garage.
Meydenbauer Center, Bellevue
11100 NE 6th Street, Ste 2,
Bellevue, WA. Tues–Sun
noon–6pm. Validated parking,
with any purchase, at the
Meydenbauer Garage.
Full-price tickets to most shows
in town are available through
Ticketmaster Northwest
Tel: 206-628 0888; or fine arts
line: 206-292 2787.

When Marion Oliver McCaw Hall
is not in use for operas, you can
enjoy performances by the
Pacific Northwest Ballet. There
are at least six productions from
October to May and an annual
production of *The Nutcracker*.

Seattle Opera Association
1020 John Street
Tel: 206-389 7676
www.seattleopera.org
This is also the place to find
out about tickets and upcoming
performances.

Seattle Symphony Orchestra
200 University Street
Tel: 206-215 4747
www.seattlesymphony.org
The Seattle Symphony Orchestra
schedules a wide variety of
concerts 11 months out of the
year. Most performances are in
Benaroya Hall Downtown. Gerard
Schwarz is the conductor.

Theaters

Seattle has a thriving theater
scene, both classical and fringe.
In fact, for such a small city, it
attracts a fine group of
performers, both professional
and amateur. Major Seattle
theaters are:

THEATRICAL ROOTS

Washington state's theatrical roots go back to the 19th century, when two local impresarios set up a series of theatres in the 1880s and 1890s. John Considine, who ran the nation's first vaudeville circuit, had theatres from Victoria to Portland. His chief competitor was a Greek man called Alexander Pantages who returned from the Alaskan goldfields having made pots of money, not by panning, but by running a playhouse. When the two teamed up, they had theatres that stretched up and down the West Coast.

ACT
700 Union Street
Tel: 206-292 7676
www.acttheatre.org
Close to Seattle Center. Seattle's leading repertory theater.
Fifth Avenue Theater
1308 5th Avenue
Tel: 206-625 1900
www.5thavenue.org
Hosts touring Broadway shows, musicals and plays in an ornate and historic building.
Freehold Theatre
1525 10th Avenue
Tel: 206-323 7499
www.freeholdtheatre.org
Intiman Theater
201 Mercer Street
Seattle Center Playhouse
Tel: 206-269 1900
www.intiman.org
Meany Theater
University of Washington
George Washington Lane and NE. 40th Street
Tel: 206-543 4880
www.meany.org
The Moore Theatre
1932 2nd Avenue
Tel: 206-443 1744
www.themoore.com
On the Boards
100 W. Roy Street
Tel: 206-217 9888
www.ontheboards.org
Cutting edge performance art.

The Paramount Theatre
911 Pine Street
Tel: 206-682 1414
www.theparamount.com
Presents well-known entertainers. For tickets call: 206-292 ARTS.
The University of Washington School of Drama
University of Washington
UW Arts Ticket Office
Tel: 206-543 4880
Seattle Children's Theater
Charlotte Martin Theatre and Eve Atford Theatre
Seattle Center
Tel: 206-441 3322
www.sct.org
Productions for children of all ages on two stages, September through to June.
Seattle Repertory Theater
155 Mercer Street
Tel: 206-443 2222
www.seattlerep.org
Located in the Bagley Wright Theater in Seattle Center, this is Seattle's flagship professional theater with productions of classic and contemporary works.

BELOW: popular Seattle nightspot.

Theater Schmeater
1500 Summit
Tel: 206-324 5801
www.schmeater.org
Housed in a former parking garage, this space offers a fun mix of serious theatre and goofball late-night shows like the popular *Twilight Zone – Live on Stage*.

Movie Theaters

Most cinemas feature first-run movies only. However, a handful of theaters will run – and sometimes specialize in – old "classics" and foreign films. Check the newspaper for theater listings and show times. In Seattle these theaters are:
Egyptian
805 E. Pine Street
Tel: 206-781 5755
The Guild 45
45th at 2115 N. 45th
Tel: 206-781 5755
The Harvard Exit
807 E. Roy Street
Tel: 206-323 8986
Metro Cinemas
NE. 45th Street and Roosevelt Avenue
Tel: 206-781 5755
Neptune
1303 NE 45th Street
Tel: 206-781 5755
Seven Gables
911 NE. 50th Street
Tel: 206-781 5755
The Uptown Cinema
511 Queen Anne Avenue N.
Tel: 206-285 1022
  College and university campuses may also show off-beat films. For typical Hollywood blockbuster films, check out the AMC Loews Meridian 16 (tel: 206-223 9600) or the AMC Pacific Place 11 (tel: 206-652 2404) Downtown.

NIGHTLIFE

Several areas are hubs for evening entertainment, with restaurants, clubs and shops open late. They are located around Lake Union, in the Pioneer Square district along the downtown waterfront, and around the university (especially along University Way), along Broadway on Capitol Hill, in Fremont and in Ballard.

In Pioneer Square the trendiest and most pleasant bars have a historical flavor, such as: **Dimitriou's Jazz Alley**, **J & M Café** and the **New Orleans Creole Restaurant**.

Bars & Music Venues

Alibi Room
85 Pike Street, Pike Place Market
Tel: 206-623 3180
Hidden in Post Alley, it draws the hip and single.

Amber
2214 1st Avenue
Tel: 206-441 9600
One of Belltown's liveliest lounges.

The Attic Alehouse and Eatery
4226 E. Madison Street
Tel: 206-323 3131
A good selection of microbrews and neighborly conversation.

Baltic Room
1207 Pine Street
Tel: 206-625 4444
A lounge where the live music is piano jazz and the words hip and cool come to mind.

Century Ballroom & Cafe
915 E Pine Street
Tel: 206-324 7263
Check to see whether it's salsa or swing night at this classy Capitol Hill joint; come early for beginner classes.

Chop Suey
1325 E Madison Street
Tel: 206-324 8000
Stylish dance club on Capitol Hill.

Conor Byrne Pub
5140 Ballard Avenue NW.
Tel: 206-784 3640
Irish pub with live Irish, Folk, Bluegrass, Alt Country, Blues and acoustic music most nights.

Crocodile Cafe
2200 2nd Avenue
Tel: 206-441 5611
Features local and international alternative rock bands.

Dimitriou's Jazz Alley
2033 6th Avenue
Tel: 206-441 9729
Presents the top names in jazz in a sophisticated atmosphere.

Doc Maynard's
610 1st Avenue
Tel: 206-682 4646
Rock 'n' roll and rhythm and blues reign supreme at this Pioneer Square bar.

Elysian Brewing Co.
1211 E. Pike Street
Tel: 206-860 1920
The beer is brewed on site and extremely good. On weekends live jazz can be heard.

Grateful Bread Café
7001 35th Avenue NE.
Tel: 206-525 3166
Folk musicians sometimes play on Sundays.

Hale's Brewery and Pub
4301 Leary Way NW.
Tel: 206-782 0737
A showcase for locally brewed ales.

Heavens Nightclub
172 S. Washington Street
Tel: 206-622 1863
Club located in Pioneer Square.

Il Bistro
93-A Pike St., Pike Place Market
Tel: 206-682 3049
A place for after work or evening rendezvous. With European flair.

Kells Irish Restaurant and Pub
1916 Post Alley
Tel: 206-728 1916
Irish restaurant and pub with inspiring Irish sing-a-longs.

Murphy's Pub
1928 N. 45th Street
Tel: 206-634 2110
Irish pub with a great selection of brews and folk music.

COMEDY CLUBS

Comedy Underground
222 S. Main
Tel: 206-628 0303
Giggles Comedy Night Club
Roosevelt & 53rd Street
Tel: 206-526-JOKE
Both clubs present nationally known comedians and local talent.

Neighbours
1509 Broadway
Tel: 206-324 5358
Everyone comes to this longtime Capitol Hill gay club to dance, dance, dance.

Neumo's
925 E. Pike Street
Tel: 206-709 9467
Capitol Hill rock club often books popular music acts and offers a good live music experience.

New Orleans Creole Restaurant
114 1st Avenue S.
Tel: 206-622 2563
Features creole, ragtime and jazz along with spicy foods.

Owl 'N' Thistle
808 Post Avenue
Tel: 206-621 7777
An Irish pub with Celtic folk bands.

The Pink Door
1919 Post Alley, Pike Place Market
Tel: 206-443 3241
A terraced place where accordion music will soften your mood while drinking and eating antipasti.

Showbox Nightclub
1426 1st Avenue
Tel: 206-628 3151
This venue has two huge dance floors, plus a live stage.

The Triangle Lounge
3507 Fremont Place N.
Tel: 206-632 0880
A Fremont haunt.

Trinity Night Club
111 Yesler Way
Tel: 206-447 4140
Multilevel Pioneer Square club offers three clubs in one, with local and national DJs.

Triple Door
216 Union Street
Tel: 206-838 4333
Located across from Benaroya Hall and below Wild Ginger (an eclectic Asian restaurant) this former vaudeville theater is beautifully reborn as a classy music venue and cocktail bar. Triple Door draws a distinctly well-heeled crowd; after work, it's a movers-and-shakers spot for appetizers and out-of-this world cocktails. Great music.

EVENTS

January

Chinese New Year
www.cidbia.com
Based on the lunar calendar, this festival is held sometime in January or February in the International District. Festivities include a parade with dragons, dancers, great food and fireworks.

February

Chilly Hilly Bike Ride, Bainbridge Island, the third Sunday in February. Hop aboard the ferry to Bainbridge Island for this 33-mile (53-km) ride sponsored by the Cascade Bicycle Club.

Festival Sundiata
Tel: 206-329 8086
www.festivalsundiata.org
At Seattle Center during Black History month.

Northwest Flower and Garden Show
Tel: 206-789 5333
www.gardenshow.com
Washington State Convention and Trade Center. On almost 5 acres (2 hectares) of the convention center floor, landscape architects, nurseries and gardeners try their best to outdo each other at over 300 booths. Admission charge.

March

25 for $25
Three-course *prix-fixe* dining deal at 25 of Seattle's best restaurants; lunch is $12.50, dinner $25. March and November Sun–Thurs.

Irish Week Festival, includes events such as the St Patrick's Day Dash, an easy 3½-mile (6-km) run along the waterfront from T.S. McHugh's on lower Queen Anne to Safeco Field.

St Patrick's Day Parade
Tel: 206-329 7224
www.irishclub.org
Parade travels from City Hall, 600 4th Avenue, to Westlake Center, 1601 5th Avenue, featuring bagpipes, Irish

ABOVE: Chinese New Year in the International District.

dancers, marching bands and the laying of the green stripe down 4th Avenue.

Whirligig
at Seattle Center
Tel: 206-684 7200
www.seattlecenter.com
Hosts this indoor carnival for kids from about mid-March to mid-April. Free entertainment; small fee for rides.

April

Daffodil Festival and Grand Floral Parade
in Tacoma
Tel: 253-863 9524
One of the largest floral parades. Parade travels through Tacoma, Puyallup, Sumner and Orting in one day.

Skagit Valley Tulip Festival
Tel: 360-428 5959
www.tulipfestival.org
Held on 1,500 acres (600 hectares) of colorful tulip fields. Bicycle and bus tours are popular.

May

International Children's Festival
at Seattle Center
Tel: 206-684 7200
www.seattleinternational.org
Children's performers and theatrical groups from around the world come to entertain at this week-long festival. Some events are free, but most charge admission.

Northwest Folklife Festival
Tel: 206-684 7300
www.nwfolklife.org
Memorial Day weekend at Seattle Center. Music, dancing, ethnic food and crafts from more than 100 countries. Many people unpack their instruments and join some of the many jam sessions which spring up all around the Center's lawns.

Opening Day of Boating Season
Tel: 206-325 1000
www.seattleyachtclub.org
Held first Saturday in May. Yachting clubs bring out a parade of boats from Lake Union to Lake Washington. Also features a rowing regatta.

Seattle International Film Festival
Tel: 206-464 5830
www.seattlefilm.com
Mid-May to mid-June at various theaters (concentrated in the University District and Capitol Hill).

University Street Fair
University Way
Tel: 206-547 4417
Held the third weekend in May, the fair features hundreds of artists' booths in a 10-block area. Mimes, clowns and street entertainment.

June

Fremont Summer Solstice Parade
Tel: 206-547 7440
www.fremontfair.com

A well-known neighborhood fair, featuring live music, local crafts, jugglers, mimes, along with a zany street parade on the Saturday closest to summer solstice.

Gay Pride Parade
Tel: 206-322 9561
www.seattlepride.org
Usually at end of June. The Northwest's largest Lesbian/Gay/Bisexual/Transgender (LGBT) Pride Parade.

Pike Place Market Festival
www.pikeplacemarket.org
Clowns, jazz musicians, and a "kids' alley" full of craft activities round out the usual entertainment at the market.

Special Olympics
At various locations depending on the event.
Tel: 206-362 4949
Olympic-style events for people with special needs.

In June, July, August and September, the **Downtown Seattle Association** sponsors lunchtime concerts in various parks and plazas. For details, call the Daily Events Line: Tel: 206-684 8582.

July

Bellevue Arts and Crafts Fair
510 Bellevue Way, Bellevue
Tel: 425-519 0770
www.bellevuearts.org
Sponsored by the Bellevue Art Museum. Features exhibits and booths throughout the mall including artists-at-work demonstration booths, musical concerts at the fountain outside Macy's and entertainment for children.

Bite of Seattle
Tel: 425-283 5050
www.biteofseattle.com
Mid-July on the grounds at Seattle Center. A taste-testers delight with over 60 restaurants participating. Pay according to your tastes.

Fourth of July-Ivar Festival and Fireworks
Myrtle Edwards Park
Tel: 206-587 6500
www.keepclam.com
A fishing derby, concerts and food at this waterfront park

during the day. A fireworks display over Elliott Bay at dusk.

Fourth of July Parades
Downtown Bothell, Issaquah, Bainbridge Island and other neighborhoods; check newspaper for listings.

King County Fair
At the fairgrounds in Enumclaw. Begins third Wednesday in July and continues for five days of music, rodeos, logger competitions, crafts and food. The oldest county fair in the state.

Lake Union Wooden Boat Festival
1010 Valley Street, south end of Lake Union
Tel: 206-382 2628
www.cwb.org
Features rowing, sailing and boat building competitions, workshops, food, crafts, and water taxis from the Center for Wooden Boats.

Seafair
Tel: 206-728 0123
www.seafair.com
Air show with amazing stunts from civilian and military aircraft. Knife-edge passes and dynamic maneuvers take your breath away.

Summer Celebration
Mercer Island
www.mercer.gov.org/summercelebration
The downtown area overflows with display booths of local artists. Sponsored by the Mercer Island Visual Arts League.

Late July–early August

Seattle's most spectacular **summer festival** is a series of events, parades and celebrations that take place over a 2½-week period (usually the third weekend in July to first week in August) in different parts of the city. Highlights include: the milk carton derby races at Green Lake, the Blue Angels Air Show (aerobatic flights), Hydroplane Races on Lake Washington, Bon Odori, festival of dances and food sponsored by the Seattle Buddhist church, Chinatown Seafair Parade, Hing Hay Park and the Torchlight Parade, a grand, nighttime parade through Downtown.

August

Camlann Medieval Faire,
Carnation. www.camlann.org
Camlann recreates the every-day experiences of a 14th-century rural village in Somerset, England. Lots of medieval festivities.

Evergreen Classic Benefit Horseshow, Redmond.
www.evergreenclassic.com

Evergreen State Fair
Monroe
Tel: 360-805 6700
www.evergreenfair.org
Held third week in August–Labor Day weekend. A country fair with big-name country stars, plus rodeos, logging competitions, carnival rides, and a chili cook-off.

Hempfest
Tel: 206-781 5734
www.hempfest.org
Myrtle Edwards Park. The nation's leading cannabis policy reform event. Live music acts, food, vendors.

Seattle Tennis Club Washington State Open
Tel: 206-324 3200
During first week in August (order tickets well in advance).

Snoqualmie Railroad Days
Snoqualmie
Tel: 425-888 0021
www.trainmuseum.org
Steam trains from the late-19th century. A 10-mile (16-km) ride from the Snoqualmie depot takes visitors up to the historic depot and quaint town of North Bend.

September

Bumbershoot
Tel: 206-281 8111
www.onereel.org
Music and arts festival at Seattle Center, Labor Day weekend. Big names and local acts perform at this music event. The entry fee entitles guests to attend hundreds of concerts in all styles throughout the Center complex.

Fremont Oktoberfest
Tel: 206-633 0422
www.fremontoktoberfest.com
Sample from more than 60 brews at Fremont, under the Aurora Bridge. Street fair with craft vendors, kids area, music, etc.

The Puyallup Fair
Tel: 253-841 5045
www.puyallupfair.com
Western Washington's largest
state fair, about 35 miles (55
km) south of Seattle. A 17-day
long country fair extravaganza.

October

Festa Italiana
Seattle Center, near Columbus
Day.
Tel: 206-684 8582
Italian dancing and food.
Greek Festival
St Demetrios Church
2100 Boyer Avenue E.
Tel: 206-325 4347
www.seattlegreekfestival.com
Held in late September or early
October at this Byzantine church
with folk dancing, arts and crafts
and Greek cuisine.
Halloween, parades, festivities
and pranks at nightclubs and
bars. Many shopping centers
offer free candy for children
roaming the malls in costumes.
Issaquah Salmon Days Festival
Main Street
Tel: 425-392 0661
www.salmondays.org
The street is closed to traffic
and open to arts and crafts
booths with artists from all over
the Northwest. Street entertainment, mime, clowns, and musicians are here as well as the
salmon jumping up to the hatchery. Big salmon cookout.

November

Seattle Marathon
Tel: 206-729 3660
www.seattlemarathon.org
Starts east of the Experience
Music Project and loops through
Downtown and along Lake
Washington, ending at the
Memorial Stadium.

December

Christmas Ships
Tel: 206-623 1445
www.argosycruises.com
Illuminated and decorated boats
parade around Lake Union and
Lake Washington, making stops
at public parks while choral

groups entertain. Check news-
papers or the website for
updated schedules.
***A Christmas Carol* performed
at the ACT Theater**
700 Union Street
Tel: 206-292 7676
An annual production of the ever-
popular, classic Dickens tale.
**Christmas tree-lighting and
caroling** in the Bavarian-style
village of Leavenworth in the
Cascade Mountains. Tel: 509-
548 5807.
**Community Hannukah
Celebration**
Stroum Jewish Center
Mercer Island
Tel: 206-232 7115
Arts and crafts, children's games
and candle-lighting.
Jingle Bell Run/Walk for Arthritis
Tel: 206-547 2707
A 5-km (3-mile) run and walk;
festive costumes and jingle bells
welcome.
New Year's at the Needle
Tel: 206-905 2100 or
1-800-937 9582
www.spaceneedle.com
The 605-ft (185-meter) landmark
offers a traditional fireworks
show, and parties on the restau-
rant and observation deck levels.
The Nutcracker presented by the
Pacific Northwest Ballet. A long-
standing tradition that runs from
early December through to New
Year. TicketMaster, tel: 206-292
2787; www.ticketmaster.com

SHOPPING

Shopping Areas

Seattle's climate and outdoor
recreational activities have
brought about the success of the
city's best-known stores such as
Eddie Bauer (now a national
chain), REI (the co-operative,
with more stores opening across
the country), the North Face and
Patagonia. Many of the traditionalists in Seattle look like they
just stepped out of one of these
sporty stores.

Several areas are well known
for shopping in Seattle. Among
them is the **Pike Place Market**,
the downtown retail district,
along **Broadway** on **Capitol
Hill**, **Fremont**, **Ballard** and the
University District. The latter
features ethnic gift shops,
specialty food markets,
restaurants, bakeries and
bookstores.
Seattle has an 8.8 percent
sales tax that is added to the
price of retail goods and food
that is served in restaurants.

Malls & Stores

Alderwood Mall
Lynnwood (near the north inter-
section of I-5 and I-405)
Tel: 425-771 1121
Features Macy's, Nordstrom, J.C.
Penney and Sears. Many furni-
ture stores and smaller malls
nearby. Upscale retailers and a
16-screen theater are found at
the village at Alderwood, the
outdoor shopping area.
Bellevue Square
NE. 8th Street and Bellevue Way
Bellevue
Tel: 425-455 2429
A 198-store mall featuring
Nordstrom and J.C. Penney.
City Centre
1420 5th Avenue
Tel: 206-624 8800
Major names include Barneys
New York and Palomino. Serves
dinner and lunch.

Country Village
23730 Bothell-Everett Highway
Bothell
Tel: 425-483 2250
A collection of country farm-houses, remodeled for shopping with brick pathways, landscaped grounds with waterfalls, gazebos and flowers everywhere in spring and summer.

Gilman Village
Gilman Boulevard
Issaquah
Tel: 425-392 6802
www.gilmanvillage.com
Country farmhouses and barns have been remodeled and made into a charming shopping village. Many stores have country-style gifts, clothing, artwork. Features several restaurants.

Lincoln Square
700 Bellevue Way NE
Bellevue
(see page 149)

Macy's
3rd Avenue and Pine Street
Tel: 206-506 6000
Formerly the Bon Marché, one of Seattle's oldest and finest department stores. Good-quality, moderately priced clothing, jewelry, toys and sundry items on nine floors. Also a post office, beauty salon, bakery and restaurants. A garage and a skywalk mean shoppers don't have to step outside on rainy days.

Nordstrom
500 Pine Street
Tel: 206-628 2111
www.nordstrom.com
Classical piano players at the baby grands are a highlight of this venerable department store which started in Seattle many decades ago. The emphasis on customer service has helped turn Nordstrom into a chain with shops throughout America.

Northgate Mall
401 NE. Northgate Way
Tel: 206-362 4777
www.simon.com
This mall features Macy's, Nordstrom, Gene Juarez Salon, restaurants and bars.

Pacific Place
600 Pine Street
Tel: 206-405 2655
www.pacificplaceseattle.com
A glitzy shopper's paradise with a glass ceiling and marble floors, Tiffany & Co. and Cartier reside here along with Club Monaco, Bebe, and more.

Pike Place Market
1st Avenue and Pike Street
Tel: 206-682 7453
(see page 94).

Rainier Square
1301 5th Avenue
Tel: 206-682 2104
www.rainiersquare.com
Top-of-the-line fashion shops are here such as Escada and David Lawrence. Rainier Square adjoins the Hilton Hotel.

Seattle Premium Outlets
10600 Quil Ceda Boulevard
Tulalip (Marysville)
Tel: 360-654 3000
www.premiumoutlets.com
There are more than 100 outlet stores in this open-air mall at the Tulalip Tribes' retail park north of Marysville. Expect to find savings of 25–65 percent off store prices. Inventory varies by store, but generally you should find in-season items and a range of regular merchandise, seconds, past-season and discontinued items.

University Village
2623 NE University Village
Tel: 206-523 0622
www.uvillage.com
Located just north of downtown Seattle, University Village is the only open-air lifestyle shopping center in the Pacific Northwest and offers a unique formula of national stores and local retailers. It is a regional destination for home furnishings, popular fashions, gifts and a selection of restaurants and cafés.

Waterfront Antique Mall
190 Sunset Ave S, Edmonds
Tel: 425-670 0770
Sells all kinds of antiques including jewelry, furniture and glass.

Westfield South Center
I-5 and I-405, Tukwila
Tel: 206-246 7400
www.westfield.com/southcenter
The largest shopping center in the metropolitan Seattle area.

CLOTHES CHART

The chart listed below gives a comparison of United States, European and United Kingdom clothing sizes. It is always a good idea, however, to try on any article before buying it, as sizes between manufacturers can vary enormously.

● **Women's Dresses/Suits**

US	Continental	UK
6	38/34N	8/30
8	40/36N	10/32
10	42/38N	12/34
12	44/40N	14/36
14	46/42N	16/38
16	48/44N	18/40

● **Women's Shoes**

US	Continental	UK
4½	36	3
5½	37	4
6½	38	5
7½	39	6
8½	40	7
9½	41	8
10½	42	9

● **Men's Suits**

US	Continental	UK
34	44	34
—	46	36
38	48	38
—	50	40
42	52	42
—	54	44
46	56	46

● **Men's Shirts**

US	Continental	UK
14	36	14
14½	37	14½
15	38	15
15½	39	15½
16	40	16
16½	41	16½
17	42	17

● **Men's Shoes**

US	Continental	UK
6½	—	6
7½	40	7
8½	41	8
9½	42	9
10½	43	10
11½	44	11

Features among others Nordstrom and Macy's. Many smaller shopping centers with furniture, electronics, clothing and food are in the vicinity of the mall.

Westlake Center and Plaza
Pine Street between 4th and 5th avenues
Tel: 206-467 1600
www.westlakecenter.com
Houses 80 specialty shops. Adjacent to Nordstrom and Macy's. Top floor features 15 fast-food stands from pizza and burgers to seafood and vegetarian cuisines. Specialty shops include Talbots, Fossil and Made in Washington.

Clothing

Baby & Co.
1936 1st Avenue
Tel: 206-448 4077
The ultimate in high-fashion wear.

Banana Republic
500 Pike Street
Tel: 206-622 2303
This branch of the always-dependable women's fashion chain is housed in the lovingly preserved Coliseum Theatre.

Some fitting rooms have theater seats in them.

Benetton
600 Pine Street, #325
Tel: 206-340 1206
Contemporary Italian fashions for men and women.

Brooks Brothers
1330 5th Avenue
Tel: 206-624 4400
High quality men's clothing.

The Coach Store
417 University Street
Tel: 206-382 1772
At the Four Seasons Olympic Hotel, the Coach Store is the maker of quality classic leather handbags, belts and accessories.

Michael's Bespoke Tailors
1203 2nd Avenue
Tel: 206-623 4785
High quality men's fashions.

Yankee Peddler
4218 E. Madison
Tel: 206-324 4218
Quality men's wear.

Photographic

Cameras West
1908 4th Avenue
Tel: 206-622 0066

One of the best places to shop for cameras and accessories.

Food

A & J Meats
2401 Queen Anne Ave N.
Tel: 206-284 3885
High-quality meats including specialty cuts and preparation.

Café Dilettante
416 Broadway E.
Tel: 206-329 6463
Makes exquisitely-rich truffles, irresistible butter-cream filled chocolates, tortes and cakes.

Great Harvest Bread Co
5408 Sand Point Way NE.
Tel: 206-524 4873
Wholewheat breads and sweets.

Honey Bear Bakery
6504 20th Ave NE
Tel: 206-525 2790
Natural foods bakery and café.

Scandinavian Bakery
8537 15th Ave NW
Tel: 206-784 6616
Scandinavian bakery with reputation for heavenly pastries.

Starbuck's
1912 Pike Place, University Village, also Bellevue, and small

SPECIALTY STORES AND GIFTS

Adelita
1422 Queen Anne Ave N
Tel: 206-285 0707
This cozy Queen Anne boutique with eclectic offerings features hard-to-find designers such as Petro Zillia and Sigal Dekai. Adelita carries trendy, feminine clothing, chic handbags, lingerie and yoga wear, bath and body products, and adorable upscale baby clothes.

Archie Mcphee
2428 NW. Market Street
Tel: 206-297 0240
A plethora of zany cheap toys that for some reason you can hardly resist. Before you know it, you've collected a dozen small neon fish, a handful of tiny, thumbtack size umbrellas and one or two wacky glow-in-the-dark dinosaurs for purchase.

Exclusively Washington
Pier 54
Tel: 206-624 2600
Works by Northwest artisans; sculpture, jewelry, clothing, pottery and Native American art.

Made In Washington
Pike Place Market (and malls)
Tel: 206-467 0788 or 1-800-338 9903
Everything in the store from crafts, local cookbooks, and wines is made in the State of Washington.

Metsker Maps
1511 1st Avenue
Tel: 206-623 8747
In need of a travel guide or map for somewhere? It's probably here. Also look at the assortment of reproductions of antique maps or globes of all sizes, including those that light up to illuminate the world.

Museum of Flight Store
9404 E. Marginal Way S.
Tel: 206-764 5720
An assortment of aviation gifts: model airplanes, selection of books, T-shirts, pins, photos. Main store at the museum, branch in Westlake Center.

Molbak's Greenhouse & Nursery
13625 NE. 175th Street
Woodinville
Tel: 425-483 5000
Almost a destination in itself, this is Washington's largest indoor nursery. Offers a huge selection of plants, trees and shrubs. Also features a café, conservatory, gift shop and patio furniture.

Sur La Table
84 Pine Street (across from Pike Place Market)
Tel: 206-448 2244
Gourmet cookware.

shops around town. Fine coffee, pastries, snacks and sandwiches from the coffee shop which started in Seattle and spread round the world.

Uwajimaya
600 5th Ave S.
Tel: 206-624 6248
Gourmet foods, records and books from Japan.

Jewelry

Ben Bridge
1432 4th Ave (various locations)
Tel: 06-628 6800
www.benbridge.com
A wide selection of jewelry, watches, gems and more.

Turgeon Raine Jewellers
1407 5th Ave
Tel: 206-447 9488
www.turgeonraine.com
High-end contemporary jewelry without the hard sales pitch.

Magazines & Books

Bulldog News
4208 University Way NE
Tel: 206-322-NEWS
Huge selection of periodicals, foreign magazines and newspapers.

Elliott Bay Book Company
101 S. Main Street
Tel: 206-624 6600
www.elliotbaybook.com
Four large rooms and two lofts with more than 150,000 titles. This large independent bookstore features readings by major authors and a café.

University Book Store
4326 University Way NE.
Tel: 206-634 3400 www.bookstore.washington.edu
Comprehensive selection of books, maps and gifts.

Wide World Books and Maps
4411 Wallingford Avenue N.
Tel: 206-634 3453
Store for the traveler or armchair traveler.

Music

Capitol Music Co.
718 Virginia
Tel: 206-622 0171
Comprehensive selection of sheet music.

Musicwerks
612 E Pine Street
Tel: 206-320 8933
www.musicwerks.org
The only store in Seattle that sells goth, industrial and electronic music exclusively.

Sonic Boom
514 15th Ave E (various locations)
Tel: 206-568-BOOM
www.sonicboomrecords.com
One of Seattle's hippest record stores for local and indie music.

Outdoor Specialists

Eddie Bauer
600 Pine Street
Tel: 206-622 2766
Also in most local malls.

The North Face
1023 1st Avenue
Tel: 206-622 4111
Backpacking clothing and gear.

REI (Recreational Equipment Inc.)
222 Yale Avenue North
Tel: 206-223 1944
www.rei.com
Downtown location features a bike path for testing potential purchases and a 65-foot (20-meter) free-standing indoor rock climbing peak. Branch stores in Lynnwood and Redmond.

SPORTS

Participant Sports

Bicycling

Seattle was rated by *Bicycling* magazine as the number one city in the US for biking.

The **Burke-Gilman Trail**, a paved road on an abandoned railroad bed, leads from Golden Gardens to Seattle's north city limits at NE 145th Street. The 15.2-mile (24.5-km) trail follows Lake Washington down by the University and is popular with people of all ages, whether biking, jogging or walking. The **Sammamish River Trail** follows the Sammamish River from Bothell, through Woodinville farmland and ends at Marymoor Park at the north tip of Sammamish Lake. This trail runs for 9½ miles (15 km) and connects with the Burke-Gilman trail.

Another popular bicycle route is the 2.8-mile (4.5-km) paved trail around **Green Lake**. It can be busy on sunny days, especially at weekends, with strollers, joggers, inline skaters and cross-country roller skiers. From Green Lake, bicyclists may choose to take the Ravenna Park Trail to the university.

Every third Sunday and second Saturday of the month from May–September, a 6-mile (9.5-km) stretch on **Lake Washington Boulevard** is closed to cars (from the Arboretum to Seward Park). Beautiful lakefront parks and scenery can be enjoyed on this paved road for family biking and hiking. Tel: 206-684 7092.

Marymoor Park in Redmond has a velodrome for racing and held the 1990 Goodwill Games bicycle races. Races are held 7:30pm Fri, Apr–Nov. Tel: 206-957 4555, www.marymoorvelodrome.org.

Numerous bicycle rides and races are held throughout the year. For information on current

events telephone the **Cascade Bicycle Club**, tel: 206-522-BIKE.
For bicycle rentals near these trails, contact the following:
Alki Bicycle Co.
2611 California Avenue SW.
Tel: 206-938 3322
The Bicycle Center
4529 Sand Point Way NE.
Tel: 206-523 8300
Gregg's Greenlake Cycle Inc.,
7007 Woodlawn Ave NE.
Tel: 206-523 1822
Sammamish Valley Cycle
8451 164th Avenue NE.
Redmond.
Tel: 425-881 8442
Also check the *Yellow Pages* directory under "Bicycle Rentals".

Boating

Canoeing, kayaking, rowing, sail boarding and sailing are all available around Lakes Union and Washington. In addition, Green Lake offers paddleboating.
University of Washington Waterfront Activities Center
Tel: 206-543 9433.
Offers canoe rentals.
Agua Verde Cafe & Paddle Club
1303 NE. Boat Street
Tel: 206-545 8570
www.aguaverde.com
Sea kayak rentals Mar–Oct. The Arboretum Gas Works are all within paddling distance of Agua Verde. Café has live music in the evenings.
Green Lake
Tel: 206-257 0171
Offers rowboats and paddleboats. Apr–Oct.
Ledger Marine Charters
1500 Westlake Ave N.
Tel: 206-283 3040
www.ledgemarinecharters.com
Moss Bay Rowing Club
1001 Fairview Avenue N. Suite 1900
Tel: 206-682 2031
www.mossbay.net
Rent kayaks, tour or take lessons. Open 8am–8pm in summer, 10am–dusk the rest of the year.
Northwest Outdoor Center
2100 Westlake Ave N.

HIKING MAPS AND INFORMATION

Mountain Madness
3018 SW Charlestown Street
Tel: 206-937 8389
www.mountainmadness.com
Offers personalized outdoor adventure tours including mountain biking, fishing, mountain climbing and hiking.
The Mountaineers
300 3rd Avenue W.
Tel: 206-284 6310
www.mountaineers.org
An outdoor recreation club that runs hiking trips.
REI, Recreational Equipment Inc
Tel: 206-223 1944
Outdoor recreational equipment

retailer that sells maps and organizes trips.
Sierra Club/Cascade Chapter
180 Nickerson Street, Suite 202
Tel: 206-378 0114
www.sierraclub.org/wa
US Forest Service/National Parks Service Outdoor Recreation Information Office
222 Yale Ave N.
Tel: 206-285 2200
www.nps.gov/ccso/oric.htm
Washington Trails Association
2019 3rd Ave, Suite 100
Tel: 206-625 1367
www.wta.org
Has most information needed on trails in the state.

Tel: 206-281 9694
www.nwoc.com
Offers sea kayak rentals, lessons and tours.

Birdwatching

Audubon Society
8050 35th Avenue NE.
Tel: 206-523 4483
www.seattleaudubon.org
The society offers a checklist of birds in the area and a list of where to purchase birdseed mixed for native species. It also conducts field trips in Seattle's parks.

Golf

Reservations to the following public golf courses are recommended as they are very popular:
Ballinger Park
23000 Lakeview Drive, Mountlake
Tel: 425-697 4653
Nine-hole, par: 34-men, 36-women.
Bellevue Municipal
5500 140th NE.
Tel: 425-452 7250
Eighteen-hole, par: 35-men, 36-women.
Foster
13500 Interurban Ave S.
Tel: 206-242 4221
Eighteen-hole, par: 69-men, 71-women.

Green Lake
5701 W. Green Lake Way N.
Tel: 206-632 2280
Nine-hole, par: 27 men and women.
Interbay Golf Center
2501 15th Ave NW
Tel: 206-285 2200
Nine-hole, par 28;
with the added bonus of heated tee stations.
Jackson Park Municipal
1000 NE. 135th Street
Tel: 206-363 4747
Eighteen-hole, par: 71-men, 73-women.
Jefferson Park Municipal
4101 Beacon Ave S.
Tel: 206-762 4513
Eighteen-hole, par: 70 men and women.
Maplewood Golf Course
4050 Maple Valley Highway, Renton
Tel: 425-430 6800
Eighteen-hole, par: 72-men, 73-women.
Seattle Golf Club
210 NW. 145th Street
Tel: 206-363 5444
Eighteen-hole, par: 27 men and women.
Tyee Valley
2401 S. 192nd Street
Tel: 206-878 3540
Eighteen-hole, par: 71 men, 73-women.

Wayne
16721 96th Avenue NE, Bothell
Tel: 425-485 6237
Eighteen-hole, par: 65-men,
66-women.

West Seattle
4470 35th Ave SW.
Tel: 206-935 5187
Eighteen-hole, par: 72-men,
74-women.

Hiking

A good pair of walking shoes, some snacks and a drink are all you need (but binoculars and camera are nice to have along) to explore the area and see what the land looked like before construction took over.

Carkeek Park (tel: 206-684 0877) offers wooded trails leading to Puget Sound beach. Playground, picnic, restrooms and high bluff views of the Sound.

Discovery Park, W. Government Way and 38th Avenue W. Tel: 206-386 4236. A 534-acre (216-hectare) park of deep wooded ravines, forest, grassy meadows and two miles of beach at the base of Magnolia Bluff. Nature trails wind their way throughout the park. The US Coast Guard's West Point Light Station is accessible by a 1½-mile (2.5-km) trail and open for tours from noon–4pm Sat–Sun, and Wed–Fri by appointment. The Daybreak Star Indian Cultural Center (tel: 206-285 4425), which includes the Sacred Circle Indian Art Gallery, features Indian arts and crafts. Open daily 10am–4pm. Admission is free. The park is open daily from 6am–11pm. Guided tours are offered, and a visitors' center is open daily 8:30am–5pm.

Foster Island Trail, from McCurdy Park or the Arboretum. An easy, level hike over wooden bridges and pontoons over Lake Washington to Foster Island.

Marymoor Park, north end of Lake Sammamish, Redmond. Extensive playing fields, playgrounds, trails, a bicycle velodrome, model plane airport and historical museum in this park.

Meadowdale Park, North Edmonds. Wooded hiking trail leads down to level, grassy picnicking area and sandy Puget Sound beach.

St Edward's Park, Juanita Drive, Bothell. Some open grassy grounds for picnicking, soccer or baseball are available on the site of this old Catholic seminary. Wooded trails lead down to still more trails along east shores of Lake Washington.

Tiger Mountain, Issaquah. There are numerous trails leading to alpine lakes and mountain vistas. Many of the trails also allow mountain biking.

Volunteer Park, E. Galer and 15th Avenue E., and E. Prospect and 14th Avenue E. (on Capitol Hill). Tel: 206-684 4743. Home of Seattle's Asian Art Museum's collection. A conservatory has collections of cacti, orchids and exotic tropical plants and is surrounded by extensive formal gardens. A 75-ft (23-meter) water tower with a steep spiral stairway provides on a clear day a panoramic view of downtown Seattle, and the surrounding lakes and mountains. Open dawn–11pm. Conservatory open 10am–7pm May 15–Sept 15; 10am–4pm the rest of the year.

For hiking trails that take up an entire day or more, try the

parks in the Cascade Mountains, especially Mount Rainier and Olympic National Park.

Horseback Riding

Some ranches offer guided tours through parks, like Bridle Trails, or mountains, like Squak and Tiger. Lengths of tours vary from one hour to all day. Call for details.

Lang's Horse and and Pony Farm
21463 Little Mountain Road, Mt. Vernon
Tel: 360-424 7630
www.comeride.com

Pets Galore Horse Rides
13659 Cedar Glen Lane SE, Olalla
Tel: 253-857 7506
www.petsgalorehorserides.com

Tiger Mountain Stables
24508 SE 133rd, Issaquah
Tel: 425-392 5090

Scuba Diving

Although not perhaps automatically associated with a US city, **Brackett's Landing** in Edmonds has a sandy beach, next to the ferry landing, which is especially designed for scuba diving. The underwater park features a sunken 300-ft (90-meter) dock and five floating rests.

Skiing

Crystal Mountain Resort
Highway 410, 40 miles (75 km) east of Enumclaw
Tel: 360-663 2265
The site of the 1972 World Cup Championships. Offers a vertical of 3,100 ft (945 meters) and 50 trails from beginner to advanced. Weekend night skiing.

Stevens Pass
Tel: 206-812 4510
Seventy miles (110 km) northeast of Seattle, 37 ski trails and a 1,800-ft (550-meter) drop.

Summit at Snoqualmie
Tel: 425-434 7669
www.summit-at-snoqualmie.com
Three ski areas atop Snoqualmie Pass – Alpental, Snoqualmie Summit and Ski Acres – joined together to offer extensive choices of trails, linked by a free shuttle bus available

Fri–Sun, and a single lift ticket. Night skiing is also available.

White Pass
Tel: 509-672 3101
Near Yakima. A vertical of 1,500 ft (460 meters) plus night skiing.

Whistler
Tel: 1-800-944 7853
This internationally renowned resort is a four-hour drive from Seattle, north of Vancouver in Canada.

Spectator Sports

Baseball

Seattle Mariners Baseball Club
Safeco Field, 1st Avenue S.
Tel: 206-346 4000
www.seattlemariners.mlb.com
Safeco Field, the $417-million ballpark, mixes tradition with high tech, with real grass on the playing field and a spectacular retractable roof, an engineering marvel unto itself. Open Apr–Sept.

The Everett Aquasox
Memorial Stadium, Everett
(Exit 192 off I-5)
Tel: 425-258 3673
www.aquasox.com
This class-A minor league team of the Mariners plays 38 games on a grass field from mid-June through early September at the outdoor Memorial Stadium in Everett. The stadium is intimate, compared to most baseball stadiums, seating only 3,600. The ballpark food here was rated one of the best in the country.

Tacoma Rainiers
Cheney Stadium, 2502 S. Tyler Street
Tel: 1-800-281 3834
www.tacomarainiers.com
The Seattle Mariners Triple-A farm club play 72 games from April through to September.

Basketball

Seattle SuperSonics
KeyArena, Seattle Center
Tel: 206-281 5800
www.sonics.nba.com/sonics/
Seattle's NBA (National Basketball Association) team. The

season begins in November and playoffs begin in May. The Key Arena, which seats 17,072, is the city team's home arena. In late 2006, both the SuperSonics and the Storm *(see below)* were sold by Starbucks founder Howard Schultz, and the future of the teams' residency in Seattle remains unclear.

Seattle Storm
Key Arena, Seattle Center
Tel: 206-281 5800
www.wnba.com/storm
Seattle's WNBA (Women's National Basketball League) team plays at Key Arena during the NBA off season.

University of Washington, Husky Basketball
Hec Edmundson Pavilion
Tel: 206-543 2200
www.gohuskies.com
The basketball season begins in November and ends in March.

Football

Seattle Seahawks
11220 NE. 53rd Street, Kirkland
Tel: 1-888-NFL-HAWK
www.seahawks.com
Seattle's NFL (National Football League) team, The Seahawks, play at state-of-the-art Qwest Field, which opened in the summer of 2002.

Husky Stadium
Southeast end of University of Washington
Tel: 206-543 2200

This 72,500-seat stadium hosts the UW's football team. The Husky Stadium has the added attraction of offering views of Lake Washington and the Cascade Mountains, while taking in the game.

Hockey

Everett Silvertips
Everett Events Center
Tel: 425-252 5100
www.everettsilvertips.com
Season runs from September to March.

Seattle Thunderbirds
Seattle Center KeyArena
Tel: 206-448-PUCK
www.seattle-thunderbirds.com
Season runs from late Sept–Mar (or May if they make the playoffs).

Hydroplane Racing

During **Seafair** hydroplane races take place north of Seward Park on Lake Washington. Boats reach speeds of over 150 mph (240 kmph) on the top of the water and follow a 2-mile (3-km) oval course. Tickets are available in advance or (more expensively) at the gate to prime viewing spots along the beach. There are very privileged seats available for large sums of money at the Captains Club, tel: 206-728 0123; www.seafair.com

Soccer

Seattle Sounders
PO Box 80966, Seattle
Tel: 1-800-796-KICK
www.seattlesounders.net
The 2005 USL First Division champions play their season from April to October. They share Qwest Field with the Seahawks football team.

TOURS

Argosy Cruises, 1101 Alaskan Way, Pier 55, Suite 201, at the foot of Seneca Street, tel: 206-623 1445, www.argosycruises.com. Offers six different narrated cruises, from one-hour trips along Seattle's waterfront and shipyards, to longer tours that pass through the Chittenden Locks into Lake Union to view the houseboats, fishing vessels and sailboats. Another cruise takes in the homes of the wealthy on Lake Washington.

Boeing's Future of Flight, Highway 526, Everett, tel: 425-438 8100 or 1-888-467 4777, www.futureofflight.org. Paine Air Field is located about 30 miles (48 km) north of Seattle, exit 189 off I-5 and 3½ miles (5.5 km) east on Hwy 526. Tours of this commercial aviation plant take place in the world's largest building, where visitors can observe the manufacture of 747s, 767s, 777s and 787s. Tours last one hour. In the summer, tickets for the day's tours can be gone by 9 or 10am. Children under 4 ft (122 cm) in height are not permitted under any circumstances.

Brewery tours: The Redhook Ale Brewery, 14300 NE. 145th Street, Woodinville, tel: 425-483 3232, www.redhook.com, brews one of Washington's more popular microbeers. Tours are given every hour Mon–Thurs 11am–10pm, Fri–Sat 11am–midnight, Sun in spring and summer 11am–9pm. **Pyramid Ale House**, 1201 1st Avenue S., tel: 206-682 3377, wwwpyramidbrew.com, offers daily tours and tastings.

Chinatown/International District Tours are run by Chinatown Discovery, tel: 425-885 3085, www.seattlechinatowntour.com. Three-hour guided tours include a six-course "dim sum" lunch at a local restaurant. Mini-tours are scheduled daily in the summer. Admission is charged.

Gray Line of Seattle, 4500 W Marginal Way, tel: 206-624 5077 or 1-800-544 0739, www.graylineof seattle.com (and the Sheraton Hotel lobby) offers numerous tours including San Juan Islands, Mount Rainier and North Bend. Tours start in the spring.

Private Eye on Seattle Mystery and Murder Tour, tel: 206-365 3739, www.privateeye

tours.com. A narrated tour of Seattle's more publicized and gruesome crime scenes. Not for the faint-hearted.

Tillicum Tours, depart between Piers 55 and 56. Tel: 206-933 8600; www.Tillicum village.com. A 4-hour tour combines harbor sightseeing with a trip to Blake Island Marine State Park. The park is host to Tillicum Village, featuring the Northwest Coast Indian Cultural Center and Restaurant. Once there, tours include an Indian-style salmon dinner and traditional tribal dances, with time left for shopping or a casual walk. Tours run daily Mar–Nov and on weekends the rest of the year. Reservations recommended.

Seattle Architectural Foundation's Viewpoints, tel: 206-667 9184, www.seattlearchitecture.org. Narrated walking tours in and around downtown Seattle have different themes: one might reveal the beauty and history surrounding a city park and another feature some of Seattle's historic buildings. A series of "lunchtime tours" offer vantage points on the city or one of its new constructions. One tour takes you to Microsoft's campus to check out the software empire. Tours run all year.

See Seattle Walking Tours, tel: 425-226 7641; www.see-seattle. com. Walks take in popular Seattle sites, including Pike Place Market, the waterfront, Pioneer Square and the Inter-national District and Smith Tower.

Underground Tours, 608 1st Avenue S., tel: 206-682 4646; www.undergroundtour.com. A three-block, one-hour walking tour of Pioneer Square, including passage through a number of basements where subterranean sidewalks and storefronts were missed by the 1889 fire before being covered by new constructions. Stairs involved and strollers not allowed; admission charged.

Washington Wine Tours PO Box 12676, tel: 206-794 0562, www.washingtonwinetours.com Specializes in guided tours to the outstanding vineyards and wineries of Washington state. There's often a Seattle pick-up point.

Train Tours

Double Decker Tours, tel: 206-624 5077 or 1-800-426 7532, www.graylineofseattle.com. Tour downtown Seattle in a double-decker bus at your own pace. Tickets are good for a day and allow visitors to hop off or on the bus at any of the Double Decker Tour's seven centrally located bus stops. Buses depart every 30 minutes. **Spirit of Washington Dinner Train**, tel: 425-227-RAIL, 1-800-876-RAIL, www.spiritofwashingtondinnertrain.com. A 45-mile (72-km) tour along the shore of Lake Washington in restored railcars/engine from the early 1900s, plus formal dinner.

Bus Tours

Bus companies that offer tours in the area (Mount Rainier, Mount St Helens, wineries, Whidbey

BELOW: Kenmore Air does tours of the city and the region.

WHALE-WATCHING TOURS

Island Mariner Cruises
Tel: 360-734 8866
www.orcawatch.com
Tours from Bellingham. The 70–90-mile (110–150-km) round trip takes about 7 hours and tours are scheduled mid-May–mid-Sept. Spotting whales is a chance endeavor but Island Mariner boasts an 85 percent success rate with the help of professional spotters.
Mosquito Fleet San Juan Orca Cruises, Everett
Tel: 425-252 6800 or 1-800-325-ORCA.

Island and San Juan Islands) include:
Contiki Holidays
Tel: 866-CONTIKI
Gray Line of Seattle
4500 W Marginal Way SW
Tel: 206-624 5077, 206-626 5208
Greyhound Travel Services
811 Stewart Street
Tel: 1-800-231 2222
Hesselgrave International
12116 Valley Ave E, Sumner
Tel: 253-863 6642
Puget Sound Coach Lines
809 W Main Street, Auburn
Tel: 253-939 5811

Boat Tours

Argosy Cruises *(see page 230)*. A variety of boat cruises.
Gray Line Water Sightseeing
Pier 57
Tel: 206-626 5208
www.graylineseattle.com/sightseeing tours.cfm
Two-hour cruises by Downtown waterfront, Elliott Bay, the Lake Washington Ship Canal and Lake Union via the Chittenden Locks.
Ride The Ducks of Seattle
Tel: 206-441-DUCK or 1-800-817 1116
www.ridetheducksofseattle.com
Tours aboard refurbished amphibious World War II vehicles go driving on the roads through Seattle before plunging with a splash into Lake Union.

Call for reservations.
www.whalewatching.com
Anacortes by Orca Search
Tel: 206-386 4320.
www.seattleaquarium.org
Affiliated with Seattle Aquarium, requires advance reservations.
San Juan Boat Rentals
Tel: 360-378 3499.
www.gonorthwest.com/washington/
Offers 3-hour tours out of Friday Harbor. Office is one block from the ferry dock, which makes it convenient for those who don't want to bring their car on the ferry.

Chartering Boats

From rowboats and kayaks to fully crewed yachts, charters are available to suit all needs.
Northwest Outdoor Center
2100 Westlake Avenue N., Lake Union
Tel: 206-281 9694.
www.nwoc.com
Offers sightseeing tours of Lake Union houseboats, sunset tours, and San Juan Island cruises. Kayak and canoe rentals available on Lake Union. Open all year.
Emerald City Charters (Lets Go Sailing)
Pier 54
Tel: 206-624 3931
www.sailingseattle.com
Runs tours in view of downtown Seattle on Elliott Bay aboard a 70-ft (21-meter) racing sloop. Sailing tours are scheduled May through October. A 2½-hour sunset trip sails daily and 1½-hour day sails.
Wind Works Sailing Center
Shilshole Bay Marina
Tel: 206-784 9386
www.windworksailing.com
Full fleet of sailboats; lessons and skippers available.

Plane Tours

Seattle Seaplanes
1325 Fairview Avenue E
Tel: 206-329 9638 or 1-800-637 5553
www.seattleseaplanes.com

Offers extensive tours of the Seattle area or destinations such as Mount Rainier, and charters to fishing camps in Canada.
Boeing Field/King County International Airport
Tel: 206-296 7380
www.metrokc.gov/airport
Call or log on for information on companies that operate at this airport.
Northwest Seaplanes
860 W. Perimeter Road, Renton
Tel: 1-800-690 0086
www.nwseaplanes.com
Scheduled and charter flights from Lake Washington and Lake Union to the San Juan Islands and BC.
Sound Flight
Renton Municipal Airport
300 Airport Way, Renton
Tel: 425-254 8063
www.soundflight.net
Floatplane tours of Seattle, the mountains, or the San Juan Islands.
Helicopters Northwest
8500 Perimeter Road, S., at Boeing Field
Tel: 206-767 0508
www.helicoptersnw.com
An on-call, round-the-clock charter service with flights throughout the US and Canada. Also offers sightseeing tours.
Kenmore Air
6321 NE. 175th Street
Tel: 425-486 1257 or 1-800-543 9595
www.kenmoreair.com
Daily flights to British Columbia, Kitsap Peninsula, San Juan and Whidbey islands and the resort inn at Semiahmoo. Also offers day excursions and overnight packages. Great scenic tours of Seattle.
Peninsula Airways
Tel: 1-800-448 4226
www.penair.com
Daily flights and charters from Seattle to Alaska.
Wings Aloft Charter Service
8467 Perimeter Road S., Boeing Field
Tel: 206-763 2113;
www.wingsaloft.com
Daily flights and charters.

A–Z

A SUMMARY OF PRACTICAL INFORMATION, ARRANGED ALPHABETICALLY

A dmission Charges

Fees to attractions can range from less than $10 to nearly $35. We've indicated whether you'll have to pay or not in the information on each attraction. On Thursdays, participating art galleries around Downtown and Pioneer Square are free. Most festivals at the Seattle Center are free, except for Bumbershoot, which charges a hefty admission price (more for the Platinum and Gold passes). Downtown is also a free zone when traveling by bus.

B udgeting for your Trip

Your budget will depend on your plans, so research your trip in advance and look for internet discounts for hotels and attractions.

Keep in mind the 2 percent car-rental tax, the 8.8 percent sales tax to all purchases and the additional half percent restaurant tax on top of the sales tax. Also expect to add a 15 to 20 percent tip on the total when dining out.

Business Hours

Most businesses in central and greater Seattle are generally open from 9am–5pm Monday–Friday and closed on Saturday, Sunday and public holidays.

Banks are usually open from 9am–6pm Monday–Friday, with many in the center opening on Saturday mornings. Most banks, government agencies such as the post office, and some other businesses close on public holidays (see page 237).

C hildren's Activities

The **Seattle Center** (see page 103) is a wonderland for children. A day or two here is well-spent. The Pacific Science Center, a hands-on museum with displays that children can manipulate to learn scientific principles, offers planetarium

AMUSEMENT PARKS

Designed for the children in all of us is Enchanted Park in Federal Way, approximately 17 miles (27 km) south of Seattle. The Wild Waves part of the park contains heated pools, including one that makes waves, and many water slides and pools for small children. The Enchanted Village has a farm, numerous cafés, a merry-go-round, ferris wheel, boat rides, train rides and more. The store inside Wild Waves sells bathing suits and any other equipment (rafts, towels, T-shirts) you may need.

**Wild Waves and
Enchanted Village**
36201 Enchanted Parkway South, Federal Way, WA 98003. (Exit 142B off I-5.)
Tel: 253-661 8000
www.sixflags.com
Open 11am–8pm last week in June–first weekend in Sept; 10am–6pm last weekend in May–third week in June, Sat–Sun, Apr, early May and Sept after Labor Day weekend.

shows, laser-light shows and nature/adventure films in the dramatic IMAX theater. At the Center House, with its fast food cafés and tourist shops, is the **Children's Museum**.

Outside, the Fun Forest offers amusement park rides, arcade games and miniature golf. The elevator up to the Space Needle is a treat, as is the view if it's not cloudy. From Center House, take a ride on the Monorail to the heart of Downtown's retail stores. Children will also enjoy the **Experience Music Project**.

Springbrook Trout Farm, 19225 Talbot Road S., Renton (tel: 253-852 0360; call for hours), is a place where anyone can catch a fish. The farm provides rods and bait and also cleans and wraps the fish for guests to take home and cook. The price depends on the size of your catch.

The **Museum of Flight**, located in Boeing airfield approximately 10 miles (16 km) south of Seattle, is one the kids won't want to miss. The central room, called the Gallery, contains 20 airplanes including an early 1900 Wright Brothers' model, fighter jets and ultra-light gliders hanging from the glass ceiling *(see page 167)*.

The **Puget Sound and Snoqualmie Valley Railroad** provides a living history adventure. The late-1800-vintage steam trains travel between North Bend and Snoqualmie for a half-hour trip through forests, farmlands and over streams. Trains run on weekends Apr–Oct; www.trainmuseum.org.

While in Snoqualmie, 30 miles (48 km) east of Seattle, a trip to **Snoqualmie Falls** *(see page 204)* is recommended. Children can explore the trails that surround the 268-ft (82-meter) falls and visit the gift shops and the visitors' center. The **Salish Lodge** next to the top of the falls has a restaurant with a deck overlooking the falls and splendid accommodation for those who wish to stay overnight.

Climate

The temperature in western Washington (west of the Cascade Mountains) is usually mild. Daytime temperatures range from 75–79°F (23–26°C) in summer and 41–48°F (4.5–9°C) in winter.

From October through April, Seattle gets 80 percent of its annual quota of rain. In summer, Seattle is frequently covered by some form of marine mist or fog in the morning that dissipates by the afternoon. Seattleites on average only receive the sun's light and warmth uninterrupted for the whole day about 55 times a year.

Snow tends to stay in the mountains, which keeps skiers and almost everyone else happy, but because of quirky weather patterns you can sometimes find yourself in a hail shower on one side of town while the other side experiences clear skies and a rainbow.

Crime & Safety

The streets of Seattle and most adjoining neighborhoods and islands are relatively safe during the day. However, as with most large cities, at night caution is advised. It is best not to walk alone at night on deserted city streets. Lock your car and never leave luggage, cameras or other valuables in view.

Never leave money, valuables or jewelry in your hotel room, even for a short time. Instead, take advantage of the hotel's safety deposit service. Carry only the cash you need, using traveler's checks whenever possible.

D isabled Travelers

Disabled travelers can obtain information about discounts, transportation, assistive technology, community resources and more from the city's Human Services website (www.seattle.gov/humanservices/aging/disability.htm) or by calling 206-386 1001.

E lectricity

The United States uses 110 volts. Electrical adaptors are readily available in stores.

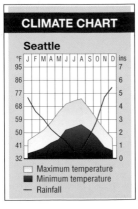

CLIMATE CHART

Seattle

	Maximum temperature
■	Minimum temperature
—	Rainfall

Embassies/Consulates

The following embassies are located in downtown Seattle. For information on other countries, contact your embassy or consulate before leaving home:

UK
UK Trade and Investment
900 4th Ave, Suite 3001
Seattle, WA 98164
Tel: 206-622 9255

Canada
1501 4th Ave, Suite 600
Seattle, WA 98101-1286
Tel: 206-443 1777

Mexico
2132 3rd Avenue Seattle
WA 98121
Tel: 206-448 3526

ABOVE: celebrating Mardi Gras.

Entry Regulations

Visas and Passports

To enter the US you must have a valid passport. Visas are required by some foreigners, and should be obtained prior to entering the country. From 2007, any Canadian or US visitor traveling to each other's countries (even for the day) will need a valid passport. Amtrak also require a valid passport if making the journey by train. Negotiations are taking place to provide travelers on a cruise that docks between the two countries with a special document; the same would be given to anyone with a sailboat or who lives near the border.

For more information, go to http://travel.state.gov/

Customs

An individual over the age of 21 is allowed to bring one bottle of liquor free of tax and 200 cigarettes duty free into the USA.

All gifts must be declared. There is a $200 exemption for visitors including US residents. For gifts worth $400–$1,000, visitors pay a 10 percent charge. Gifts worth upwards of $1,000 are charged a "duty right" tax variable by item.

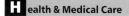

Gay & Lesbian Travelers

Capitol Hill Travel
410 Broadway East 110, Seattle, WA 98102
Tel: 206-726 8996
www.capitolhilltravel.com
Vacation planning for gay and lesbian travelers.

Seattle LGBT Community Center
1115 East Pike Street, Seattle, WA 98122
Tel: 206-323-LGBT (5428)
www.seattlelgbt.org
Open Mon–Sat 10am–9pm, Sun 11am–8pm.

Health & Medical Care

Innoculations and Documentation

Vaccinations are not required for entry unless the visitor is from, or has passed through, an infected area. In this case, a health record may be necessary. Other documents that are invaluable are a driver's license and any type of health or travel insurance card. If you intend to do any driving, obtain an International Driving Permit. It's a useful accessory to your own country's driving document, which may be viewed by local authorities as less than real.

Medical Services

The medical care in Seattle is excellent, but it is prohibitively expensive if a long hospital stay is required.

To avoid unwelcome bills, you should ensure that you have adequate health insurance before traveling to the US. Check with your current insurance provider that you are covered.

Most hospitals have a 24-hour emergency room service. Here are some major hospitals in the Seattle area that can provide emergency care:

In Seattle
Children's Hospital and Medical Center
4800 Sand Point Way, NE.
Tel: 206-987 2000
Harborview Medical Center
325 9th Avenue (corner of Jefferson Street)
Tel: 206-731 3000
Swedish Medical Center
747 Broadway
Tel: 206-386 6000
Swedish Medical Center, Ballard
5300 Tallman Ave NW
Tel: 206-782 2700
Swedish Medical Center, Providence Campus
500 17th Avenue
Tel: 206-320 2000

**University of Washington
Medical Center**
1959 NE Pacific Street
Tel: 206-598 3300
Virginia Mason Hospital
925 Seneca Street
Tel: 206-624 1144

**In Bellevue
Overlake Hospital Medical
Center**
1035 116th Ave NE, Bellevue
Tel: 425-688 5000

**In Kirkland
Evergreen Hospital Medical
Center**
12040 NE 128th Street, Kirkland
Tel: 425-899 1000

**Referrals
King County Medical Society**
Tel: 206-621 9393 (physician
referral).
**Seattle-King County Dental
Society**
Tel: 206-443 7607 (dentist
referral).

Pharmacies

Certain drugs can only be pre-
scribed by a doctor and purchased at a pharmacy. Bring any
regular medication with you and
check the *Yellow Pages* under
"Pharmacies" for listings.

I nternet & Websites

Wi-Fi (wireless internet facility) is
available in Columbia City, the
University District and several
Downtown-area parks. Select
Community Transit and Metro
buses also have Wi-Fi, as do many
of the ferries that ply back and
forth across Puget Sound. E-mail
can be sent from most branches
of FedEx/Kinko's copy shops, as
well as coffee shops around town.
For a small fee, one-hour internet
access is available at all branches
of Seattle Public Library.
    There are also several internet
cafés, including:
Aurafice Internet & Coffee Bar,
616 E Pine Street, www.aurafice.com
Cyber-Dogs, 909 Pike Street,
www.cyber-dogs.com

ABOVE: surfing in the Central Library.

Online Coffee Company, 1720 E.
Olive Way, www.onlinecoffeeco.com
Uncle Elizabeth's Internet Café,
1123 Pike Street.

L ost Property

If valuables are lost or stolen,
report them to the local police
department. A description of
the items will be filed, and if the
items turn up the police will
return them as soon as possible.

Lost luggage

Most airlines and other transportation companies have insurance
for lost customer luggage, but it
doesn't hurt to ask the company
what its policy is. Be sure to
mark all luggage with identification tags. If luggage left at the airport is turned in to Sea-Tac's lost
and found *(see page 209)*, someone from that department will
usually bring the luggage to your
hotel if returning to the airport is
inconvenient.

M edia

Print

The major daily newspapers in
Seattle are the *Seattle Post-
Intelligencer* and *The Seattle
Times*. On Sunday, the two com-
bine into one large edition. Friday tabloid sections in both
papers are useful guides to
weekend events. *Seattle*

Weekly, a tabloid news-
magazine, and *The Stranger*
both print guides to the week's
recreation and entertainment,
including visual arts, theater,
music and film. Also included is
dining and shopping information. *Puget Sound Business
Journal* is a weekly newspaper
that covers business activities
in the Puget Sound area.
    Foreign language newspapers
include the *North American Post*,
a Japanese daily, the *Northwest
Asian Weekly*, and *Hispanic News*
(weekly).
    Public libraries offer reading
rooms stacked with periodicals
and, often, a good selection of
foreign newspapers and magazines. Libraries also tend to have
terminals and internet access.
    Newsstands that sell foreign
publications include:
Bulldog News
4208 University Way NE.
and 401 Broadway Avenue
Tel: 206-632 6397
J & S News
204 Broadway E.
Tel: 206-324-READ
**Read All About It International
Newsstand**
93 Pike Street (in Pike Place
Market)
Tel: 206-624 0140

Television & Radio

Excluding cable television, seven
major stations serve the Seattle
area. The public broadcast
station is KCTS. It does not air
commercials, but supports itself
through public donations and
grants.
    There are numerous radio
stations in the city to cater to all
tastes *(see opposite)*.

Money

Traveler's Checks

American dollar traveler's checks
are the safest form of currency. If
lost or stolen, most can be
replaced. In addition, they are as
acceptable as cash in many
stores, restaurants and hotels.

Banks will generally cash large amounts of traveler's checks. Always keep a record of the check numbers separate from the checks themselves. Remember to take your passport with you in case you are asked to produce it as identification.

To report stolen or lost traveler's checks call:
American Express
Tel: 1-800-221 7282
MasterCard
Tel: 1-800-223 9920
Thomas Cook Mastercard
Tel: 1-800-223 7373
Visa
Tel: 1-800-227 6811

Currency & Credit Cards

Foreign currency exchange is available at Sea-Tac (see page 208), major Seattle banks and at some major downtown hotels. Daily newspapers print exchange rates for most major currencies.

Having a credit card can be valuable for emergencies and transactions such as renting a car. Visa and MasterCard are widely accepted throughout the United States. In case of a lost or stolen card, use their toll-free numbers to report the incident immediately:
Visa Tel: 1-800-336 8472
MasterCard Tel: 1-800-826 2181.

P ostal Services

The main post office in Seattle is located at 301 Union. Tel: 206-748 5417. Open Monday–Friday 7:30am–5:30pm. Travelers uncertain of their address in a particular town may have mail addressed in their name, sent care of General Delivery at the main post office of that town. Mail will be held there for you to pick up (be sure to bring current identification).

Be sure to include a five-digit zip code for all addresses within the US. Information about zip codes may be obtained from any post office. Overnight delivery service and Express Mail is also provided by the post office and some private companies. Check in the Yellow Pages under "Delivery Service."

Stamps may also be purchased from vending machines which can often be found in hotels, stores, airports, and bus and train stations.

Public Holidays

New Year's Day January 1
Martin Luther King's Birthday 3rd Monday in January
President's Day 3rd Monday in February
Memorial Day last Monday in May
Independence Day July 4
Labor Day 1st Monday in September
Columbus Day 2nd Monday in October
Veteran's Day November 11
Thanksgiving 4th Thursday in November
Christmas December 25
(See page 222 for a calender of festivals and events.)

R eligious Services

For referrals of religious services by denomination, contact:
The Church Council of Greater Seattle
4 Nickerson, Suite 300
Tel: 206-525 1213
www.churchcouncil.org

SEATTLE TELEVISION & RADIO CHANNELS

Television:
4 KOMO	ABC affiliate
5 KING	NBC affiliate
7 KIRO	CBS affiliate
9 KCTS	PBS
11 CW11	independent
13 KCPQ	Fox
22 KTWB	independent

Radio – AM stations:
570 KVI	Talk
630 KCIS	Christian
710 KIRO	News/sports/talk
770 KTTH	Talk
820 KGNW	Christian
880 KIXI	Nostalgic pop hits
950 KJR	Sports/talk
1000 KOMO	News
1050 KBLE	Religious
1090 KPTK	Liberal talk
1150 KKNW	CNN News
1210 KNWX	Business/investing

1250 KKDZ	Radio Disney
1300 KOL	Talk
1330 KENU	Electronic dance
1360 KKMO	Spanish
1380 KRKO	News/talk – Everett
1420 KRIZ	Classic soul/R&B
1540 KXPA	Spanish
1560 KZIZ	Gospel
1590 KLFE	Christian
1620 KYIZ	Urban contemporary
1680 KTFH	International programming

Radio – FM stations:
88.5 KPLU	Jazz/news/NPR
89.5 KNHC	Top 40/dance
89.9 KGRG	Alternative rock
90.3 KEXP	Alt/world music
90.7 KSER	Public affairs/world music
91.3 KBCS	Jazz/folk/world music

92.5 KQMV	'70s, '80s, '90s pop hits
93.3 KUBE	Rhythmic Top 40
94.1 KMPS	Country
94.9 KUOW	News/NPR
95.7 KJR	'60s/'70s hits
96.5 KJAQ	'80s popular music
97.3 KBSG	Oldies
98.1 KING	Classical
98.9 KWJZ	Smooth jazz
99.9 KISW	Rock
100.7 KKWF	Country
101.5 KPLZ	Today's
102.5 KZOK	Classic rock
103.7 KMTT	Adult alternative
104.5 KMIH	Contemporary hits
105.3 KCMS	Christian
106.1 KISS	Pop rock
106.5 KWPZ	Contemporary praise music
106.9 KRWM	Soft rock
107.7 KNDD	Modern rock

Smoking

There is currently a no-smoking law in effect in practically all Seattle bars, restaurants and offices. Smokers must be at least 25 ft (7.6 meters) away from doors, windows and vents when smoking. Be sure to request a smoking room when booking a place to stay.

Telephones

For long distance calls within the **206**, **425** and **253** area codes, the ten-digit phone number must be preceded by a "1."

For long-distance calls outside the above local area codes, first dial a "1", then the area code and then the phone number.

For assistance in long distance dialing, first dial zero and an operator will assist you. Phone numbers that are preceded by 1-800, 1-866, 1-877 and 1-888 are free of charge only when dialed from within the US.

Public libraries have terminals for web-based pick-up, and a few coffee shops also have terminals. For more information on internet and email facilities, *see page 236*. If all else fails, find a Kinko's copyshop. Large Kinko's stay open late, have both Macs and PCs, and facilities for printing.

Telegraph and Fax

Telegraph services are available through Western Union. Tel: 1-800-325 6000.

Fax machines can be found at most hotels and at the airport and are located throughout the city. See the *Yellow Pages* under "facsimile" for information.

Time Zones

Seattle is within the Pacific Standard Time Zone (the same as California), which is two hours behind Chicago and three hours behind New York City. From 2007, Daylight Saving Time was extended by several weeks and for most of the United States

begins at 2am on the second Sunday of March and ends at 2am on the first Sunday of November.

On Pacific Standard Time, when it is **noon in Seattle** it is:

• 3pm in New York and Montreal
• 8pm in London
• 4am (the next day) in Singapore and Hong Kong
• 5am in Tokyo; and
• 6am in Sydney

Tipping

Tips are intended to show appreciation for good service and should reflect the quality of service rendered. The accepted rate is 15–20 percent of the bill in restaurants for waiting staff (10 percent for barstaff), 10–15 percent for taxi drivers and hairstylists. Porters and bellhops generally warrant 50 cents to $1 per bag; valets $1 to $2.

Tourist Information

A wealth of information on attractions, activities, accommodations and restaurants is available from the **Seattle Convention and Visitors Bureau** in the Washington State Convention Center at One Convention Place, 701 Pike Street, Suite 800, Galleria Level. Tel: 206-461 5840. Open Monday–Friday 8:30am–5pm, in summer daily 9am–5pm.

The bureau also operates an **information center** at **Sea-Tac Airport**, located on the baggage level. Tel: 206-431 5906. Open daily 7am–2am.

Useful Numbers

Emergency Services

For police, fire or medical emergencies, dial **911**.

AAA of Washington
Tel: 206-448 5353
Bainbridge Island Information
Tel: 206 842 3700

Coast Guard Emergencies
Tel: 206-217 6000
Crisis Clinic
Tel: 206-461 3222
FBI
Tel: 206-622 0460
Hostelling International of Seattle
Tel: 206-622 5443
Mountain Road Conditions
Tel: 1-800-695-ROAD
Seattle's Convention and Visitors Bureau
Tel: 206-461 5840
Seattle Post-Intelligencer
Tel: 206-448 8000
The Seattle Times
Tel: 206-464 2121
Transitional Assistance
(formally Travelers Aid)
Tel: 206-315 2996
Weather
Tel: 206-526 6087

WEIGHTS & MEASURES

The US uses the imperial system of weights and measures.
1 inch	= 2.54 centimeters
1 foot	= 0.3048 meter
1 mile	= 1.609 kilometers
1 quart	= 0.9464 liter
1 ounce	= 28.3 grams
1 pound	= 453.5 grams
1 yard	= 0.9144 meter

WHAT TO READ

General

The Battle in Seattle: The Story Behind and Beyond the WTO Demonstrations by Janet Thomas. Fulcrum Publishing (2000).

Inside the Pike Place Market: Exploring America's Favorite Farmer's Market by Braiden Rex-Johnson, Paul Souders (photographer). Sasquatch Books (1999).

King: The Bullitts of Seattle and Their Communications Empire by O. Casey Corr. University of Washington Press (1996).

Native Peoples of the Northwest: A Traveler's Guide to Land, Art and Culture by Jan Halliday. Sasquatch Books (2000).

North Bank Road: The Spokane, Portland and Seattle Railway by John T. Gaertner. Washington State University Press (1991).

1001 Curious Things: Ye Olde Curiosity Shop and Native American Art by Kate C. Duncan. University of Washington Press (2001).

Redhook: Beer Pioneer by Peter J. Krebs. Four Walls Eight Windows (1999).

Red Man's America: A History of Indians in the United States by Ruth Murray Underhill. University of Chicago Press (1971).

Roadside Geology of Washington by David D. Alt and Donald W. Hyndman. Missoula, Montana: Hyndman Mountain Press Publishing Company (1984).

Seattle Cityscape by Victor Steinbrueck. University of Washington Press (1973).

Sexless Oysters and Self-tipping Hats: 100 Years of Invention in the Pacific Northwest by Adam Woog. Seattle: Sasquatch Books (1991).

Skid Road: An Informal Portrait of Seattle by Murray Morgan. University of Washington Press (2002).

Washington State Place Names by James W. Philips. University of Washington Press (1976).

Wet and Wired: A Pop Culture Encyclopedia of the Pacific Northwest by Randy Hodges and Steve McLellan. Taylor Publications (2000).

History

The American Fur Trade of the Far West by Hiram M. Chittenden. University of Nebraska Press (2006).

American Workers, Colonial Power: Philippine Seattle and the Transpacific West, 1919–41 by Dorothy B. Fujita Rony. University of California Press (2002).

Boeing: In Peace and War by Eugene E. Bauer. Taba Publishing (1991).

BEST BOOKS TO READ

Ten Little Indians by Sherman Alexie. Grove Press (2003).

Waxwings by Jonathan Raban. Pantheon Books (2003).

Half Asleep in Frog Pajamas by Tom Robbins. Bantam Books 1994).

The Body of David Hayes by Ridley Pearson. Hyperion (2004).

Broken for You by Stephanie Kallos. Grove Press (2004).

Longtime Gone by J.A. Jance. William Morrow (2005).

Hannah West in the Belltown Towers by Linda Johns. Sleuth Puffin (2006).

Seattle and the Demons of Ambition by Fred Moody. St Martin's Griffin (2003).

Boeing Trivia by Carl M. Cleveland. Seattle: CMC Books (1989).

Columbia by Stewart Holbrook. Columbia Textbook Publishers (2003).

Eccentric Seattle: Pillars and Pariahs Who Made the City Not Such a Boring Place After All by J. Kingston Pierce. Washington State University Press (2003).

Exploring Washington's Past: A Road Guide to History by Ruth Kirk and Carmela Alexander. University of Washington Press (1995).

Ivar: The Life and Times of Ivar Haglund by Dave Stephens. Seattle: Dunhill Publishing (1988).

Native Visions: Evolution in Northwest Coast Art from the 18th Through the 20th Century by Steven C. Brown, Seattle Art Museum. University of Washington Press (2003).

Puget's Sound: A Narrative of Early Tacoma and the Southern Sound by Murray Morgan. Seattle and London: University of Washington Press (2003).

Rites of Passage: A Memoir of the Sixties in Seattle by Walt Crowley, William Crowley. University of Washington Press (1997).

Seattle: Past to Present by Roger Sale. Seattle and London: University of Washington Press (2003).

Shaping Seattle Architecture: A Historical Guide to the Architects by Jeffrey Karl Ochsner, editor. University of Washington Press/American Institute of Architects (2003).

Washington: A Bicentennial History by Norman H. Clark. W.W. Norton (1976).

The Wisdom of the Native Americans: edited by Kent Nerburn. New World Library (1999).

Women & Men on the Overland Trail by John Mark Faragher. Yale University Press (2001).
Women in Pacific Northwest History (Revised Edition) by Karen J. Blair, editor. University of Washington Press (2001).

Nature

The Great Northwest Nature Factbook: A Guide to the Region's Remarkable Animals, Plants & Natural Features by Ann Saling. WestWinds Press (1999).
Hiking the North Cascades by Fred T. Darvill. Stackpole Books (1998).
Nature Walks in and around Seattle: All-Season Exploring in Parks, Forests and Wetlands by Cathy M. McDonald and Stephen R. Whitney. Mountaineers Books (1997).
The Northwest GreenBook: A Regional Guide to Protecting and Preserving Our Environment by Jonathan King. Seattle: Sasquatch Books (1991).
Of Men and Mountains: The Classic Memoir of Wilderness Adventure by William O. Douglas. The Lyons Press (2001).
Pacific Salmon and Steelhead Trout by R.J. Childerhose. Seattle: University of Washington Press (1981).

Trees of Seattle by Arthur Lee Jacobson. Arthur Lee Jacobson (2006).

Other Insight Guides

Other Insight Guides, Pocket Guides and Fleximaps which highlight destinations in this region include:

Insight Guide: Pacific Northwest. Assembled by a team of over 30 local writers and photographers, this volume is bold, beautiful and packed with information.

Insight Pocket Guide: Seattle. A local resident leads the reader through the sites and sounds of Seattle.

Insight Fleximap: Seattle and *Insight Fleximap: Vancouver* are easy to use, contain lots of information and have a laminated, wipe-clean finish.

Insight CityGuide: Vancouver is an in-depth look at the city and the region, written by experts and photographed by a local.

FEEDBACK

We do our best to ensure the information in our books is as accurate and up-to-date as possible. The books are updated on a regular basis, using local contacts, who painstakingly add, amend and correct as required. However, some mistakes and omissions are inevitable and we are ultimately reliant on our readers to put us in the picture.

We would welcome your feedback on any details related to your experiences using the book "on the road". Maybe we recommended a hotel that you liked (or another that you didn't), or you have found an interesting new attraction, or some facts and figures we didn't mention. The more details you can give us (particularly with regard to addresses, e-mails and tele-

phone numbers), the better. We will acknowledge all contributions, and we'll offer an Insight Guide to the best letters received.

Please write to us at:
Insight Guides
PO Box 7910
London SE1 1WE
United Kingdom
Or send e-mail to:
insight@apaguide.co.uk

SEATTLE STREET ATLAS

The key map shows the area of Seattle covered by the atlas section. An index of street names and places of interest shown on the maps can be found on the following pages. For each entry there is a page number and grid reference.

Map Legend

Freeway with Junction		Airport		Bus Station	
Freeway (under construction)		Church (ruins)		Tourist Information	
Divided Highway		Monastery	Freeway	Post Office	
Main Road		Castle (ruins)	Divided Highway	Cathedral/Church	
Secondary Road		Archeological Site	Main Roads	Mosque	
Minor Road		Cave	Minor Roads	Synagogue	
Track		Place of Interest	Footpath	Statue/Monument	
International Boundary		Mansion/Stately Home	Railway	Tower	
Province/State Boundary		Viewpoint	Pedestrian Area		
National Park/Reserve			Important Building		

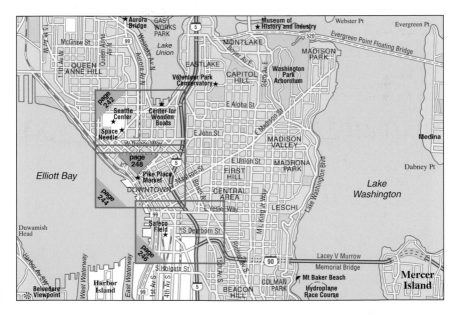

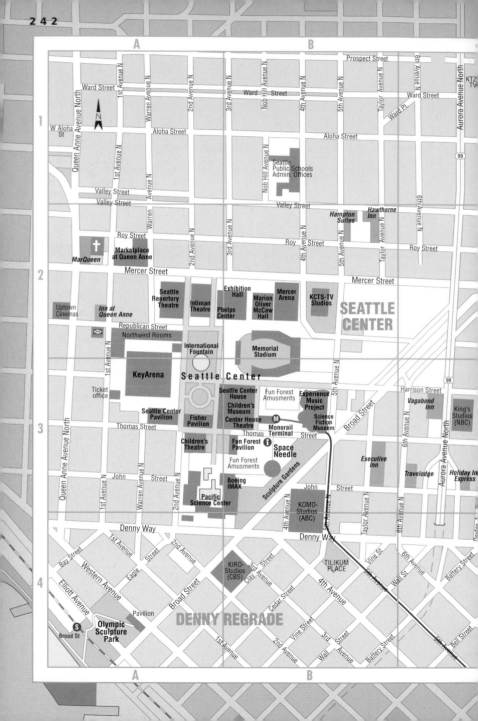

Lake Union

Yale Street
Landing

Silver
Cloud Inn

Prospect St

Fred Hutchinson
Cancer
Research
Center

Chandler's
Cove

SOUTH LAKE
UNION PARK

Aloha Street

Valley St

Maritime
Heritage Center,
Center for
Wooden Boats

Courtyard
by Marriott

Marriott
Residence
Inn

Roy Street

Valley Street

Shurgard
Building

Broad Street

Roy Street

Mercer Street

Mercer Street

Republican Street

Republican Street

CASCADE

Harrison Street

Harrison Street

CASCADE
PLAYGROUND

Thomas Street

Thomas Street

Seattle Times
Building

REI

John Street

John Street

DENNY
PARK

DENNY
PLAYFIELD

Denny Way

Denny Way

Denny Way

Loyal
Inn

Eighth
Avenue
Inn

Travelodge
Downtown

Stewart Street

Lenora St

Days Inn
Town Center

Lenora St

Library

Police Dept.
West Precinct

King Cat
Theatre

Virginia

0   300 yards

0   300 m

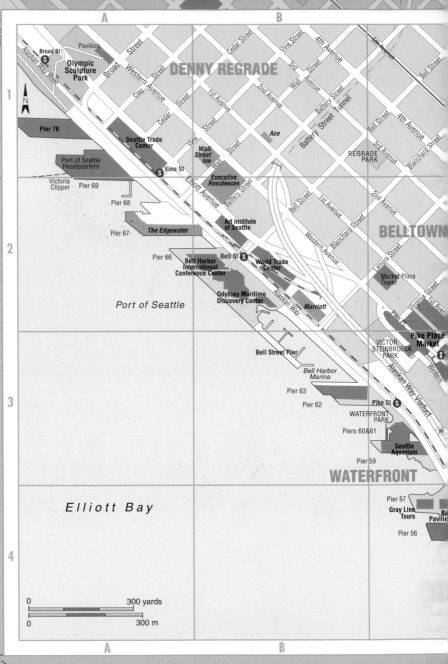

A

B

1

N

Broad St

Alaskan Way West

Pavilion

Olympic
Sculpture
Park

Broad Street

Western Avenue

Clay Street

Cedar Street

Cedar Street

Vine Street

Wall Avenue

Battery Street

Battery Street Tunnel

Bell Street

4th Avenue

5th Avenue

Vine Street

3rd Street

2nd Avenue

DENNY REGRADE

Ace

Bell Street

3rd Avenue

4th Avenue

Blanchard Street

**REGRADE
PARK**

Pier 70

Seattle Trade
Center

Port of Seattle
Headquarters

Victoria
Clipper

Pier 69

Vine St

Pier 68

Elliott Avenue

Wall
Street
Inn

Wall Street

Executive
Residences

Battery Street

1st Avenue

Bell Street

Blanchard Street

2nd Avenue

BELLTOWN

Pier 67

The Edgewater

Art Institute
of Seattle

Western Avenue

Lenora Street

2

Pier 66

Bell Harbor
International
Conference Center

Bell St

World Trade
Center

Market Place
Tower

Virginia Street

1st Avenue

Port of Seattle

Odyssey Maritime
Discovery Center

Alaskan Way

Marriott

Pike Pl

**Pike Place
Market**

VICTOR
STEINBRUECK
PARK

Bell Street Pier

Alaskan Way Viaduct

Western

Bell Harbor
Marina

Pier 63

Pier 62

3

Pike St

WATERFRONT
PARK

Piers 60&61

99

Pier 59

Seattle
Aquarium

WATERFRONT

Elliott Bay

Pier 57

Gray Line
Tours

Bay
Pavilion

Pier 56

4

0 ———————— 300 yards

0 ———————— 300 m

A

B

A · B

1

Pier 54
Madison St
Ye Olde
Curiosity Shop
Pier 53
Pier 52
Washington
State Ferries
Pier 51

Waterfront
Place
Maritime
Building
Federal Office
Building

Alaskan Way Viaduct

99

Elliott Bay

Norton
Building
2nd Ave

FINANCIAL
DISTRICT

Marion Street

Western Ave

Post Avenue

1st Avenue

Columbia

3rd Avenue

4th Avenue

5th Avenue

Columbia
Center

Arctic
Building

Cherry Street

Public
Safety
Building

City
Hall

James Street

King County
Jail

King County
Admin

Jefferson Street

Underground
Tour

Pioneer
Building

Pioneer
Square

King County
Courthouse

PIONEER
PARK PLACE

James Street

Smith
Tower

CITY HALL
PARK

Yesler
Building

Yesler Way

Merchant's
Cafe

Best Western
Pioneer Square

PIONEER SQUARE

Prefontaine Pl

Prefontaine
Building

Washington St

Pier 50

S Washington Street

S Washington Street

2
Pier 49

Pier 48

Princess
Marguerite III

Grand
Central
Arcade

Merrill
Place

Klondike
Gold Rush
National
Historic Park

38 King
Street

OCCIDENTAL
PARK

Occidental
Park

Globe
Building

WATERFALL
GARDEN

S Main Street

Fire
Station

S Jackson Street

Police
Museum

Court
in the
Square

S King Street

Occidental Avenue S

1st Avenue S

2nd Avenue

Jackson St
Station

Internation
District

International
District Stati
Metro Transi

AMTRAK
King Street
Station

4th Avenue South

5th Avenue S

Pier 47

Pier 46

Pier 44

Alaskan Way Viaduct

Railroad Way S

519

3

Seattle Port

Alaskan Way South

S Dearborn Street

1st Avenue South

Occidental Avenue S

Qwest Field
Stadium

Airport Way Su

US Immigratio
& Naturalizatic
Service (INS)

Salvation
Army

3rd Avenue S

4th Avenue South

5th Avenue S

90

4

Marginal Way South

Alaskan Way Viaduct

99

Qwest Field
Event Center

South Royal Brougham Way

Safeco Field

1st Avenue South

519

3rd Avenue S

4th Avenue South

S Atlantic Street

0 _____ 300 yards
0 _____ 300 m

N

A · B

STREET INDEX

ART & PHOTO CREDITS

Bruce Bernstein Collection/
Courtesy of the Princeton
University Library 25
Bodo Bondzio 165
britishcolumbiaphotos.com/
Alamy 194
Barry Broman 202L
Jerry Dennis 79T, 81, 81T, 97,
98T, 114T, 115T, 126, 129,
129T, 130, 136T, 137T, 170,
174, 174T, 182T, 185T, 188L,
188R, 188T, 189L, 189R, 200,
205T, 210, 215, 229, 230
Natalie B. Fobes 12/13
Lee Foster 153T
Dennis Frates 186, 190, 191
Historical Society of Seattle and
King County/Museum of History
and Industry 23, 27, 29
Image Works/Topham 32L
Catherine Karnow 1, 2/3, 3BR,
4T, 4C, 5T, 5B, 6CL, 6CR, 6B,
7CL, 7R, 8TR, 8CL, 8BR, 9TR,
9CL, 10/11, 14, 15, 16L, 16R,
17, 18L, 18R, 19, 20, 21, 28,
30, 32R, 33, 35, 36/37, 38/39,
40, 41, 43, 44, 45, 46, 47, 48L,
48R, 49L, 49R, 50, 51, 54, 55,
56, 57, 58, 59, 60, 64/65,
66/67, 68, 72, 73, 74T, 75,
75T, 76, 76T, 77, 78, 79, 80,
82L, 82R, 83, 83T, 84, 85, 88,
89, 91L, 91R, 91T, 92, 93, 93T,
94, 95, 95T, 96, 96T, 98R, 99,
100, 101, 102, 103, 104T,
104/105, 105T, 106, 107,

107T, 108, 108T, 109, 112,
113, 115, 116, 116T, 117, 118,
118T, 119, 120, 121, 122, 123,
124T, 125, 125T, 126T, 127L,
127R, 128L, 128R, 130T, 131,
132, 132T, 133, 134, 135, 138,
138T, 139, 140, 140T, 141T,
142/143, 146, 147, 148, 149T,
150, 151, 151T, 152, 153L,
153R, 154, 155, 155T, 156,
156T, 157, 161, 162, 162T,
164, 164T, 166, 167, 168, 169,
169T, 170T, 171, 172, 172T,
173T, 181, 182, 184T, 191T,
192T, 195, 196, 197, 197T,
199T, 201T, 202R, 209, 214,
216, 220, 222, 224, 227, 231,
233, 235, 236, 238
Kirkendall-Spring Photographers
204
Joel W. Rogers 31
Seattle Art Museum/Paul
Macapia 34
Michael T. Sedam/Corbis 175
Charles Shugart 199
Smithsonian Institution, National
Anthropological Archives 21
Tim Thompson 61, 62, 160, 163,
173, 176/177, 180, 183, 184R,
185, 187, 192, 193, 198, 201,
203, 202T, 205
Courtesy of Underground Tours
24
Jamie Wakefield 63, 137, 149
R.F. Zallinger/Museum of History
and Industry 26

Pages 52/53: Natalie B. Fobes
52/53, 52CR, 52BR, 53CL; Peter
Newark's American Pictures 52TL,
52BL, 53TR, 53CR, 53BC
Pages 86/87: all images
Catherine Karnow
Pages 110/111: Mick Hutson/
Redferns Music Picture Library
111TR; Catherine Karnow
110/111, 110BR, 111CL, 111BL,
111BR; Marc Sharrat/Rex
Features 110BL
Pages 158/159: Daniel J. Cox/
OSF 158BR; Jeff Foott/OSF
158/159; David C. Fritts/
OSF 158CR; Mark Hamblin/OSF
159CL; Richard Herrmann/OSF
158BL; T. Kitchin & V. Hurst/NHPA
158TL; Lon Lauber/OSF 159BR;
Kevin Schafer/NHPA 159TR
Pages 206/207: Gary Braasch/
Corbis 206/207; Natalie B. Fobes
207CL, 207BL; Kerrick James
207BR; Buddy Mays/Travel Stock
206CR; Andrea Pistolesi 206BL,
207TR, 207CR

Map Production: Mike Adams,
James Macdonald and
Stephen Ramsay

©2007 Apa Publications GmbH & Co.
Verlag KG, Singapore Branch

Production: Linton Donaldson

GENERAL INDEX

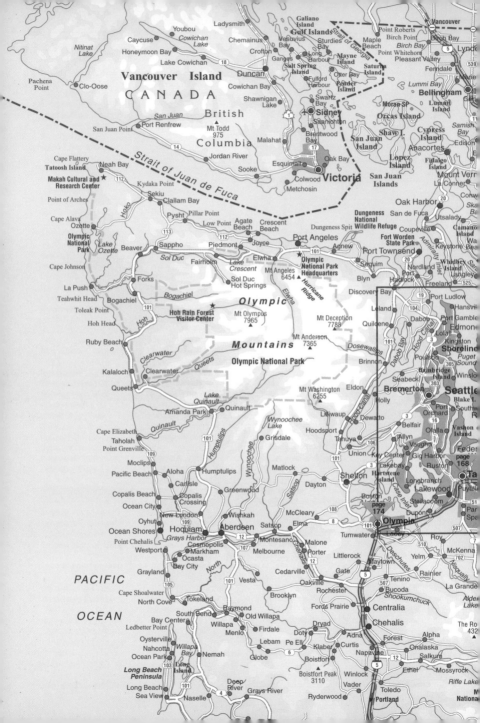

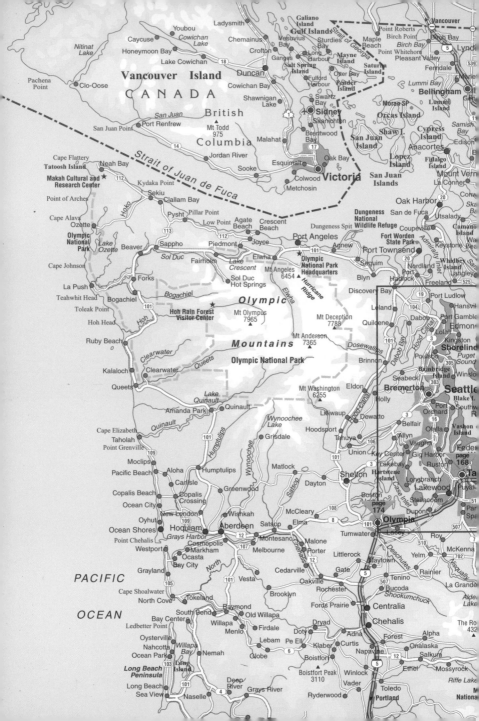